Nothin' But
MUSCLE

199 Radical Rides

Published by

Krause Publications, a division of F+W Media, Inc.
700 East State Street • Iola, WI 54990-0001
715-445-2214 • 888-457-2873
www.krausebooks.com

To order books or other products call toll-free 1-800-258-0929
or visit us online at www.krausebooks.com or www.Shop.Collect.com

Library of Congress Control Number: 2010931155

ISBN-13: 978-1-4402-1549-0
ISBN-10: 1-4402-1549-9

Designed by Sharon Bartsch
Edited by Brian Earnest

Printed in the United States of America

CONTENTS

TIMELESS MUSCLE

The term "muscle car" really has no strict definition. Some muscle cars are small, like the Corvettes and AC Cobras. Some are big, like the Buick Gran Sports or Chevy Impala SS's.

Some do the quarter-mile in 11 seconds, some take more like 17. Some are "Plain Jane" sedans that truly qualify as wolves in sheep's clothing — who would ever know by looking at it that an early Chevy "409" Impala could blow the doors off almost anything on the road at the time? On the other hand, there are an equal number of muscle cars that carried all kinds of wild paint jobs, hood scoops and menacing accessories that made them look as fast as they ran. C'mon, has there ever been anything harier-looking than a winged Plymouth Superbird or technicolor Pontiac Judge, with color-coordinated "eyebrows" over the wheel wells?

In "Nothin' But Muscle," we go back and revisit the best of the high-testosterone machines — the cars that everybody wanted to drive, and nobody wanted to race against. Not every muscle car made our cut. We stuck to the cars that were the most influential and most memorable. A lot of great cars missed out. We go as far back as the 1950s with some Hudsons and Chevys that were true forerunners of the machines that followed. In the early 1960s, the star performers on the streets and strips of America were the 409 Chevys, 421 Super-Duty Pontiacs, 426 Max Wedge Mopars, and powerhouse 427 Fords.

The 1964 model year brought us the legendary Pontiac GTO, considered by many car buffs to be the first true muscle car — a midsize car with a big-block stuffed under the hood.

The late 1960s were clearly the salad days for great muscle machines: big-block Mustangs, Shelbys, Chevelles, Firebirds, Camaros, Chargers, Challengers, Super Bees, AMXs, Gran Sports, 4-4-2s... Every automaker seemed to be making cars that could satisfy even the heartiest appettite for horsepower.

The 1970s were "the lost years" for muscle car fanatics, as the gas crunch and squirrelly insurance companies combined to turn down the music on the hi-po party.

Good things have a way of coming back around, however, and the 1980s rebounded with a new era of 5-liter Mustangs and menacing black Buicks that gave a new generation of horsepower freaks something to lust after.

Since then, we've seen the arrival of the Dodge Vipers, 500-hp Corvettes, new-generation Mustangs and even the return of the Camaro. Sure, these modern wonders are light years ahead of those spartan pavement pounders of the 1960s. Shoot, some of them even get great gas mileage! But for all their differences, really fast, scary, spectacular machines from all eras seem to share a common spirit. Whether you're talking about a 1970 LS6 Chevelle, or a 2006 Z06 Corvette — the cars in our list were the gnarliest things around for their time.

It's these "Muscle Car Hall of Famers" that we celebrate in the pages that follow.

Here's hoping the high-octane gas never stops flowing.

1951-1952 HUDSON HORNET

If there was ever a car that was unlikely to dominate American stock car racing, it was the "Step-Down" Hudson Hornet. With a 124-inch wheelbase, a 77-inch width and a shipping weight around 3,600 lbs., the Detroit-built Hornet was a big car. Under the hood was an inline, L-head six — not a V-8.

The Hornet had made its bow in 1951, the same year that the Chrysler Firepower Hemi V-8 was introduced. Few observers thought that, even with 308 cubic inches, the new Hudson product could ever set the pace in the recently formed sport of stock-car racing.

Marshall Teague, the owner of a garage in Daytona Beach, Florida, saw the Hornet's potential. He figured out that the car's low center of gravity, its great handling and its big, "torquey" six were just what was needed to beat the racing-winning Olds 88.

Teague outran the Olds drivers and was then able to get the attention of Hudson's top brass. He convinced management to add "heavy-duty" parts to their options list. With extras like "Twin H" carburetion (a setup using two single-barrel carburetors) the Hudsons were virtually unbeatable on the nation's racetracks.

The Hornet got only minor changes in 1952, but by then the "roundy-round" boys had all they needed to keep the Hudsons out front. A number of top NASCAR drivers switched to the brand and 27 out of 34 Grand National races went to Hudson Hornets that year.

Teague took the checkered flag at Daytona. He then switched to AAA-sanctioned racing up north and won half of the 14 races on the schedule. Other Hudson drivers took five more, giving the nameplate 39 wins in 48 major 1952 events.

Hornets were not low-priced cars. The popular coupe sold for $2,742, the Hollywood two-door hardtop cost $3,095 and the convertible was priced at $3,342.

For those not involved in stock car racing, the Hudsons didn't seem all that fast in straight-line acceleration testing. *Motor Trend* magazine reported a 0-to-60 time of 16.8 seconds. However, ace automotive writer Tom McCahill tested a Teague-tuned Hornet and found it could achieve the same speed in 12.8 seconds. McCahill recorded a maximum speed of 107 mph, versus *Motor Trend*'s under-100 mph top speed.

Tom Glatch

1954 HUDSON HORNET

The 1954 Hudson Hornets were still the stars of the racing world, but in the end all those checkered flags weren't enough to keep the nameplate alive.

Even with the midyear introduction of the low-priced Hornet Special series, sales did not pick up. In all, 24,833 Hornets were made. Only 11,603 of the smaller Wasps were put together.

The base Hornet engine, still at 308 cubic inches, was rated at 160 hp and the Twin-H option brought that figure to 170 hp for $86 more. However, the stock-car racers used the specially built 7-X engine, which was available through the company's parts operation for $385. This high-performance engine reportedly produced 210 hp.

Hudson won 17 out of 36 NASCAR Grand Nationals, again more than any other make, and driver Marshall Teague wrapped up another AAA title with five wins.

Other Hudson drivers took three more victories to account for half the AAA events that season. Ironically, Teague's last win came September 12, at Milwaukee, Wis., not far from where the 1955 Hornets would be constructed in Kenosha.

Hornet prices in 1954 ranged from the Hornet Special Club Sedan at $2,571 to the convertible Brougham at $3,288.

This year the big cars were restyled to look more like the compact Jet introduced the year before. The grille had a heavy, bowed molding tracing the upper radiator opening. There was a full-width, flat horizontal loop surrounding the wedge-shaped parking lights at each end. The main bar (top of the loop) was ribbed towards the middle and held a triangular Hudson medallion in a finned housing at its center. Behind this bar was an angled plate with four additional, wide-spaced ribs. Block letters spelled out the Hudson name below the scoop on the nose of the hood. Despite a new one-piece curved windshield, new sheet metal from the belt line down, a modernized interior and the most powerful flathead sixes ever installed in a passenger car up to that time, the public and the critics voted that the Hudson was outdated and sales were dismal.

After long talks, Hudson and Nash-Kelvinator merged on May 1, 1954, to form American Motors Corporation. Hudson production would end in October, with the name being transferred to a variation of the Nash.

Doug Mitchel

1957 RAMBLER REBEL

Viewed in retrospect, the first Rebel ranks as one of the finest muscle cars ever made. It was offered in this format for just the single season and is now a rarity that AMC enthusiasts covet for their collections.

Under its hood was an enlarged version of the V-8 introduced a year earlier. The 4.00 x 3.25-inch bore and stroke, 327-cube engine featured five main bearings, a forged-steel crankshaft and a 9.5:1 compression ratio. Large cast-iron exhaust manifolds were hooked to dual exhaust pipes with straight-through mufflers.

AMC had originally planned to use a Bendix "Electrojector" electronic fuel-injection system in the Rebel. The system proved problematic and it's unlikely that any fuel-injected Rebels were ever turned out. A Carter WCFB four-barrel carburetor was used on 1,500 production units instead. Instead of 288 hp and fuel injection, the cars that left the assembly line had 255 carbureted horses.

Another thing in the original plan was limited production. AMC expected to manufacture Rebels on a made-to-order basis and to offer only two options: EFI and Hydra-Matic transmission. Extras added later included Solex tinted glass and 6.70 x 15 Goodyear Blue Streak racing tires.

The Rebel's standard transmission was a three-speed manual gearbox, with overdrive, linked to a Borg & Beck 10-inch clutch. The extra-cost "Flashaway" Hydra-Matic transmission was essentially the same unit used by Oldsmobile and Pontiac.

The Rebel came only as a four-door hardtop and only in a solid silver-gray color scheme. Its special full-length body side trim featured a bronze-gold anodized aluminum insert with a "Rebel" nameplate on each front fender.

AMC promoted "amazing acceleration and speed" for the new car and road testers substantiated such claims. Motor Trend said that the only car capable of outrunning the Rebel from 0-to-60 was the fuel-injected Corvette.

A Rebel with overdrive and the 4:10 axle was made available for short acceleration runs at Daytona Beach in February 1957. *Motor Trend*'s Joe Wherry reported a best time of 7.5 seconds from 0-to-60. *Hot Rod* magazine obtained a 9.4-second 0-to-60 time in a Rebel with Hydra-Matic and reported that the stick-shift version with 4.10 gears could break 8 seconds flat. The car with Hydra-Matic did the quarter-mile in 17 seconds at 84 mph.

1965 RAMBLER MARLIN

The 1965 Marlin was probably the closest thing the AMC family offered to the Ford Mustang, and it really was a overlooked performer on the muscle car landscape.

The distinct Marlin roofline bowed on the 1964 Tarpon show car, which utilized the compact Rambler American's 106-inch stance. The Tarpon seemed to take aim at Plymouth's Valiant-based Barracuda and the '65 Ford Mustang, but the AMC brass blew Dick Teague's design up in size and sat it on the mid-size Rambler Classic chassis. From the beltline down, the two had the same body.

The 112-inch-wheelbase Rambler Classic was restyled for 1965 and grew about 5 inches longer. It now had distinctions from the upscale Ambassador, which got four additional inches of wheelbase and more individual styling.

Instead of stressing go-power, the Marlin emphasized comfort and roominess. It featured an Ambassador instrument panel and could be had with individually reclining front seats or slim bucket-type seats with a center console or center cushion.

Tucked under the hood was the same new 232-cid/155-hp Torque Command six used in the Ambassador. A pair of Gen-I AMC V-8s were optional. The first was a mild 287-cid/198-hp version. The second was the 327-cid/270-hp V-8 that had been around since the days of the 1958 Ambassador.

Writer Tom McCahill found a 327 Marlin, with automatic transmission capable of 0-to-60 mph in 9.7 seconds.

The factory base price for the Marlin was $3,100. There was sufficient curiosity in it to draw 10,327 orders in the short first-year run that followed its February 1965 introduction. That would be a high-water mark, so to speak, as the 1966 Marlin, minus the Rambler nameplate, some previously standard equipment and with the addition of an optional four-speed manual gearbox, found only 4,547 customers.

"Do Rogues really come with rally stripes?"

"No, but with the new engine they drive that way."

'66 Rambler American Rogue

1966-67 RAMBLER ROGUE

The smallish 1966 Rambler Rogue packed lot of whallop under the hood, especially for an AMC, which wasn't really a player in the muscle car game at the time.

The Rambler Rogue Typhoon V-8 arrived on April 7, 1966. A year earlier, the first V-8 powered U.S. compacts had been made, but the near-300-hp Rogue was a definite "break-the-mold" machine for AMC.

A V-8 stuffed in the 106-inch-wheelbase Rambler American was exciting enough. On top of that, it was the debut of the newly designed AMC V-8, an engine that would be a standard bearer for the independent automaker in coming years.

The old AMC V-8 — not used in Americans — dated back to 1956 and didn't have much room to grow. It was somewhat heavy and generally didn't take well to attempts to extract more ponies. In fact, 270 hp was the max for the 327-cid version of 1958-1966.

The new 290-cid "Typhoon" V-8 had a 3.75 x 3.28 bore and stroke, giving it plenty of growing room. It was rated at 200 hp with a two-barrel carburetor and 225 hp with a four-barrel. Eventually, 304-, 343-, 360-, 390- and 401-cid V-8s came out of the same thin-wall-casting design. This engine gave both satisfactory service on the road and a good accounting of itself in racing and street performance. It wangled its way into some of the most interesting AMC muscle cars made after 1966.

The 290-cid V-8 was first slated to go into 1,500 special Rogue two-door hardtops with black tops and rear decks and Sungold lower bodies.

Fewer than 1,500 Rogue V-8s were made. Since the option came in other Rambler Americans, there were leftover Rogue Typhoon pieces that went on six-cylinder cars and this doesn't help those hunting or restoring these cars today.

1968 AMX "390"

From its inception as a prototype in '66, through its 2 1/2-year production run, to its ever-rising status as a collector muscle car today, the two-passenger AMX has always blazed new trails for a gets-no-respect corporate parent,

AMX stood for "American Motors Experimental." The car with that name was Step 2 in AMC's image revitalization program. The goal was to attract young car buyers who were scooping up high-performance models from other automakers. In the attempt to do this, designer Dick Teague created the first steel-bodied, two-seat American production model since the '57 Ford T-Bird.

The first AMX was a non-running fiberglass concept car that let auto show attendees know that ultra-conservative AMC could design a car with pizzazz. A later running model had a "Ramble Seat" in place of the rear deck.

The AMC Javelin pony car bowed in the fall of 1967 as a 1968 model. The two-place AMX — which was a foot shorter in wheelbase and length — came out as a 1968-1/2 model. Along with it came a 390-cid Gen II AMC V-8, which was rated at 315 hp.

The short 97-inch wheelbase cut the 390-powered AMX's curb weight to 3,205 lbs. That gave the little coupe a 10.8 lbs.-per-horsepower ratio when equipped with the 315-hp version of the 390-cid V-8. *Car and Driver* found this combination good for a 6.6 second 0-to-60 mph time. The 390 AMX did the standing-start quarter-mile in 14.8 seconds at 95 mph. Top speed was an estimated 122 mph.

Many buyers were happy with the performance of the standard 290-cid/225-hp V-8 or the one-step-up 343-cid/280-hp V-8, but the "390" was the most muscular engine option.

The '68 AMX was base-priced at $3,245, but Road & Track estimated the price of the 390-cid version at $3,500. Each AMX built in calendar year 1968 had a metal dashboard plate bearing a special serial number from 000001 to 006175. However, the first 550 cars, which were assembled in 1967, did not have this feature. That means that total production was 6,725 units.

In February 1968, on a test track in Texas, race driver Craig Breedlove established 106 world speed records with an AMX. About 50 special red-white-and-blue "Craig Breedlove" editions were then built. They had 290-cid V-8s and a four-speed manual transmission.

Jerry Heasley

1969 SC/RAMBLER

It may not have found many buyers, and it might not get mentioned in the same breath as the Chevelles, GTOs, Mustangs and Chargers of the period, but one of the most eye-catching vehicles from the golden age of muscle cars was a small hardtop with a patriotic color scheme and a massive scoop dominating the front portion of its hood. This AMC Hurst SC/Rambler represented one of the company's most unique models and the swan song for the Rambler American compact car.

Every muscle car lover knows the name of Hurst Performance Products. So, in 1969, American Motors hooked up with the Pennsylvania performance parts company to surprise everyone with the SC/Rambler (or "Scrambler" as some folks call it). Hurst actually thought up the idea and AMC bought it.

Based on the two-door Rogue hardtop coupe, the SC/Rambler stressed the big-engine-in-little-car format to the max. Below the hood went a 390-cid/325-hp V-8 linked to a Borg Warner four-speed manual gearbox with a Hurst shifter. A 3.54:1 rear axle with Twin-Grip differential was included, too. With a curb weight of about 3,000 lbs., the hot little car had a power-to-weight ratio of 10.03 lbs. per horsepower.

The AMC factory estimated low 14-second quarter-miles at 98 mph. *Road Test* magazine clocked 14.4 at 100.44 mph and managed to hit 109 mph without topping out. Modified SC/Ramblers have run the quarter-mile in the 9-second bracket.

The SC/Rambler interior was done in plain-looking gray vinyl, but it had red-white-and-blue headrests. This color scheme was carried onto the body, in several variations. Full carpeting was another selling feature. The first 500 cars built had red center body side panels and thick blue horizontal racing stripes on the hood, roof and deck. A blue arrow pointed towards the scoop, which had large letters spelling the word "AIR" and calling out the engine size. This was the "A" type graphic treatment.

When the cars sold quickly, another batch was made with new "B" type trim. These had a mostly white exterior with narrow red and blue stripes. Then, a third batch of cars was made, reverting to the type "A" trim, but lacking all of the elements. The A-finished cars seem to be the more common of the 1,512 SC/Ramblers built.

Jerry Heasley

1970 AMX

A two-seater with 290 ponies under the hood is nothing to take lightly in any Saturday night stoplight showdowns, and it's likely that 1970 AMX owners didn't find too many eager takers when it came time to line 'em up.

The AMX came with a new 360-cid V-8 as standard equipment. The 290 hp was 65 more than last season's 343-cid base engine. Other standard features included courtesy lights, a heavy-duty 60-amp. battery, rear torque links (traction bars), a tachometer, a 140-mph speedometer, 14 x 6-inch styled steel wheels, fiberglass-belted Polyglas wide profile tires, an energy-absorbing anti-theft steering column, a Space-Saver spare tire, heavy-duty shocks and springs, an Autolite Model 4300 four-barrel carburetor and dual exhausts.

Base-priced at $3,395 (and advertised as "the only American sports car that costs less than $4,000") the new AMX had a production run of 4,116 units, which made it the rarest of the three two-seat editions — 1968, 1969,1970 — that AMC offered. The height of the fastback coupe was reduced about one inch. While the wheelbase remained at 97 inches, the car's over-

all length grew about 2 inches to 179 inches. The increase gave it a longer nose and made it look more like its Mustang-Camaro-Firebird-Cougar-Barracuda-Challenger competitors, which should have helped sales, but didn't. It sold better when it was a totally distinct car. At 3,126 lbs., it was the heaviest AMX yet, but only by 29 lbs., so with the bigger engine the effect on performance was negligible.

Appearance-wise, the AMX got new rear lamps and a completely restyled front end that was shared with Javelin performance models. TThe restyled hood had a large ram-induction scoop that took in cold air for the engine.

Eric Dahlquist wrote up the '70 AMX in the December 1969 edition of *Motor Trend* and summed it up as "one of the better constructed cars around." The test car had the optional 390-cid V-8 that produced 325 hp at 5000 rpm and 420 lbs.-ft. of torque at 3000 rpm. It drove through the Borg-Warner four-speed gearbox to a 3.54:1 rear axle. Zero-to-60 mph took 6.56 seconds and Dahlquist did the standing-start quarter-mile in 14.68 seconds at 92 mph. Top speed in fourth gear was recorded as 109 mph.

Phil Kunz

1970 REBEL "MACHINE"

The 1970 AMC Rebel Machine couldn't exactly hide — at least not with that crazy red-white-and-blue color scheme — but it's still largely overlooked among killer pony cars and muscle machines from the era. It had AMC's biggest, most powerful 390 V-8. It produced 340 galloping ponies at 5100 rpm. The "standard stuff" list was filled with a four-speed, close-ratio tranny, a Hurst shifter, a lighted 8000-rpm hood tach, Ram Air, 3.54:1 or 3.91:1 rear axles, heavy-duty shocks and springs, a low-back-pressure dual exhaust system, front and rear sway bars, 15-inch white-letter tires, styled wheels, high-back bucket seats and power disc brakes.

"Standing before you is the car you've always wanted," AMC teased in a two-page introductory ad in the December 1969 issue of *Hot Rod* magazine. The ad copy warned, "Incidentally, if you have delusions of entering the Daytona 500 with the Machine, or challenging people at random, the Machine is not that fast. You should know that. For instance, it is not as fast on the getaway as a 427 Corvette, or a Hemi, but it is faster on the getaway than a Volkswagen,

a slow freight train, and your old man's Cadillac." Which meant it was plenty fast enough.

All this came at a price of $3,475 in a car with a 114-inch wheelbase and curb weight of 3,640 lbs. and produced performance in the range of 14.4-second quarter-miles at a 98-mph speed. It also produced sales of 2,326 cars.

The first 100 "Machines" delivered from the AMC factory in Kenosha, Wisc., were finished in white. Hurst Performance Products did up the lower beltline stripes and hood in blue and then added red stripes on the upper body sides. At the rear, red-white-and-blue stripes ran across the fender tips and deck. Special "The Machine" emblems were tacked on the front fender sides and on the rear trim panel's right-hand side.

For buyers who didn't like the patriotic paint scheme, AMC advertised, "If you like everything about it except for the paint job, which admittedly looks startling, you can order the car painted in the color of your choice." When buyers did this, they got silver striping and a blacked-out hood. The original color scheme became a $75 option.

Phil Kunz

1965 SKYLARK GS

"There is mounting evidence that our engineers have turned into a bunch of performance enthusiasts," said one ad. "First they stuff the Wildcat full of engine. Then the Riviera Gran Sport. And now this, the Skylark GS, which is almost like having your own, personal-type nuclear deterrent."

With a 400/325 V-8, a four-barrel carburetor and a 10.25:1 compression ratio, the Skylark GS tested by *Motor Trend* in May 1965 cranked out .81 hp per cubic inch and fed it through a two-speed Super Turbine 300 automatic transmission with a floor-mounted shifter. (A floor-mounted three-speed stick shift was standard.) The magazine reported that its 3,720-lb. test car reached the 60-mph mark in a mere 7.8 seconds. It did the quarter-mile in 16.6 seconds at 86 mph and had a top speed of 116 mph.

Buick engineers said that the Skylark GS was completely different than the regular Specials because all three body styles — coupe, hardtop and convertible — used a beefed-up

convertible-type frame that resisted torque flexing. Naturally, it was fitted with heavy-duty shocks and springs and a stiffer anti-roll bar up front. Other features of the first Skylark GS included heavy-duty upper control arm bushings, dual exhausts, 7.75 x 14 tires and a choice of 2.78:1, 3.08:1, 3.23:1, 3.36:1, 3.55:1 and 3.73:1 rear axle ratios. To show what a Skylark Gran Sport could do set up with 4.30 gears and cheater slicks, *Motor Trend* mentioned that Lenny Kennedy's race-prepped example clocked a 13.42-second, 104.46-mph quarter-mile run at the Winternational Drags.

"It seems to us that Buick has another winner in the Skylark Gran Sport," said Bob McVay, *Motor Trend*'s assistant technical editor. "The point is that better cars are being built— and Buick is building them!"

V-8, Super Turbine automatic and other options that raised its price to $3,978.04. It covered the quarter-mile in 14.92 seconds at 95.13 mph.

1970 GRAN SPORT 455

The 1970 GS 455 was one of the great muscle cars of its era, and one of the fiercest Buicks ever produced. Its 455-cid engine was derived from the earlier 430-cid V-8 and produced 350 hp at 4600 rpm. Torque output was a strong 510 ft.-lbs. at 2800 rpm. It featured a 10.0:1 compression ratio and a Rochester four-barrel carburetor. This engine could push one of the approximately 3,800-lb. well-equipped Skylark bodies from 0-to-60 mph in about 6.5 seconds.

Available once again was the Stage I option. In fact, *Motor Trend* opined, "Buick's Stage I was interesting in 1969, now with the 455 mill it's an engineering tour de force." In addition, with a price of just $199.95, the engine option package was a bargain. It included extra-large nickel-chrome stellite steel valves, big-port cylinder heads with special machining and valve relieving, stronger valve springs, a high-lift cam, a carburetor with richer jetting, blueprinted pistons (notched for valve clearance) and an advanced-performance distributor. As in the past, the Stage I V-8 was available with either a special shift-governed automatic or a heavy-duty four-speed manual with a beefed-up clutch.

A Stage I GS 455 with automatic transmission could do 0-to-60 mph in 5.5 seconds and took just less than 14 seconds to zip down the quarter-mile. One magazine did it in 13.39 seconds at 105.5 mph and *Motor Trend* clocked 13.79 seconds at 104.50 mph as it flew through the traps. The stick-shifted version was just a little slower in reaching 60 mph from a standing start.

On top of its super performance, the GS 455 was a real handler and hugged the road even better when equipped with Rallye Ride package for $15.80 extra. It gave *Motor Trend*'s press car extra stability at high speed. The test car had four-wheel manual drum brakes that could slow it from 60 mph in 139.1 ft. Senior editor Bill Sanders said the brakes "held up exquisitely without fade after repeated stops from over 100 mph."

The Gran Sport 455 option could be ordered for two body styles. The two-door hardtop cost $3,283 and 8,732 were put together. Buick built only 1,416 of the convertible versions, which sold for $3,469 and up.

1970 SKYLARK GSX

"Buick's GSX. A limited edition," said the teaser headline on a Buick ad in the April 1970 issue of *Motor Trend*. The automaker called it "another light-your-fire car from Buick." As things turned out, not too many people had their fires lit, but you have to admit that with a total production of 678 copies, the GSX is a limited-edition muscle car.

Deep down inside, there wasn't too much of a difference between a 1970 GS 455 and a GSX of the same vintage. The latter carried a $1,196 options package as standard equipment. The package included a 455 four-barrel V-8, a hood-mounted tach, a Rallye steering wheel, power front disc brakes, a four-speed manual transmission, a 3.42:1 posi- rear axle, G60-15 "billboard" Wide-Oval tires, a special front stabilizer bar, front and rear spoilers, black vinyl bucket seats, heavy-duty front and rear shocks, a rear stabilizer bar, rear control arms and bush-ings, Firm Ride rear springs and GSX ornamentation. The hood-mounted tach was specific to the GSX model and the four-speed gearbox had a Hurst shifter. The GSX ornamentation included a special graphics package with hood stripes and side panel stripes.

For 1970, the GSX came only in two exterior colors, called Saturn Yellow and Apollo White. Buick built 491 of the Saturn Yellow cars. The other 187 cars were Apollo White. Black vinyl interior trim, code 188, was used with both colors. Other special features included a distinctive padded steering wheel, a trunk tension bar designed to support the spoiler and a baffle incorporated into the rear spoiler. Of the 678 cars manufactured, 278 had standard 455-cid/315-hp V-8s, and 400 had the 345-hp Stage 1 engine option. All of the cars were built between February and May of 1970, but the VIN numbering appears to be assigned randomly.

Jerry Heasley

1971-1972 SKYLARK GSX

The 1971-72 GSX was a special-order muscle car that remains somewhat of an oddity today. Only 168 of the cars were reportedly produced.

While not as muscular as 1970 editions, the 1971-1972 Skylarks with the GSX package and the Stage 1 engine option are still tremendous performance cars and, since they were rare when new, are extremely hard to find today.

A GSX package was an option for 1971-1972 Buicks and could be ordered for any Skylark GS from the GS 350 to the GS 455 Stage 1. To order a 1971 or 1972 GSX, customers had to get their Buick dealer to check off the Special Car Order, or SCO, section of the order form.

The 1971-1972 cars varied widely in color and came with an unlimited range of options. The Buick GSX Registry stated that very little is known about them. Apparently, the option was added to 124 cars in 1971 and 44 cars in 1972.

Like other 1971-1972 Buicks, the GSX editions used de-tuned engines, all of which had an 8.5:1 compression ratio and less horsepower and torque than in 1970. However, when equipped with Buick's potent 455 Stage 1 engine, the GSX was still one of the hottest muscle cars in town. In fact, Buick fans insist that the Stage 1s can run down the quarter-mile faster than an LS6 big-block Chevelle.

In 1971 it was possible to put the GSX package on a car with the 350-cid/260-hp four-barrel V-8 that was standard in Grand Sports. This motor generated 360 lbs.-ft. of torque at 3000 rpm. Another option was the standard 455-cid/315-hp V-8 with 450 lbs.-ft. of torque at 2800 rpm. The 1971 version of the 455-cid Stage 1 engine produced 345 hp at 5000 rpm and 460 lbs.-ft. of torque at 3000 rpm.

In 1972, the engines were further choked by government emissions rules and the output numbers looked even worse because they were presented in SAE net horsepower (nhp) terms. The 350 produced 195 nhp at 4000 rpm and 290 lbs.-ft. of torque at 2800 rpm. The base 455 produced 225 nhp at 4000 rpm and 360 lbs.-ft. of torque at 2600 rpm. The 455 Stage 1 produced 270 hp at 4400 rpm and 390 lbs.-ft. of torque at 3000 rpm. At the rear of the cars, 3.08:1 or 3.42:1 axles were standard, depending on the engine and transmission combination.

Both 1971 and 1972 GSXs used a special frame, a computer-designed rally-tuned-suspension and large-diameter sway bars.

1971 GRAN SPORT 455

Buick combined the Gran Sport and the GS 455 into one series for 1971. This gentleman's muscle car — the Gran Sport Buick — was one of the few potent performance packages that was tractable in all kinds of driving. It could even be ordered with air-conditioning. Gran Sport equipment included a blacked-out grille with bright trim, bright wheelhouse moldings and bright rocker panel moldings with red-filled accents. Dual, functional hood scoops sat in the center of the hood. GS monograms appeared on the front fenders, deck and grille. Cars equipped with the 455 or 455 Stage 1 options had additional engine identification emblems. Standard equipment was the same as on the Skylark Custom, but bucket or notchback front seats in vinyl trim were optional.

For 1971, General Motors listed all its engines with SAE net horsepower ratings, along with gross horsepower ratings that reflected a reading without accessories. The SAE method was known as the "installed" output — the final output figure of the engine within a car carrying all necessary operating accessories. This may have been GM's way of mollifying insurance companies that were starting to impinge on the salability of muscle cars.

The GS 455 cid V-8 had a gross rating of 330 hp and an installed rating of 265 hp. The 455-cid Stage 1 engine had a 275 SAE hp rating, but its gross output rating was 345 hp at 5000 rpm. This 345-hp rating was down from that of the 1970 Stage 1, which produced 360 hp at 4600 rpm. The reason was a lower 8.5:1 compression ratio, which was down from a 10.0:1 compression ratio in 1970. A functional Ram-Air induction system helped feed the engine cold air.

Buick's trademark — a high torque rating — was also down from 510 lbs.-ft. at 2800 rpm in 1970 to 460 lbs.-ft. at 3000 rpm for 1971. Still, if one averaged all 1971 GS 455 road tests, the elapsed time for the quarter-mile was 14.25, which compares favorably to an average ET of 14.02 for the 1970 model.

Production figures show that 8,268 GS and GS 455 two-door hardtops were built. Of these, 801 had the Stage 1 option. Convertibles accounted for 902 total GS and GS 455 assemblies. A number of highly desirable options were offered, such as a Hurst-shifted Muncie M20 transmission and code RPO E6 through-bumper exhaust extensions.

Jerry Heasley

1972 SKYLARK GS 455 STAGE 1

According to *Motor Trend*'s A. B. Shuman, "Buick, it seems, has an indisputable knack for making singularly sneaky cars."

The Skylark-based muscle car was champion in the Stock Eliminator category in Pomona, Calif., and went on to beat all the other stock class winners to become overall category winner. In Shuman's hands it did 0-to-60 mph in 5.8 seconds, while the quarter-mile took 14.10 seconds (with a 97-mph terminal speed). With open exhausts, fatter tires and a few "tweaks" allowed by NHRA rules, weekend drag racer Dave Benisek set an elapsed time record of 13.38 seconds, at Pomona, with the same car.

By coincidence, the 1970 GS 455 Stage 1 also did the quarter-mile in 13.38 seconds, but that was because it had a higher compression ratio (10.0:1), more horsepower (360 at 4600 rpm) and a taller (numerically lower) 3.64:1 rear axle.

By 1972, the no-lead version of the car ran an 8.5:1 compression ratio, produced 275 hp at 4400 rpm and came linked to a 4.30:1 rear axle. Shuman opined that the car ws "the best example of the Supercar genre extant."

Despite such a positive appraisal, Buick made only 7,723 GS hardtops and 852 GS convertibles in model year 1972 and that included GS 350, GS 455 and Stage 1 production. In addition to a 350- 455- or 455-cid Stage 1 V-8, all 1972 Gran Sports had four-barrel carburetors, dual exhausts, functional hood scoops, and a heavy-duty suspension. GS monograms appeared on the front fenders and rear deck and bright moldings trimmed the rocker panels and wheel lips.

Capacity of both the engine and the turbo unit was increased and hot air, rather than the hot water used earlier, was used to warm the induction system. Buick engineers also relocated the knock sensor and linked it directly to the electronic control module (ECM). The diameter of the turbine outlet pipe was increased from 2 to 2 1/2 inches to nearly eliminate backpressure. Two other performance

1984 REGAL GRAND NATIONAL

There weren't many cars from the 1980s that reached icon status, but the Regal Grand National was definitely one of them — and probably at the top of the list.

After showcasing its turbo-engine technology at the 1984 new-car shows, Buick brought out a new model it advertised as "the hottest Buick this side of a banked oval." This new Regal Grand National coupe was, according to Buick, "produced in limited numbers for those who demand a high level of performance." Its stated purpose was to give young and young-at-heart Buick buyers much of the feeling of a NASCAR racer. Buick built 2,000 copies of this car.

"A little chrome and a lot of power in basic black attire, that's what the Buick Regal Grand National coupe is all about," said the ad copywriters. The cost of the option—$1,282—was quite modest, considering that it had a host of appearance and equipment extras. To begin with, Grand Nationals carried the 231-cid (3.8-liter) turbocharged V-6 with sequential fuel injection (SFI). This code LM9 engine produced 200 hp at 4000 rpm and 300 lbs.-ft. of torque at 2000 rpm. It came linked to a four-speed auto-matic transmission and a 3.42:1 rear axle.

Ingredients of the GN option included black exterior finish on the body, bumpers, bumper rub strips, bumper guards, front air dam, windshield wipers, rear deck lid spoiler, taillight bezels and aluminum wheels. The paint code was No. 19. Grand National identification was carried on the front fenders and the instrument panel. A sport steering wheel, a tachometer, a turbo-boost gauge, a 94-amp alternator, power brakes and steering, dual exhausts and a special hood with a turbo bulge were also included in the package. The code 995 Lear Siegler seats (sand gray cloth with charcoal leather inserts) were embroidered with the Grand National model's distinctive "6" (for V-6) logo.

Individual options available from Buick included a hatch top (RPO CC1), an Astroroof with silver glass (RPO CF5), a theft-deterrent system (RPO UA6), cruise control (RPO K34), electronic touch climate-control air conditioning (RPO C68), a rear window defogger (RPO C49), a remote trunk release (RPO A90), electronic instrumentation (RPO U52) and a lighted vanity mirror on the passenger-side sun visor.

1985 REGAL GRAND NATIONAL

Why change a good thing? The Regal GN wasn't selling in big numbers (2,102 built in 1985), but it was pulling enthusiasts into Buick showrooms where some of them bought other models. With oodles of image and oomph, the "new" GN certainly did not require a drastic overhaul, but it still got a facelift.

The forward-slanting nose of all '85 Regals carried a new grille. On the GN, it was finished in black. So was nearly everything else, including the windshield wipers. There were minor updates to the upholstery and ornamentation. Still, the ultra-high-performance version of the Regal T-Type was basically unchanged on the outside.

Under the hood once again was the turbocharged 3.8-liter V-6 with sequential fuel injection. The system (introduced in 1984) provided more precise fuel delivery. Metered fuel was timed and injected into the individual combustion ports sequentially through six Bosch injectors. Each cylinder received one injection per every two revolutions, just prior to the intake valve opening.

A nine in the eighth position in the VIN number indicated the use of the 3.8-liter turbo, which carried option code RPO LM9 as it did in 1984. This engine was rated for 200 hp at 4000 rpm and 300 lbs.-ft. of torque at a slightly higher 2400 rpm.

The '85 GN stuck with a monotone black exterior treatment and was identified by special model badges. The Grand National package retailed for $675, so prices for the high-performance model started at $12,640. The package included the turbo V-6, quick-ratio power steering, an instrumentation group, sport mirrors with left-hand remote control, a four-speed automatic transmission, air conditioning and P215/65R15 black sidewall tires.

There were some interior revisions for 1985. A new two-tone cloth interior with front bucket seats carried code 583 soft trim. Underneath the car was a specific Gran Touring suspension.

Buick reported production of 2,102 Regal Grand Nationals in 1985.

1986 REGAL AND LESABRE GRAND NATIONALS

The 1986 Buick Regal Grand National package was a $558 option for the sporty T-Type, which itself listed for $13,714. The Grand National package included all Regal T-Type features, plus black (code 19) finish on the body, bumpers, bumper rub strips, bumper guards, rear spoiler and front air dam, Grand National and Intercooler identification trim, front bucket seats (trim code 583), a full-length-operation console and a performance-tuned suspension. Buyers had a choice of new standard chrome-plated steel wheels or new aluminum wheels. A high-mounted stop lamp became a part of the standard General Motors safety equipment package for 1986. Regal Grand National production climbed to 5,512 during the model run.

While overall appearance of the '86 Regal Grand National was very similar to the second (1984) and third (1985) Grand Nationals, Ron Yuille and his Buick Turbo Engine Group worked out some significant engineering upgrades for 1986 models. They included the use of an intercooler that lowered the temperature of the air charge between the turbo and the intake manifold. Airflow was also improved over 1985 by using a two-piece aluminum intake manifold with an open-plenum chamber. This change alone was good for a 10-percent horsepower boost to 235 hp at 4400 rpm. Torque increased to 330 lbs.-ft. at 2800 rpm. Another new-for-1986 item was an electric, temperature-controlled cooling fan.

A very different kind of Buick bearing the Grand National seal was introduced in conjunction with the 1986 Daytona 500. The 1986 1/2 LeSabre Grand National also featured monotone black finish, a front air dam, Buick's Level III suspension system, Electra T-Type wheels, Goodyear Eagle GT tires, unique rear quarter window trim and special GN badges. The LeSabre Grand National was built exclusively for promotional purposes only. It did not have a turbocharged V-6 or the performance of a Regal Grand National. Only 112 were made.

Jerry Heasley

1987 GNX

The 1987 GNX just might be the gnarliest ride to come out of American car factories in the 1980s. Even gear heads who don't want anything to do with that decade's cars often admit to secretly admiring the menacing GNX, with its bad-ass reputation and pavement-scorching performance.

To commemorate the end of Grand National production in 1987, Buick joined with ASC/McLaren to build a high-performance car called the GNX. The concept behind the GNX was to merge basic high-performance techniques with the latest in electronics and turbocharging technology to create the ultimate production modern muscle car. It was to be the kind of car enthusiasts and collectors would want to own. Almost overnight, the GNX achieved a memorable spot in the "muscle car roll of honor."

Along with rear-wheel-drive Regals, the hot Grand National was to go out of production in June or July 1987. When enthusiasts realized these would be the last turbocharged, rear-wheel drive Buicks, orders picked up. The model got an extension on life and approximately 10,000 assemblies were scheduled between August 3, 1987 and December of that year. The 547 GNXs

built were made as a part of this total.

The car was outlined in an April 25, 1986, document detailing a plan to build the "quickest GM production supercar. Ever!"

The heart of the GNX became a turbocharged and intercooled 3.8-liter SFI V-6 that developed 276 hp at 4400 rpm and 360 lbs.-ft. of torque at 3000 rpm. It was blueprinted and fitted with such things as special bearings, shot-peened rods and a high rpm valvetrain.

Outwardly, the GNX got a "high-intensity" image with glossy paint, low-gloss Vaalex fender louvers, cast aluminum wheels and flared fenders. The hood had a power bulge, the deck had an airfoil and the body had little identification. ASC/McLaren supplied the option package at a cost of $10,995, which gave the GNX an MSRP of $29,900. According to Buick, 0-to-60 performance was 5.5 seconds and the quarter-mile took 13.43 seconds at 104 mph. Top speed was a claimed 124 mph. *Car & Driver* published test results of 4.7 seconds for 0 to 60 mph and 13.5 seconds for the quarter-mile at 102 mph. The magazine reported top speed to be "120 mph limited by a cut-off."

Jerry Heasley

1987 REGAL GRAND NATIONAL

The 1987 Grand Nationals were capable of doing 0-to-60 mph in the low 6-second bracket, which is really moving for a car from the 1980s. And you were still one of the coolest guys on your block if you had one.

Cars Illustrated magazine published quarter-mile performance of 13.85 seconds and 99.22 mph. *Musclecars* magazine's test Buick was just a little slower, if you can call 13.90 seconds at 98.16 mph "slow." Collectors today like the superior performance of the 1987 Grand National model, even though the '86 is a whole lot rarer.By the end of the summer of 1987, Grand National sales had practically doubled over those of the entire previous year. This was due largely to the massive publicity exposure the hot, high-performance model was receiving in enthusiast publications. Buick dealers then pressured the company to make more of the cars, since dealers were marking them up an additional $3,000 per unit.

Grand National production had originally been slated to halt in July 1987, when Buick was supposed to stop making rear-wheel-drive Regals. On Aug. 3, company executive W.H. Lotts decided to extend production of only the Grand National model through December. By the end of the year, total production had risen to 20,193 cars.

All of the approximately 10,000 cars built after August 3 came with 17 required options. These included black exterior finish, gray interior trim code 583, the 3.8-liter turbocharged V-6, the Grand National equipment package, Soft-Ray tinted glass, door edge guards, two-speed wipers, an electric rear window defogger, a visor vanity mirror, remote-control mirrors, a limited-slip differential, a tilt steering column, tungsten halogen headlights, headlight warning chimes, a heavy-duty battery, an RPO UM6 Delco radio and a front license plate mounting bracket. Buyers could add two option packages and five stand-alone options, but other regular Buick Regal options were unavailable.

1956 "POWER-PACK"

"The Hot One's Even Hotter," said the Chevrolet's fiery ads. The American auto industry was having a horsepower race and Chevy was stepping up to the starting line. The Bow Tie brand transitioned, at least a little, from a "family" car to a performance car with the release of its 265-cube "small-block" V-8 in 1955.

The number of optional "small-block" V-8s was expanded to four — and two of those were rated above 200 hp. The Power-Pack engine of 1955 became the "Turbo-Fire 205" V-8, which had a 9.25:1 compression ratio, a single four-barrel carburetor and dual exhausts. It developed 205 hp at 4600 rpm and 268 lbs.-ft. of torque at 3000 rpm. The most powerful option was a Corvette engine that cranked up 225 hp at 5200 rpm and 270 lbs.-ft. of torque at 3600 rpm.

The Chevrolet V-8s weighed less than the division's six-cylinder engines, which resulted in an outstanding power-to-weight ratio — one reason why the 1956 Chevrolet V-8s were called the "Hot Ones." Jim Wangers, an advertising executive employed by Chevrolet's ad agency, Campbell Ewald, was an avid high-performance enthusiast. Wangers was instrumental in establishing Chevrolet's 1956 "The Hot One's Even Hotter!" advertising campaign. He promoted the idea of driving a '56 Chevy up Pikes Peak to set a new record. Afterwards, Wangers wrote: "Just point this new '56 Chevy uphill and ease down on the gas. In the merest fraction of a second you sense that big bore V-8 lengthening out its stride. And up you go with a silken rush of power that makes a mountain road seem as flat as a roadmap. For nothing without wings climbs like a '56 Chevrolet!"

Base One-Fifty models had minimal trim, a two-spoke steering wheel with horn ring, one sun visor, a lockable glovebox, a dome light, cloth-and-vinyl upholstery (all-vinyl on station wagons), black rubber floor mats and small hubcaps. These "stripper" cars were plain-looking, but popular with high-performance buffs. Less equipment meant less weight, but you could still get any engine option. The hot ticket for weekend drag racing was the lightest model (One-Fifty two-door sedan) with the Corvette V-8.

With a 115-inch wheelbase and 197.5-inch length, the Chevy V-8 was a well-balanced machine. Chevrolet model-year production of 1,574,740 units in 1956 was enough to give the brand the crown for being America's number one automaker.

Performance on the street and on the track had a lot to do with achieving strong sales.

1957 "FUELIE" COUPE

The youth movement was in motion and Americans weregetting "hipper" in 1957. American Bandstand, beatniks and Brigette Bardot were now part of the culture.

The 1957 Chevys were in tune with the times. They had a more youthful, tail-finned look that was "radical" for a once-upon-a-time bread-and-butter car. "'57 Chevrolet! Sweet, smooth and sassy," said one ad.

All V-8 models, except those with stick shift, carried a new 283-cid V-8, which offered up to 283 hp in "super" fuel-injected format. All Chevrolets with a V-8 had large, V-shaped hood and deck lid ornaments (which were gold on Bel Airs). Very few cars carried the "fuel-injection" nameplate.

A total of seven V-8s were available and some were quite rare. Five of the 283s ranged from fairly hot to scalding. A four-barrel carburetor and dual exhausts gave the 220-hp Turbo-Fire 220 more muscles to flex. Dual four-barrel carbs were featured on the Turbo-Fire 245 V-8. Fitted with a Rochester mechanical fuel-injection setup, the Ramjet 250 version of the 283 engine was another choice. Next in horsepower was the Super Turbo-Fire 270, which combined dual Quadrajet carbs with a higher 9.5:1 com-

pression ratio. Chevy's legendary one-horsepower-per-cubic-inch Super Ramjet 283 was the top option combining the Rochester F.I. system with a 10.5:1 compression ratio. It was awesome and Chevrolet promoted this solid-lifter fuel-injection V-8 as the first American production-car engine to provide one horsepower per cubic inch of displacement.

Chevy tried to stay conservative when hyping horsepower in 1957 and there was a good reason for this. On April 10, a New Hampshire state senator made national news with charges that the auto industry was "engaged in a ridiculous and dangerous horsepower race." By June 6, the board of directors of the Automobile Manufacturers Association recommended to member companies that they take no part in auto racing or other competitive events involving tests of speed and that they refrain from suggesting speed in passenger car advertising or publicity. So, Chevy ads mentioned "V-8s up to 245 hp" and then footnoted information about the 270-hp high-performance engine and 283-hp Ramjet fuel-injection engine in small print.

Model-year production for 1957 peaked at 1,515,177 cars.

Jerry Heasley

1961 IMPALA SS AND 409

When it comes to big Chevy muscle cars, the first Impala SS with optional 409-cube big-block V-8 might be the purest strain of the breed. A big engine stuffed in a small car is the classic formula for a muscle car and the '61 Chevy Impala was, in relative terms, a downsized car. This gave the big-block versions super-high-performance abilities. For example, the SS two-door hardtop with a 409-cid/360-hp engine was good for 0-to-60 mph in 7.8 seconds and a 15.8-second quarter-mile.

The very first SS option could be ordered for Impala two-door sedans, four-door sedans and hardtops and no "factory assembly" was required. The package was strictly a dealer-installed item, costing around $54 for a few basic ingredients like "SS" emblems, a padded dash, spinner wheel covers, power steering, power brakes, heavy-duty springs and shocks, sintered metallic brake linings, a 7,000-rpm tachometer, 8.00 x 14 narrow whitewall tires, a dashboard grab bar and a chrome shift housing for the floor-shifted four-speed gear box.

Two V-8 engines were available at prices between $344 and about $500. The Turbo-Thrust 348-cid big-block came with 11:25 compression in 340-hp (four-barrel carburetor) and 350-hp (three two-barrel carburetor) versions. A new 409-cid Turbo-Fire engine was available with 360 hp (four-barrel), 380 hp (three two-barrel) or 409 hp (dual quad) options. It had 11:1 compression. A four-speed close-ratio transmission was $188 extra.

Some Chevy experts warn that the 1961 Impala SS is not the easiest car to restore. Only 456 Impalas were fitted with the "SS" package (including 142 with 409-cid engines), so parts are hard to find. This is something to consider if you have your heart set on becoming a Super Sport buyer. But take heart, because a 409-cid '61 Chevy without SS equipment is also a desirable muscle car.

According to the Standard Catalog of Chevrolet 1912-2003, a 1961 Bel Air sport coupe with the 409-cid/409-hp engine zipped down the quarter-mile in 12.83 seconds. Don Nicholson was also Top Stock Eliminator at the 1961 National Hot Rod Association's Winternationals behind the wheel of a 409/409 Chevy.

Jerry Heasley

1962 BEL AIR 409

"She's so fine my 409!" Remember the song? "Gonna save my pennies and save my dimes. Gonna buy me a 409, 409, 409."

What yearning that Beach Boys pop hit lit in teenagers of the early 1960s. Save your pennies and save your dimes and buy yourself a 409, could it be true? Not really, but put in enough hours in the grocery store or as a pump jockey at the local Esso station, mow a few lawns on the side, get a little help from Dad on the down payment and maybe, just maybe, you could buy one. That is, if your dealer would sell a kid a 409. Most local dealers refused. They didn't want a kid getting killed in a car they had sold. A 409 was killer fast!

The 409 engine could be ordered in about anything Chevrolet built, even station wagons, but the heart-stopping combination was a 409 in a "bubble top" Bel Air two-door hardtop. This body style got its nickname from the vast sweeps of front and rear window glass and was a better pick than the imitation convertible Impala hardtop due to its lighter weight. Fit the

409 with a close-ratio four-speed manual transmission, and in the stoplight grand prix nobody else would even come close (unless you missed a shift or your contender had slipped a Chrysler Hemi into that chopped Ford coupe). Take that 409 to the Saturday night drags and you'd get your car's value, that and a documented race with some pretty impressive times—like 115 mph at the end of a standing-start quarter-mile.

A 409 would go! Its power rating? How about 409 hp for the dual four-barrel carburetor version. OK, so it's 1962 and you're not into drag racing. You're looking for a car to take out on the highway and eat up the miles. You'll stop a little more often to fill up the fuel tank, but a 409 fitted with tall gears, Chevrolet's optional heavy-duty suspension and sintered metallic brakes would easily cruise with the top European sports sedans. On a long straight stretch you might even get the speedometer needle to nudge the 150-mph mark (the bubble-top body was fairly aerodynamic).

1962 CORVETTE FUEL-INJECTED SEBRING 327

The last straight-axle Vette was the first to offer a 327-cid small-block V-8. There were three versions of the engine and the hottest was part of a package nicknamed after the sports car races at Sebring, Florida. In this format, Vette enthusiasts got the sole fuel-injected version of the new engine. But, that was cause for excitement. It churned out an unbelievable — for the time — 360 hp!

Some say that the high-performance equipment offered for Corvettes of this era were related to the AMA racing ban of 1957 and its effect on Zora Arkus-Duntov. As the story goes, with these competition restrictions, the Corvette's "father" could no longer continue his racing with official factory backing. Therefore, he began to slip some serious racing equipment into the options bin. The story seems plausible, too, when you look at the 1962 Corvette options list. You could not get power steering, power brakes or air conditioning. However, you could add hot "Duntov" camshafts, thermo-activated cooling fans and aluminum-cased transmissions.

Other competition-oriented Corvette "Sebring" extras included 15 x 5.5-inch wheels (no charge), a direct-flow exhaust system (no charge), a 24-gallon fuel tank ($118.40), a four-speed manual gearbox ($188.30), a positraction rear axle ($43.05), sintered-metallic brake linings ($37.70) and heavy-duty suspension ($333.60). The 327-cid/360-hp Rochester fuel-injection engine was $484.20 by itself.

With a 3,080-lb. curb weight, the fuel-injected '62 Vette carried just 8.6 lbs.-per-horsepower (the lowest ratio ever up to that point) and could scat from 0-to-60 mph in just 5.9 seconds. It did the quarter-mile in 14.9 seconds. Until the arrival of the Ford-powered Cobra in late 1962, Corvettes dominated B-production racing in Sports Car Club of America (SCCA) events. This period, in fact, has been called the first "Golden Age" of Corvette racing.

The high-performance image didn't hurt in the showroom. An all-time high of 14,531 Corvettes were manufactured in 1962. However, few had the ready-to-race Sebring package with all the competition-oriented options.

Phil Kunz

1963 IMPALA Z11 427/ IMPALA SS 409

The 1963 Chevrolets promised Jet-Smooth comfort, Jet-Smooth luxury and Jet-Smooth driving excitement. Then there was the Z11. It went like a jet, but it wasn't exactly smooth as it blasted from the "Christmas tree" and left other super stockers coughing in its dust. The Z11 was a monster and it gobbled up the quarter-mile with brutality, rather than the smooth sailing of normal, street-performance Chevy models.

Chevrolet dropped the Bel Air "bubbletop" in 1963. After that, the Impala coupe, with its squared-off roof, became the basis for the RPO Z11 drag-racing package. Only about 57 of these cars were built. All were made specifically for Super/Stock drag-racing competition. Twenty-five Z11s were released by Chevrolet on December 1, 1962. An additional 25 were released on New Year's Day. Seven more were sold later on.

The Z11 option included an aluminum hood, aluminum front fenders, aluminum fender brackets and other lightweight parts. The cars also had no center bumper backing and bracing. All extra insulation was deleted to cut total weight by about 112 lbs. Under the hood was a 427-cid/430-hp V-8 with dual four-barrel carburetors.

Also in 1963, Chevrolet built five Mark II

NASCAR 427 "mystery" engines and used them in racing cars at Daytona Beach. The cars the engines went in won the two 100-mile preliminary races and set the track's new stock-car record. These engines were closely related to the Z11 engines and were also prototypes for the 1966 Chevy 396-cid V-8. The cylinder block deck surfaces were angled to parallel the piston domes. The engines also used a staggered or "porcupine" valve layout. Early in the 1963 model year, General Motors ordered all of its divisions to halt factory support of racing and the mystery-engine project came to a close.

Since most Chevy buyers were not in the market for a Mark II "mystery" engine or a Z11 package, the best option for those interested in a muscular street car was the Impala SS with the extra-cost 409 V-8.

Motor Trend technical editor Jim Wright tested two versions of the Impala SS in the magazine's March 1963 issue. One had the 327-cid V-8. The other had the 409-cid/340-hp engine hooked to a Powerglide two-speed transmission. Even at that, it did 0-to-60 mph in 7.7 seconds and covered the quarter-mile in 15.9 seconds at 88 mph.

It was no Z11, but it was fast for 1963.

Jerry Heasley

1963 CORVETTE STING RAY Z06

Chevrolet's all new Sting Ray for 1963 was hot. It had a glorious new body, broadened in scope with the first Corvette coupe. It had an independent rear suspension and fuel injection and even knock-off wheels. Plus, it had the Z06 racing option.

The Z06 Corvette was impressive for its day and would possibly be as legendary as the L88 is today, except for the superiority of the Cobra, which unexpectedly destroyed Duntov's 1963 Sting Ray party. Ready for sale in October of 1962 — and available strictly on the coupe — the Z06 option consisted of a fuel-injected 327-cid engine, a 36.5-gallon fuel tank, heavy-duty brakes, heavy-duty suspension and knock-off wheels.

The heavy-duty brakes consisted of drums with sintered metallic linings, power assisted and backed by a dual circuit master cylinder. "Elephant ear" scoops rammed fresh air to the drums and cooling fans spun with the hub. Early in the 1963 calendar year, Z06 was expanded to include the really necessary racing part, the 36.5-gallon fuel tank, which fit the back of the coupe body like a pea in a pod. Coded N03, the "big tank" helped make the Corvette competitive in long-distance endurance racing events, such as Daytona.

Curiously, the knock-off wheels, which have become almost synonymous with the 1963 split-window Corvette, leaked due to the porosity of the aluminum and poor sealing at the rims. No more than a dozen coupes and roadsters actually got them. Futhermore, only one Corvette has been documented original with original knock-offs. It was originally picked up at the factory by an independent racer. Edward Schlampp Jr. raced the car in the SCCA A-production class.

Later in the model year, N03 was not mandatory with Z06, so only about 60 of the 199 Z06 Corvettes ended up with the big tank. N03 Corvettes also came with their inner wheel well housings modified to fit larger-than-stock tires.

In 1963, no RPO option was hotter than Z06.

Jerry Heasley

1964 CHEVELLE MALIBU SS 327

Life started out simple enough for the 1964 Chevelle. It was the lowest-priced of the four all-new A-body intermediates from General Motors that model year. The others were the Pontiac Le-Mans, the Olds Cutlass and the Buick Skylark.

A variety of models was offered with the top-of-the-line Malibu two-door hardtop and convertible available with the $170 Super Sport option. This package included bucket seats, a console and appropriate SS badges.

Initial power-plant offerings included the standard 194-cid six, an optional 230-cid six and a pair of old reliable 283-cid V-8s. In V-8 models, the 195-hp two-barrel version was standard. An L77 220-hp version with a four-barrel carburetor was $54 extra.

Nostalgia for the earlier models was fine, but when Pontiac shoved its big 389-cid/325-hp V-8 into GTO-optioned Tempests, the pressure was on to keep up. Oldsmobile answered quickly with a 330-cid/310-hp "police" option for its F-85, which soon evolved into the 4-4-2.

GM had just been through one of its soul-cleansing anti-performance purges in 1963 and Chevrolet, at first, was turned down when it requested that the 327-cid small-block V-8 be approved for use in the Chevelle. GM brass relented and, in quick order, the 250-hp L30 and 300-hp L74 327 V-8s were added to the Chevelle options list at midyear. The former was only $95 over the base 283-cid V-8 and the latter added another $138. Chevy literature even advertised the 365-hp L76 out of the Corvette and some back-door drag racing specials most likely got them.

It seemed that the Chevelle lived right, from its introduction through its value today as a collectible car. A Malibu two-door hardtop listed for $2,484 in base, V-8 form and the convertible at $2,587. Today, show condition convertibles sell for over 10 times their original price and the hardtops only slightly less. Models with four-speed manual gearboxes and SS trim do even better.

Jerry Heasley

1964 CORVETTE L84 "FUELIE"

If you really wanted to burn rubber in an American car in 1964, you wanted a Corvette. And if you wanted to max out your Corvette's potential for outrunning the law, you wanted the L84 option.

This was basically the 300-hp L75 V-8 fitted with Ram-Jet fuel injection. It was good for 375 hp at 6200 rpm and 350 lbs.-ft. of torque at 4400 rpm.

Chevrolet made 8,304 fuel-injected Sting Ray coupes. They sold for $4,252 and up and weighed 2,945 lbs. The $4,037 convertible weighed in at 2,960 lbs. and had a 13,925-unit production run.

Seven exterior colors were available for 1964: Tuxedo Black, Ermine White, Riverside Red, Satin Silver, Silver Blue, Daytona Blue and Saddle Tan. All body colors were available with a choice of black, white or beige soft tops.

All Corvettes built in 1964 had a 327-cid V-8 block with a 4.00 x 3.25-inch bore and stroke. Only 3.2 percent of 1964 Corvettes were sold with the standard three-speed manual transmission. Most — 85.7 percent — were equipped with a four-speed manual transmission. An L84-powered 1964 Corvette could go from 0-to-60 mph in 6.3 seconds and from 0 to 100 mph in 14.7 seconds. It had a top speed of 138 mph.

A "Fuelie" Corvette in 1964? You couldn't beat it, man.

Jerry Heasley

1965 CORVETTE STING RAY

You could make a strong case that the 1965 Corvettes were the high point of the "Sting Ray" era. The 1965 is, most assuredly, a memorable Corvette.

1965 was the only year you could buy a fuel-injected, disc-braked Sting Ray. It was the first year for the big-block and side-mounted exhausts. And with prices starting at $4,106, the 1965 Corvette Sting Ray was also quite a bargain.

Options few European sports cars could match included power steering, power brakes, power windows, air conditioning, AM-FM radio, telescopic steering column and a wood-rimmed steering wheel.

But the performance enthusiast was usually drawn first to the engine and power-train specifications sheet. Standard equipment — and meant for the boulevardiers — was Chevy's tried-and-true 327-cid/250-hp Turbofire V-8. The next step up was a 300-hp version of the 327 and new for '65 was the precursor to the famous LT1. This L79 version of the 327 developed an impressive 350 hp, combining "sizzle with calm, cool behavior." Up next was the most

powerful carbureted 327, putting out 365 advertised horses.

A legend since 1957, Ram-Jet fuel injection made its final appearance in 1965. At $538, fuel injection was an expensive option, but it made the 327-cid V-8 a 375-hp world-class stormer. It was the ultimate small block.

The introduction, in April 1965, of the 396-cid big-block V-8 marked the beginning of a new era for the Corvette. The 396 was made available at the same time in full-sized Chevrolets and Chevelles. Rated at 425 hp and priced at only $292.70, the 396 made the fuel-injected Corvette seem superfluous in those days of cheap, high-octane gasoline.

The big-block Corvettes could be immediately identified by the "power bulge" on the hood. Introduced at the same time as the 396 was a new $134.50 option, side-mounted exhausts.

Although the fuel-injected Corvette remained through the end of the 1965 model year, it was not widely available and was quietly dropped when the '66s made their appearance.

Jerry Heasley

1965 CHEVELLE Z16

The '65 Chevelle Z16 was an awesome muscle car that kind of sneaked out in the style of the first GTO. At first, it looked like Chevy was ignoring the clamor for a big-block Chevelle when it made a new 396-cid engine available for two other bow-tie products.

The announcements took place at the General Motors Proving Grounds in Mesa, Arizona, Chevy's all-new Caprice luxury car got a 325-hp version. At the same time, a 425-hp, solid-lifter 396 was made optional in the Corvette.

It seemed like the Chevelle had been overlooked, but nothing could be further from the truth. Through a "secret" program, Chevrolet made a 375-hp 396 available in a special Chevelle Malibu SS 396 model. Chevrolet chose not to advertise this hot car at first, since extremely limited production was anticipated.

Why was production so limited, when the latest GTO was setting sales records and Chevy enthusiasts were wild for a 396-powered muscle Chevelle? Well, the new Malibu SS 396 (RPO Z16) was a hurry-up car that pushed the Chevelle into the big-block muscle car leagues, but its special engineering came at a high cost.

On the surface, the Z16 looked, quite simply, like a big-block Chevelle with the new porcupine-head 396 dropped in. In reality, the Z16 was much more. Underneath, it was a heavy-duty machine that was much more like a big car than an intermediate model. Chevrolet wasn't quite ready to turn it out in mass quantities.

The SS 396 coupe used a convertible frame filled with rear suspension reinforcements and two additional body mounts. Its big power-assisted brakes came from the larger cars, with 11-inch-diameter drums front and rear.

Every Z16 came out as a Chevelle Malibu SS Sports Coupe (Fisher Body style No. 13837). All of the cars were coupes — there were no convertibles. The 375-hp 396 was the L37 engine option, with special left- and right-side exhaust manifolds to fit the engine bay. The engine was linked to a four-speed Muncie gearbox with a 2.56:1 first gear. No cars with an automatic transmission were built.

Exactly 201 of the Chevelle Z16s were built for 1965. In 1966, Chevrolet was "geared up" with an SS 396 Chevelle that was easier to order and available to the general public.

Jerry Heasley

1966 CHEVY II NOVA SS

A Chevy II with a big motor stuffed in it was the quintessential 1960s muscle car: not big on exterior flashiness; no big styling bells and whistles to take your breath away; no hint that it was capable of blowing the leaves off the trees.

But these were some "Plain Jane" machines that could fight!

In the early '60s compact-car race, Ford's Falcon was hot and Chevrolet's Corvair was not. By '62, Chevy had a more conventional Chevy II to fight the Falcon with. A lot of folks compared it to the '55 Chevy, but it didn't have a hot motor to go with its just-right size and looks.

By '63, Chevrolet offered a Super Sport option for the Nova sport coupe and ragtop. The SS package included amenities such complete instrumentation, an electric clock, a deluxe steering wheel, bucket seats and full wheel covers, plus special trim and emblems.

The '66 Chevy II was significantly restyled and engines available for SS Novas included a 327-cid/350-hp V-8 with a staggering 11.0:1 compression ratio. In essence, this was a "factory hot rod."

Racecar tuner Bill Thomas had constructed a hot rod Nova two years earlier. He dubbed it the "Bad Bascomb." It had Corvette indepen-dent rear suspension. The factory car had a stock chassis, but it was still hot enough to make your eyes water.

The 327 was a small-block engine derived from the 283. It had a 4.00 x 3.35-inch bore and stroke. The 275-hp RPO L30 edition had a 10.51 compression ratio, hydraulic valve lifters and a single four-barrel carburetor. It generated 275 hp at 4800 rpm and 355 lbs.-ft. of torque at 3200 rpm. The hotter RPO L79 version featured an 11.0:1 compression ratio teamed with the hydraulic lifters and single four-barrel. It cranked out peak horses at 5200 rpm and developed 360 lbs.-ft. of torque at 3600 rpm.

Car Life magazine (May 1966) tested the L79 Nova equipped in true muscle-car-era fashion with a four-speed manual gearbox, limited-slip differential, power steering and brakes, heavy-duty suspension, air conditioning, deluxe bucket seats, a console and full instrumentation. The Corvette engine and other options raised the price from $2,480 to $3,662.

The car did 0-to-60 mph in 7.2 seconds and handled the quarter-mile in 15.1 seconds at 93 mph. The magazine criticized steering and braking, but not its all-out performance and top speed of 123 mph!

Jerry Heasley

1966 CHEVELLE SS 396

The SS 396 wasn't Spartan by any means, but it certainly seemed to be built more for "go" than "show."

Like other Chevelles, the SS models — coupe and ragtop — had a new cigar-shaped body with "lean-forward" front fenders. Two-door Chevelles rode on a just-right-size 115-inch wheelbase and had an overall length of 197 inches. The front and rear tread were both 58 inches wide.

The SS 396s were clearly aimed at muscle car fans willing to spend $2,276 for a sport coupe (two-door hardtop) or $2,984 for a convertible. Together, the two body styles accounted for 72,272 assemblies. More than one enthusiast magazine made comparisons between the SS 396 and hot-rodded '55 Chevys.

The 396-cid V-8 belonged to Chevy's big-block engine family. Essentially a de-stroked 409 with a 4.09 x 3.76-inch bore and stroke, this size engine was standard equipment in the muscular SS. However, it was offered in three configurations.

The standard SS 396 engine was the RPO L35 version with 325 hp at 4800 rpm and 410 lbs.-ft. of torque at 3200 rpm. It had a 10.25:1 compression ratio and single exhausts. The SS kit also included twin simulated hood intakes, ribbed color-accented sill and rear fender lower moldings, a black-out style SS 396 grille, black rear cove accents and "Super Sport" script plates on the rear fenders. An all-vinyl bench seat interior was standard.

Next up the rung was the RPO L34 version of the 396, which shared its cylinder head and compression ratio with the L35 version, but had certain upgrades such as a forged-alloy crankshaft, dual exhausts, a higher-lift cam and chrome piston rings. These helped raise its output to 360 hp at 5200 rpm and 420 lbs.-ft. of torque at 3600 rpm. The 360-hp SS 396 Sport Coupe did 0-to-60 mph in 7.9 seconds and the quarter-mile in 15.5 seconds.

Top option in the SS 396 lineup was the RPO L78 engine, a midyear release that was probably installed in less than 100 cars. It had an 11.0:1 compression ratio, fatter tailpipes, a hotter slide-lifter cam and other go-fast goodies that jacked its output number to 375 hp at 5600 rpm and 415 lbs.-ft. at 3800 rpm. Cars with this engine could do 0-to-60 mph in about 6.5 seconds.

Jerry Heasley

1966 CORVETTE 427

If there was one car that seemed specially designed to make the cops look slow in the mid-1960s, it was the big-block Corvette.

And one thing is for sure: if you decided to put your foot down to the floor on this insane little beast, you'd best hang on. This was not a car for the faint of heart.

When *Car Life* magazine did a comparison between two '67 Corvettes, it picked one car with a 327-cid V-8 and automatic and a second car with the 427-cid big-block V-8 and a four-speed manual gearbox. The latter vehicle was accurately described as, "a muscular, no-nonsense, do-it-right-now hustlecar." The editors added, "A drive in the 427 can convince anyone with a drop of sporting blood in his veins that an over-abundance of power can be controllable and greatly invigorating."

The basic format of the Corvette Sting Ray had been established by the classic 1963 model. For 1967, the overall appearance was cleaned up and the front fender had five functional, vertical air louvers that slanted forward towards their upper ends.

The new 427-cid V-8 came in 390- and 425-hp versions. *Car Life* tested the heftier version

and found that it had power peak at a lower rpm and a wider range of torque delivery. This made the maximum muscle option more compatible to everyday driving, but didn't seem to hamper its quarter-mile capabilities. The 425-hp engine featured strong cam timing, special exhaust headers, a transistorized ignition system, solid lifters and a big four-barrel Holley carburetor. The 390-hp big-block initially came hooked to a mandatory wide-ratio four-speed manual gearbox and the 425-hp job came attached to a close-ratio four-speed stick. A modified Powerglide automatic was scheduled as a midyear option for the 390-hp engine only.

Car Life's 427/425 Corvette was a ragtop to boot. Its as-tested price tag of $5,401 included a Positraction rear axle, tinted windshield, transistor ignition, AM/FM radio, telescoping steering shaft, 7.75-15 UniRoyal Laredo gold stripe nylon tires, the close-ratio four-speed, power brakes, power steering and power windows. With a curb weight of 3,270 lbs. it had an 8.5:1 weight-to-power ratio. Zero-to-60 mph came in just 5.7 seconds and the quarter-mile was covered in 14 seconds with a terminal speed of 102 mph.

Jerry Heasley

1967 CAMARO SS 350/SS 396

Was there a cooler car in 1967 than the new Camaro SS, with its hot engine menu, sweet pony car profile and killer nose stripe?

Just as the Mustang was based on the Falcon, the Camaro was based on the Chevy II Nova. That meant it could accommodate all kinds of muscular Chevy V-8s. To Chevy lovers, the term Super Sport equated to a muscle car, so the high-performance Camaro utilized the same "SS" designation as its bigger brothers.

An extensive lineup of engines was offered for Chevy's late-breaking contender in the pony car market and the initial offering for muscle car maniacs was a hot new small-block RPO L48 V-8 with 350 cubic inches and 295 hp. You could order it only with the SS 350 package, which included a raised hood with non-functional finned louvers, nose stripe, special ornamentation, fat red-stripe tires and a stiff suspension. Best of all, you got all this for $211.

A heavy-duty three-speed manual transmission was standard in the Camaro SS and options included a two-speed Powerglide automatic or a four-speed manual gear box. There was also a wide variety of rear axle ratios including 2.73:1, 3.07:1, 3.31:1, 3.55:1, 3.73:1, 4.10:1, 4.56:1 and 4.88:1. *Car and Driver* tested an SS 350 at 0-to-60 mph in 7.8 seconds and the quarter-mile in 16.1 seconds at 86.5 mph. *Motor Trend* needed 8 seconds to get to 60 mph, but did the quarter in 15.4 at 90 mph.

On November 26, 1966, Chevy released a pair of 396-cid big-block V-8 options: The RPO L34, which was priced at $235 with the SS package, produced 325 hp. The RPO L78 ($550 including SS goodies) produced an advertised 375 hp.

Motor Trend tested an L35 SS 396 Camaro with four-speed gearbox at 6 seconds for 0-to-60 mph and a 14.5-second quarter-mile at 95 mph. Car Life (May 1967) drove a similar car with Powerglide and registered a 6.8-second 0-to-60 time and 15.1-second quarter-mile at 91.8 mph.

Since a total of 34,411 Super Sports were built and 29,270 were SS 350 models, that leaves 5,141 that were built as SS 396s.

1967 CAMARO Z/28

"Win on Sunday, sell on Monday" was the automakers' creed in the super '60s. In the Camaro's case, in '67, the Sports Car Club of America's new Trans-Am "sedan" racing series was the place to strut your stuff.

In Trans-Am Cup competition, engine size was capped at 305 cubic inches, so the various companies strived to develop the most muscular motor they could within this "formula." Chevy's Vince Piggins decided the answer was to create a Camaro powered by a maximum-output small-block V-8. The Z/28 was the result of this effort.

RPO Z/28 was a performance equipment package designed to make the Camaro a contender in Trans-Am events. It was introduced November 26, 1966, during the American Road Race of Champions at Riverside Raceway in California.

Chevrolet used a 283-cid V-8 in the pilot version, but that was too far below the 305-cid engine-displacement limit to be a winner. In the production car, Chevrolet combined the 327-cid block with the 283-cid crankshaft and came up with a 302-cid V-8. By playing with other high-performance parts like a giant four-barrel carb, an aluminum high-rise intake and L79 Corvette heads, they got this motor to crank out about 350 hp and 320 lbs.-ft. of torque at 6200 rpm. However, to play it safe, the Z/28 was advertised at 290 hp at 5800 rpm and 290 lbs.-ft. of torque at 4200 rpm.

The basic Z/28 package listed for $358, but other options were mandatory with the car and jacked the price up to where a typical Z/28 sold for at least $4,200. The price included a heater, but air conditioning was not available. And for those with serious racing in mind, even the heater could be deleted.

The Z/28 performed very well and, since it was designed for competitive road racing, it had terrific handling and braking to go with its impressive straight-line acceleration. The 1967 first-year model could move from 0-to-60 mph in 6.7 seconds and did the quarter-mile in an amazing 14.9 seconds at 97 mph. Its top speed was 124 mph.

Jerry Heasley

1967 IMPALA SS 427

In 1967, with Chevelle sales soaring on the SS 396's muscle reputation, Chevrolet concluded that high performance could help to sell big cars. This led to the Impala SS 427, a full-size juggernaut that looked big enough to trample any little coupe or pony car it could catch.

To understand the SS 427's role in the product mix, it's important to remember that the Chevelle SS 396 was more than a Malibu with Super Sport trim. Malibus were not available with the big Turbo-Jet V-8, while SS 396s came only that way. That made the SS 396 exclusive. Its real job was establishing a high-performance identity that would spur sales of the less costly Chevelles it resembled.

Similarly, the Impala SS 427 was intended to be an "image" car, though one of larger proportions. While the 427-cid engine was made available in other Chevrolets, only the SS 427 came with a full assortment of muscle-car goodies. They included special badges and engine call-outs, a Corvette-inspired power dome hood, larger wheels, a stiffer suspension and standard red-stripe tires.

When first introduced, SS 427 features were optional for two body styles in the separate 1967

Impala SS series. Regular Super Sport equipment included vinyl-clad Strato bucket seats, black grille finish, wheelhouse moldings, black lower body and deck lid accents, badges and specific wheel covers. A second option, coded RPO L36, turned the SS into an SS 427. This $316 package included the SS 427 trim and a 385-hp 427 Turbo-Jet V-8.

Ordering this option required the buyer to add at least the heavier-duty M13 three-speed manual gearbox. For additional go-power, an M20 four-speed or Turbo-Hydra-Matic could be specified, as could a more powerful 425-hp engine. Out of a total run of 76,055 Impala Super Sports, only 2,124 were SS 427s.

Viewing any SS 427 as a muscle car depends on one's definition of the species. The '67 version was road tested at 8.4 seconds for 0-to-60 mph and 15.8 seconds for the quarter-mile. That's just slightly slower than a 1970 SS 396 Chevelle with 350 hp, which isn't bad at all for a full-sized Chevy

Simply put, if you wanted a big car that screamed, the 427 Impala SS was right in your wheelhouse.

Jerry Heasley

1967 CHEVROLET II NOVA SS

This boxy, but neat-looking Chevy compact continued to make an excellent muscle car when equipped with the right extras. In the January 1967 *Motor Trend*, "Tex" Smith noted, "The fattest parts catalog of all is authored by Chevrolet, but with it comes the sad tale of yanking power options from some of the lines, notably Corvair and Chevy II, to the extent that one wonders if Ralph Nader has been secretly elected to the board of directors."

Smith pointed out that the maximum output engine for the '67 Nova SS was a 327-cid/275-hp V-8 that had 75 hp less than the top 1966 engine option. This four-barrel motor with 10.25:1 compression generated peak horsepower at 4800 rpm and put out 355 lbs.-ft. of torque at 3200 rpm. Tex did point out, however, that the Nova SS retained all of its 1966 gearing selections and was "surprisingly alert," despite all the changes Chevrolet had made.

The Nova got only minor changes for its second year in the marketplace. There was a new anodized aluminum grille that had a distinct horizontal-bars motif with a Chevy II nameplate on the driver's side. The Super Sport — or SS — series continued to be available as an upper line in the Nova model range.

The Nova SS sport coupe had a suggested base price of $2,467 and weighed 2,690 lbs. Appearance items included with the SS ranged from a special black-accented grille and specific Super Sport full wheel covers to body and wheelhouse moldings. Naturally, there were SS badges in several locations. The interior featured all-vinyl trim with front Strato bucket seats, a three-spoke steering wheel and a floor shift trim plate.

The motivation for the power reduction was the new Camaro, which was actually based on the Chevy II/Nova. Chevrolet did not want a hot, Corvette-engined Nova stealing muscle car fans away from the new pony car. In the end, the people spoke and a lot of parts managers were kept busy ordering Camaro bits for smart Nova owners. Total production of the Nova SS was 10,100 units.

Jerry Heasley

1967 CHEVELLE SS 396

Gearheads were digging the power-packed Chevelles in the late 1960s. Even in an "off" year like 1967, Chevy cranked out more than 63,000 copies of its midsize favorite.

The mid-size 1967 Chevelle continued on with a cigar-shaped body and forward-thrusting front fenders. The radiator grille had more prominent horizontal bars. The prices for the SS 396 coupe jumped to $2,825 and the SS 396 convertible's price increased by the same amount to $3,033. Annual production of Chevelle SS 396s fell a bit, with 63,006 being made.

Chevelle Super Sport models again had twin simulated hood air intakes, ribbed color-accented sill and rear fender lower moldings, a black-out style SS 396 grille and rear cove accents and "Super Sport" script plates on the rear fenders. Specific SS wheel covers were included, along with red-stripe tires. An all-vinyl bench seat interior was standard.

The 325-hp engine (RPO L35) was carried over as the base choice in 1967. The RPO L34 version was also offered again, but its horse-power rating dropped to 350 hp at 5200 rpm. The L78 375-hp version of the 396-cid V-8 was not listed on Chevy specifications sheets, but it was possible to purchase the components needed to "build" this option at your Chevy dealer's parts counter. The total cost of everything needed to upgrade a 350-hp engine to a 375-hp job was $475.80.

SS 396 buyers could get the 325-hp engine with a standard heavy-duty three-speed manual transmission, a four-speed manual gearbox, Powerglide automatic (or later in the year, Turbo-Hydra-Matic). There was a choice of nine axle ratios from 3.07:1 to 4.10:1, but specific options depended upon transmission choice. The 350-hp engine came with the heavy-duty three-speed manual, wide- or close-ratio four speeds or Powerglide. There were eight rear axle ratios from 3.07:1 to 4.88:1, but you could not get all of them with every engine and transmission setup.

The 1967 SS 396 sport coupe with 375 hp did 0-to-60 mph in 6.5 seconds and did the quarter-mile in 14.9 seconds.

Jerry Heasley

1967 CORVETTE 427

In 1967, if you spotted a Corvette with a big old hood scoop facing forward ... well, you probably didn't want to doing any racing for money. Unless you had a big-block Corvette yourself!

Some consider the 1967 the best looking of the early Sting Rays. Its styling, although basically the same as in 1966, was a bit cleaner. The same egg-crate style grille with Argent Silver finish was carried over. The same smooth hood seen in 1966 was re-used. The crossed flags badge on the nose of the 1967 Corvette had a widened "V" at its top. On the sides of the front fenders were five vertical and functional louvers that slanted towards the front of the car.

The Corvette "427," with its own funnel-shaped, power bulge on the hood, had been introduced in 1966. Its big-block V-8 was related to Chevrolet's 427-cid NASCAR "mystery" racing engine and the production-type Turbo-Jet 396. A 427-cid/435-hp 1967 Corvette convertible carried on 7.7 lbs. per horsepower. It could hit 60 mph in 5.5 seconds and do the quarter-mile in 13.8 seconds. Three four-speed manual gearboxes—wide-ratio, close-ratio and heavy-duty close-ratio—were optional. A desirable extra was side-mounted exhaust pipes.

Cars with 427s got a different power bulge hood and more top horsepower (435) when fitted with three two-barrel carburetors. The special hood had a large, forward-facing air scoop, usually with engine call-outs on both sides.

There were four versions of the 427 in 1967. The regular L36 was nearly unchanged from mid-1965. Next came the L68, with 400 hp. The Tri-Power L71 delivered 435 hp. Extremely rare (only 20 were built) — and off in a class by itself — was the aluminum-head L88. This powerhouse was officially rated at only 430 hp, but really developed nearly 600 hp!

Jerry Heasley

1968 CAMARO SS 396

It takes an expert to tell the difference between the first Camaro and the second one at a glance. Only minor changes were made for '68. The front end received subtle changes and ventless side windows were introduced. A new Astro-Ventilation system was relied on to bring fresh air into the cockpit. Rectangular parking lamps replaced the square ones of 1967 and side marker lamps, required by new federal laws, were added. The grille insert was finished in silver instead of black. Front and rear spoilers were now optional.

Chevrolet expanded the number of Camaro SS options to five. The SS 350 had the same hood as in 1967, but the SS 396s had a unique hood with four non-functional intake ports on either side. The SS 396 represented the ultimate Camaro production car for muscle car lovers and it came in four versions. The L35, which produced 325 hp at 4800 rpm and 410 lbs.-ft. of torque at 3200 rpm, was the most popular with 6,752 installations. Second in popularity was the L78 edition, which 4,889 buyers ordered. It produced 375 hp at 5600 rpm and 415 lbs.-ft.

at 3600 rpm. The L34 version, which generated 350 hp at 5200 rpm and 415 lbs.-ft. of torque at 3600 rpm went into 2,018 cars. Rarest was the L89 version with aluminum heads. It was conservatively rated for 375 hp at 5600 rpm and 415 lbs.-ft. at 3600 rpm, but due to its high $896 price tag drew only 311 orders.

In 1968, the L35 option cost $63.20 over the base 350-cid Camaro SS engine. The L34 was $184.35 extra and the L78 was $316 extra. Other desirable SS options included the M20 and M21 four-speed manual gearboxes, both for $195.40, the M22 heavy-duty four-speed manual gearbox for $322.10, M40 Turbo-Hydra-Matic transmission for $221.80, a ZL2 cowl-induction hood for $79, a JL8 four-wheel disc brakes package for $500.30, a U16 tachometer for $52.70, U17 special instrumentation for $94.80 and G80 Positraction for $42.15.

Car Life magazine road tested a 375-hp SS 396 with cold-air induction and other muscle car hardware. It did 0-to-60 mph in 6.8 seconds and the quarter-mile in 14.77 seconds at 98.72 mph. Its top speed was 126 mph.

Jerry Heasley

1968 CAMARO Z/28

Even though only 602 copies were made, the Chevrolet Camaro Z/28 Special Performance Package made a strong impact on muscle car fans in 1967, especially considering that it was made primarily for road racing and had only half of a selling season in the marketplace. While it did not catch the Ford Mustang in sales, the Camaro was not that far behind the original, four-year-old pony car in racing results and that's something that rapidly enhanced the Z/28's appeal to enthusiasts.

As in its first year, the 1968 Z/28 came only as a two-door sport coupe. You could not order it with air conditioning or with an automatic transmission. In fact, you had to order a four-speed manual gearbox, as well as optional power-assisted front disc brakes. Also included was a dual exhaust system, deep-tone mufflers, special front and rear suspensions, a heavy-duty radiator, a temp-controlled de-clutching fan, quick-ratio steering, with 15 x 6-inch wheel rims, E70 x 15 white-letter tires and special body striping.

Below its hood, the Z/28 featured the same hot 302-cid Chevy small-block V-8 that had been used in 1967. This engine had an easy-to-remember 4.0 x 3.0-inch bore and stroke. It carried a single 800-cfm Holley four-barrel carburetor on top of a special intake manifold and had 11.0:1 compression pistons. Maxium horsepower was 290 at 5800 rpm and it generated 290 lbs.-ft. of torque at 4200 rpm.

In addition to the standard Muncie four-speed, a Muncie close-ratio four-speed gearbox was the only option. A 3.73:1 rear axle was standard and six other ratios were optional: 3.07:1, 3.31:1, 3.55:1, 4.10:1, 4.56:1 and 4.88:1.

The 1968 Camaro Z/28 was road tested by three major magazines. It was written up in the June issue of *Road & Track*, which recorded a 0-to-60 time of 6.9 seconds and a 14.9-second quarter-mile at 100 mph. *Car Life* did its test in July '68 recording a 7.4-second 0-to-60 run and a 14.85-second quarter-mile at 101.4 mph. *Car and Driver* really caught the attention of enthusiasts with its 5.3-second 0-to-60 and a 13.77-second quarter-mile at 107.39 mph! No wonder Z/28 sales started to take off. Chevrolet put together 7,199 examples of its Camaro road racer.

Phil Kunz

1968 NOVA SS 396

The "Gen II" Chevy II/Nova is becoming one of the hottest collectible Chevrolets in today's youth-oriented enthusiast marketplace. Starting in '68, Chevy's "senior compact" was restyled to resemble a small Chevelle. The re-skinned Nova was perched on a 111-inch wheelbase and you would need a 183.3-inch long measuring tape to gauge the distance between the front and rear bumpers. The new "Coke-bottle" body was 72.4 inches wide and 52.6 inches high. The coupe weighed about 2,850 lbs.

The new Nova appeared to be anything but a real muscle car when it made its first appearance in the fall of 1967. At that time, only two body styles were offered and Super Sport equipment was now considered an option package.

But the car's image began to change by the time the sales year was half over. The Nova's new stub frame was borrowed from the Camaro parts bin and, by January 1968, Nova buyers were being offered some new engine options, since big-block V-8s fit comfortably in the new power plant cradle.

For small-block performance fans, the milder 327-cid V-8 with 275 hp was carried over from the last two years. Joining it were two hotter small-block-based options. These were the new 350-cid/295-hp V-8 with a 10.25:1 compression ratio and a 325-hp version of the 327 with 11.0:1 compression. However, the really big news was the availability of the 396-cid V-8, which was now being offered for serious muscle-car lovers.

Sharing 4.094 x 3.76-inch bore and stroke dimensions and a single four-barrel carburetor setup, the 396-cid big-block V-8s came two ways. The first version had a 10.25:1 compression ratio. It generated 350 hp at 5200 rpm and 415 lbs.-ft. of torque at 3200 rpm. The second version had an 11:1 compression ratio and delivered 375 hp at 5600 rpm and 415 lbs.-ft. of torque at 3600 rpm. Chevrolet didn't advertise this engine, which provided 6-second 0-to-60 mph performance and was good for 14-second quarter-mile runs.

The Nova's standard transmission was a column-mounted three-speed. Options included a three-speed with floor shifter, a four-speed stick (commonly ordered by muscle car fans) and Powerglide automatic.

The Nova SS had a base price of about $2,995. Chevrolet built a total of just 5,571 cars carrying the Nova SS package this year. Of those, only 234 had the milder 396-cid engine and 667 had the 396-cid/375-hp option.

Phil Kunz

1968 CHEVELLE SS 396

"To say Chevelle is all-new is an understatement," boasted the 1968 sales catalog for Chevy's hot mid-sized model. "It is brilliantly original for '68! Out-of-the-ordinary roof lines, front fenders and taillight arrangements. The latest look in long-hood/short deck styling. Two wheelbases: 112 inches for coupes and convertibles, 116 inches for sedans and wagons. An expansive grille to emphasize wider tread."

The new '68 Chevelle body had a "wrapover" front end to give it a distinctive character. It also had the long-in-front-short-in-back styling that was all the rage in this era. As with other '68 GM intermediates, the use of two wheelbases allowed for sportier-looking Chevelle coupes and ragtops.

The high-performance SS 396 was a separate series in 1968. It included a sport coupe base-priced at $2,899 and a convertible priced at $3,102. Both had the shorter wheelbase, of course. Overall length, at 197.1 inches, was just a tad longer than in 1967, even though the wheelbase was downsized by 3 inches. Front and rear tread widths were also up an inch to 59 inches. The new Chevelle was also nearly an inch taller at 52.7 inches.

The SS 396 models were made even more distinctive by the use of matte black finish around the full lower perimeter of the bodies,

except when the cars were finished in a dark color. Other SS features included F70 x 14 wide-oval red-stripe tires, body accent stripes, a special twin-domed hood with simulated air intakes, "SS" badges, vinyl upholstery and a heavy-duty three-speed transmission with floor-mounted shifter.

The standard engine was the RPO L35 version of the 396-cid V-8, which had an advertised 325 hp. The RPO L34 version with 350 hp was $105 extra and was the only option early in the year. That situation didn't last long, as competitors like the 375-hp Dodge Charger R/T and 350-hp Olds 4-4-2 were soon stealing sales away from Chevrolet based on horsepower alone.

At midyear, Chevy re-released the RPO L78 version of the 396 with 375 hp. This option cost $237 more than a base V-8. A '68 SS 396 with this engine and the close-ratio four-speed manual gearbox was road tested from 0-to-60 mph in 6.6 seconds and did the quarter-mile in 14.8 seconds at 98.8 mph.

As in the past, Chevrolet continued to offer the SS 396 with a wide range of transmission and rear axle options. Also standard were finned front brake drums and new bonded brake linings all around. About 57,600 Chevelle SS 396s were made and this total included 4,751 with the L78 engine and 4,082 with the L34 option.

Doug Mitchel

1968 CORVETTE 427

"Corvette '68 . . . all different all over." That's what it said in the sales brochure. It was the Chevy sports car's first major restyling since 1963. The fastback was replaced by a "tunnel-roof" coupe. It featured a removable back window and a two-piece detachable roof section or T-top. The convertible's optional hardtop had a glass rear window.

The front end was more aerodynamic than those on previous Corvettes. As before, the headlights were hidden. They were now vacuum operated, rather than electrically operated. The wipers also disappeared from view when not in use.

Except for the rocker panels, the body sides were devoid of chrome. Conventional door handles were eliminated. In their place were push buttons. The blunt rear deck contained four round taillights with the word Corvette printed in chrome in the space between them. The wrap-around, wing-like rear bumper and license-plate holder treatment resembled that used on the 1967 models.

Chevrolet's big-block, 4.251 x 3.76-inch bore and stroke, 427-cid V-8 was available in the Corvette in four different muscular versions. The least powerful was RPO L36. It had hydraulic valve lifters, a 10:25:1 compression ratio and a single Holley four-barrel carburetor. Its output was 390 hp at 5400 rpm and 460 lbs.-ft. of torque at 3600 rpm.

The second-most powerful 427 was the L68 version, which featured a 10.25:1 compression ratio and three Holley two-barrel carburetors. It produced 400 hp at 5400 rpm and 460 lbs.-ft. of torque at 4000 rpm. Car and Driver tested one of these cars, with a four-speed manual gearbox and 3.70:1 rear axle, in its May 1968 issue. It did 0-to-60 mph in 5.7 seconds and the standing-start quarter-mile in 14.1 seconds at 102 mph. Its top speed was estimated to be 119 mph.

Next came RPO L71, which was a step up the performance ladder with its special-performance, solid-lifter camshaft, three Holley two-barrels and an 11.0:1 compression ratio. It was good for 435 hp at 5800 rpm and 460 lbs.-ft. of torque at 4000 rpm. The L71-powered Corvette could go from 0 to 30 mph in 3.0 seconds, from 0 to 50 in 5.3 seconds and from 0-to-60 in 6.5 seconds. An L71 with a four-speed manual transmission and 3.55:1 rear axle was tested by *Car Life* in June 1968. It did the quarter-mile in 13.41 seconds at 109.5 mph. Its top speed was 142 mph.

The ultimate option was the super-powerful RPO L88 aluminum-head V-8, a $947 option intended primarily for racing. With a 12.50:1 compression ratio it produced an advertised 430 hp at 5200 rpm. However, some said its actual output was 560 hp at 6400 rpm.

Jerry Heasley

1968 SUPER YENKO CAMARO 427

If you wanted a fast, hairy bad-ass car that was ready to go racing right out of the box for 1968, all you had to do was ring up Don Yenko.

Yenko, of Canonsburg, Pa., operated Yenko Sportscars. He was one of the first Chevy dealers to turn Camaros into hot rods. Yenko had previously turned out race-modified Corvettes and Corvairs. After the Camaro was introduced, he dreamed up the "Yenko Super Camaro."

The Yenko SC was essentially a new Camaro V-8 that had the factory small-block replaced with an L72 Corvette engine. This 427 dropped right in the Camaro chassis, then Yenko's racing team mechanics added some heavy-duty bits and did some performance tuning.

Yenko Sportscars offered 427-powered Camaros with two horsepower ratings, 435 or 450. Most cars also received a Yenko data plate, special Yenko badges, 427 emblems and a clone of the "Yenko Stinger" Corvette hood. The basic '67 Yenko Camaro sold for about $3,800. The exact number made that year is unknown. For years, it was thought that 54 cars were made the first year, but some experts feel the total may have been closer to 100.

Don Yenko helped to establish a distributorship called Span, Inc., based in Chicago, that marketed the muscular Camaros nationally. It is likely that many of the cars were actually modified in Chicago. When they were shipped to Canonsburg, Yenko added decals, badges and other special features. To help sell the cars, Yenko supplied sales literature to other performance-car dealers like Fred Gibbs Chevrolet in LeHarpe, Illinois. Drag racer Dickie Harrell, who had previously worked for Nickey Chevrolet of Chicago, became Yenko's Midwest distributor.

Today, Yenko Camaros are worth big bucks in the collector car hobby, and they belong on any list of the best muscle cars ever to prowl the pavement.

Jerry Heasley

1969 CAMARO COPO/427

If you knew the right Chevrolet dealer to see in 1969, you could order up a really nasty Camaro right from the factory.

In '69, the Central Office Production Order (COPO) remained the key to doing an "end run" around GM's anti-performance policies. By quietly using this system, dealer Don Yenko was again able to offer his SYC (Super Yenko Car) Camaro in '69 trim. These cars could be ordered through Yenko's showroom or from two dozen other selected Chevy dealers. The '69s were built as COPO 9561 and 9737 cars.

The '69 edition of the big-block 427 Camaro could be ordered with either the M22 four-speed manual gearbox or the Turbo-Hydra-Matic transmission. In either case, it listed for $4,245. Yenko Camaros were available in a limited range of six body colors: LeMans Blue, Hugger Orange, Olympic Gold, Daytona Yellow, Rallye Green and Fathom Green. Some had vinyl roofs. The base price was around $4,000.

Chevrolet first agreed to building 50 cars,

but dealers asked for more and supposedly 69 of these monsters were made. In '69, $4,000 was considered a huge sum of money for any Chevy and the COPO cars were difficult to move. This was especially true of the famous ZL-1 version created by Fred Gibb Chevrolet. The ZL-1 carried a 430-hp factory rating (565 actual horsepower) and cost more than $7,000. Gibb ordered 50, but had to return them because he couldn't sell the cars. Some sat on the lot for over two years.

Experts estimate that between 199 and 201 COPO cars were built, but some enthusiasts believe that as many as 350 Yenkos were made. There is an old photo of Don Yenko standing in front of a transporter truck and he is holding a handwritten sign that reads "Our 350th Camaro." Hard evidence is lacking, though. The total of 350 could be for all cars built since 1967. No one knows for sure. However, people are beginning to research all of the high-performance dealerships more closely.

Jerry Heasley

1969 CAMARO RS/SS 396

Although not the hottest muscle Camaro of 1969, (some 427-powered COPO cars were also built by the factory) the 396-powered Indy Pace Car is one of the most collected Camaros of all time.

After making a hit at the Indianapolis Motor Speedway during the 1967 Indy 500 race, Chevy was invited to bring the '69 Camaro back for a repeat performance. This time the company decided to take better advantage of sales promotion opportunities by releasing the Z11 pace car replica option package for the model 12467 ragtop.

The genuine Indianapolis 500 Pace Cars were 375-hp SS 396 convertibles with "hugger" orange racing stripes, rear spoilers and black and orange hound's-tooth upholstery. About 100 were built to pace the race and transport dignitaries and members of the press around Indianapolis.

Chevrolet then released the Indy Pace Car replica option and sold 3,674 copycat cars to

the general public. The Z11 was actually just a $37 striping package for convertibles only. But other extras, such as the $296 Super Sport option and the special interior, were also required. Buyers could order the pace car treatment on either RS/SS 350 or RS/SS 396 ragtops. The 350-powered versions are much more common. They had 300 hp.

To qualify as a collectible muscle car, a pace car replica has to have the big-block, which came in four variations. These were the L35 ($63) with 325 hp, the L34 ($184) with 350 hp, the L78 ($316) with 375 hp and the L89 ($711) with aluminum heads and 375 hp. It isn't hard to guess which is rarest and most valuable.

The 375-hp ragtops were good for 7-second 0-to-60 acceleration and could do the quarter-mile in just about 15 seconds, so they have some real muscle to go with their good looks.

The Indy coupes were all built at Norwood, Ohio, and about 200-300 may have been put together.

Jerry Heasley

1969 CAMARO Z/28

By 1969, Chevrolet and the American public were both beginning to catch on to how great the Z/28 was.

Chevy built 602 Camaros with the Z/28 package in the first year of the option — 1967. The Z/28 package was popular from the start and sales leaped to 7,199 cars in 1968. But even divisional brass weren't ready for 1969's larger increase to 20,302 assemblies of Camaros with the Z/28 Special Performance Package.

The Z/28 package was offered only for the Camaro coupe. Some sources say that it came in a basic version priced at $458 and a version with dealer-installed headers for $758. However, there were actually at least six variations. The basic package released September 26, 1967, included the 302 V-8, dual exhausts with deep-tone mufflers, special front and rear suspensions, rear bumper guards, a heavy-duty radiator with a temperature-controlled fan, quick-ratio power steering, 15 x 7 rally wheels, E70 x 15 special white-lettered tires, a 3.73:1 rear axle and special hood and trunk stripes. On October 18, bright engine accents and Z/28 emblems for the grille, front fender and rear panel were added and rally wheels were no longer specified, but wheel trim rings were added.

The 1969 model had an extended model-year run and on September 18, 1969, the package was revised again, with the price going to $522. New ingredients included bright exhaust tips. The final documented changes came on November 3, 1969, and were very minor.

There are many variations between Z/28s, as well as between original cars and the written factory specifications. For example, very-early-in-the-run cars were manufactured with the 1968-style stripes and 15 x 6-inch rally wheels. Buyers ordering a spoiler on the early cars got the 1967-1968 style spoiler. And these cars were the only ones to carry the chambered dual exhaust system.

A well-equipped Z/28 set up for racing could be purchased for under $4,000. *Hot Rod* magazine drove a stock Z/28 through the quarter-mile in 14.34 seconds at 101.35 mph. The editors then bolted on some aftermarket hardware and did it in 13.11 seconds at 106.76 mph.

1969 CAMARO ZL1

In 1968, Chevrolet dealer Fred Gibb was well known to drag racing enthusiasts for his energetic support of their sport. Gibb, the owner of the Fred Gibb Agency of La Harpe, Illinois, talked to Vince Piggins about constructing the "ultimate" muscle car. The idea was to use an all-aluminum 427-cid V-8 in the compact Camaro body to create a Super Stock racing car. Piggins, who is now a high-performance legend, was in charge of such projects for Chevrolet Motor Division.

National Hot Rod Association (NHRA) rules said that a minimum of 50 cars had to be built to qualify the super-hot ZL1 Camaros for competition. Chevrolet General Manager E.M. "Pete" Estes gave Fred Gibbs his word that Chevrolet Motor Division would build the first ZL1s before the end of the year, on the condition that the Illinois dealer would take 50 of the cars at a proposed price of $4,900.

Gibbs accepted Estes' offer and General Motors Central Office Production Order system was utilized to order the cars. The first ZL1s built were a pair of Dusk Blue cars made at the Norwood, Ohio, assembly plant on December 30, 1968. They arrived at the Le Harpe, Illinois, dealership the next day, covered with snow. Unfortunately, the factory invoice price had climbed to $7,269!

All 50 cars that were shipped to Gibbs were virtually identical, except for the choice of color and transmission. They had the COPO 9560 option with the aluminum 427 V-8. Nineteen additional cars were also built for other Chevrolet dealers around the country. The equipment on all 69 cars included the Z22 Rally Sport package, J50 power brakes, N40 power steering, a V10 tachometer, racing style outside rearview mirrors, exhaust resonators, a dual exhaust system with tailpipe extensions, a special steering wheel, F70-15 black sidewall tires with raised gold letters, special lug nuts, special wheel center caps, special identification decals on the hood, grille and rear panel, a special instrument cluster and an extra-wide front valance panel.

According *Super Stock* magazine, the ZL1 Camaro in racing trim could cover the quarter-mile in as little as 10.41 seconds at 128.10 mph. That was with the "stock" Holley 850-cfm carburetor. Driver Dickie Harrell, who raced for the Fred Gibbs dealership, traveled around the country campaigning a ZL1. He took four wins and registered a best performance of 10.05 seconds at 139 mph.

Jerry Heasley

1969 CORVETTE ZL1

There were only two of these awesome beasts ever built, and they are two of the gnarliest American ever built during they heyday of the American muscle car.

The ZL1 was an all-aluminum, 427-cid, Chevy "Rat" engine. Just 69 engines were installed in '69 Camaros, and two somehow wound up in Corvettes.

There were 10-12 engineering test Corvette "mules" built with ZL1s. They were used in magazine road tests, engineering and track evaluations and driven by the likes of Zora Arkus-Duntov and GM VIPs. Of course, these ZL1 evaluation vehicles had to be destroyed — eventually.

In the process, two 'Vettes went out the door as RPO ZL1s. They included a Canary Yellow car with side pipes and a Can-Am White T-top coupe with black ZL1 side stripes.

In 1989, the yellow car, also a T-top, was confiscated by the U.S. government. It had been in the possession of a convicted cocaine dealer serving a sentence in an Alabama prison. Earlier, someone had paid $225,000 for the car, which had 55,317 original miles. The government es-

timated its value at around $500,000, but sold it for the minimum reserve bid of $300,000.

Greg Joseph, a Ph.D of history at Long Beach College, in California, researched ZL1 history. This led him to *Hot Rod* magazine (December 1968), with a cover story on Chevy's new all-aluminum 427. The article told of a "painted-block ZL1" engine in a test Corvette driven by the automotive press. A parenthetical statement added: "And all those guys at the '69 Chevy preview thought it was an L88. Forgot your pocket magnets, right, guys?"

Chevrolet had painted the ZL1s, possibly to hide them from the press, as had been the case with one of the test cars spotlighted in *Hot Rod*.

To the journalists, the ZL1 (a $3,010 assortment of aluminum cylinder block and heads) was a $1,032.15 RPO L88 package. The L88 engine itself was a race option, but in ZL1 metal, it featured thicker walls and main webbing, along with dry-sump lubrication provisions.

It's hard to believe there was a step above the L88 in the muscle-car era, but the ZL1 filled the bill. It still ranks, today, as the wildest RPO engine of its time.

Jerry Heasley

1969 CHEVELLE SS 396/SS 427

You could get two kinds of Chevelle SS's for 1969: cool and fast, or cooler and faster.

There was no separate SS 396 series this year. The Super Sport equipment package became the Z25 option, which was ordered for 86,307 cars.

The popular high-performance option package included the 396-cid/325-hp engine, dual exhausts with oval tailpipes and bright tips, a black-painted grille, bright wheel opening and roof drip moldings, a black-painted rear cove panel, Malibu-style rear quarter end caps, Malibu taillights and taillight bezels, a twin power dome hood, special "SS 396" emblems on the grille (as well as front fenders and rear deck lid) and 14 x 7-inch Super Sport wheels with F70 x 14 white-letter tires.

Three regular production engine options were available and all of these were based on the 396-cid block. The mildest choice was the L34 version, which put out 350 hp and added $121 to the car's window sticker. Next came the L78 version of the 396 with 375 hp and a $253 price tag. A variation of the L78 was the new L78/L89, which was jokingly advertised at 375 hp. The engine's actual output was much higher, thanks to special hardware like a pair of high-performance aluminum cylinder heads.

An extremely rare 1969 engine was a 427-cid V-8 that was made available, in very limited numbers, on a special Central Office Production Order (COPO) basis. These engines came from GM's Tonawanda, New York, factory. Only 358 of the 427s were assembled and most or all of them went to dealer Don Yenko, who had them custom installed in cars sold at his Yenko Sports Car dealership in Canonsburg, Pennsylvania.

A road test of the 1969 SS 396 with 375 hp proved it to be a tad slower than earlier editions, probably due to a slight increase in the car's weight. It moved from 0-to-60 mph in 7.6 seconds and covered the quarter-mile in 15.4 seconds.

Jerry Heasley

1969 CHEVROLET CORVETTE 427

After a year's absence, the Stingray name (now spelled as one word) re-appeared on the Corvette's front fenders in 1968.

By any name, the Corvette with a big block was still a stone cold killer!

The 427-cid/390-hp RPO L36 V-8 was again the starting-point engine for muscle car enthusiasts. Then came RPO L68 for $326.55 extra. It was the same 10.25:1 compression V-8 fitted with three two-barrel carburetors, which upped its output to 400 hp. The 427-cid 435-hp RPO L71 Tri-Power engine also returned in much the same form as 1968. Its price tag was $437.10.

Three ultra-high-performing options began with the RPO L88 V-8. It again included a "power blister" hood. Hot Rod magazine tested an L88 and described it as a "street machine with soul." This year the basic package was $1,032.15 and also required heavy-duty brakes and suspension, transistor ignition and Positraction. The test car — a Stingray convertible — was base priced at $4,583.45, but went out the door at $6,562 as an L88 with a beefy Turbo-Hydra-Matic and 3.36:1 rear axle. It did the quarter-mile in 13.56 seconds at 111.10 mph.

There was also the RPO L89 V-8 for $832.05. This was a solid-lifter version of the 427 with aluminum cylinder heads on the L71 block. It had a 12.0:1 compression ratio, a 435 hp at 5800 rpm rating and produced 460 lbs.-ft. of torque at 4000 rpm.

The ultimate 1969 power option was the aluminum block and aluminum heads RPO ZL1 V-8, which is listed separately. Other 1969 Corvette muscle options included an RPO M20 four-speed manual transmission for $184.80, an RPO M21 four-speed close-ratio manual transmission for $184.80, an RPO M22 heavy-duty close-ratio four-speed manual transmission for $290.40 and an RPO M40 Turbo-Hydra-Matic automatic transmission for $221.80. And of course, what muscle Corvette fan would be caught dead without an RPO N14 side-mount exhaust, which sold for $147.45 in 1969?

For the top engines listed here, the L71 and the L88 were the closest in performance. The L71 made the trip down the quarter-mile in 13.94 seconds at 105.63 mph and the L88 did it in 14.10 seconds at 106.89 mph. The L88 had a top speed of 151 mph.

Jerry Heasley

1970 CAMARO RS/SS 396

Ask some Camaro buffs what their favorite Camaro is, and chances are you'll find someone making an argument for the beloved early-1970s RS models. If they are not the most beloved Camaros ever, they are at least in the conversation.

Due to slow sales of the 1969 Camaros and delays in the design of an all-new replacement, the 1970 model arrived in showrooms very late in the game. In the fall of 1969, Chevrolet dealers had to continue selling leftover '69s until all of the cars were gone. Some of these units were delivered with 1970 titles (depending on state laws), but the true 1970 models — sometimes called "1970 1/2 Camaros"— did not go on sale until Feb. 26, 1970.

When it arrived, the 1970 Camaro had completely revamped styling that made it seem like a GT coupe crafted in Europe. It featured high-intensity headlights, a semi-fastback roofline, a snout-style grille carrying an "egg crate" insert and a much smoother looking rear end. The convertible was gone and the only available body style was the sport coupe. Standard equipment included all General Motors safety features, Starto-Bucket front seats, an all-vinyl interior, carpeting, an Astro-Ventilation system, a left-hand outside rearview mirror, side marker lights and E78-14 bias-belted black sidewall tires. The base V-8 was a 307-cid small block V-8.

RPO Z27 was the Camaro SS option package. It included a 350-cid/300-hp V-8, bright engine accents, power brakes and special body ornamentation.

RPO Z22 was the Rally Sport option package. It included a black-painted grille with a rubber-tipped vertical center bar and resilient body-color grille frame, and the "split" bumper treatment with independent left and right front bumpers,.

The SS 396 Camaro substituted a big-block V-8 for the 350. The 396-cid engine had a 4.126 x 3.76-inch bore and stroke and actually displaced 402 cubic inches, although Chevrolet promoted it as a "396." This engine's advertised horsepower was 350 at 5200 rpm.

Jerry Heasley

1970 MONTE CARLO SS 454

Chevrolet's all-new Monte Carlo was a luxury-personal-performance car based on the 116-inch-wheelbase Chevelle sedan. Even though the Monte Carlo had its own 8-inches-longer frame, many of its chassis parts were interchangeable with those of the Chevelle. The reason for the longer frame was the Monte Carlo's 6-foot-long hood, which was there to enhance its classic look more than anything else. The length wasn't needed to accommodate optional big-block V-8 engines, which fit easily in the new car's engine bay.

Due to the body and frame changes, the Monte Carlo had different weight distribution characteristics than the Chevelle and Chevrolet engineers had to beef up the springs and shocks and install heavier stabilizers. The front stabilizer bar was larger than the Chevelle's and the rear stabilizer bar was of a type available only as an option on the Chevelle SS 396. The SS 454 version of the Monte Carlo came standard with an automatic leveling control system in which the rear shocks had pressurized air bags that extended the shocks as more weight was added to the rear of the car. The Monte Carlo's 60.3-inch front track and 59.3-inch rear track were both wider than those of the Chevelle.

Chevrolet's new 454-cid version of the Turbo-Jet big-block V-8 was available with the SS 454 package only.

The new 454-cid engine had a 4.251 x 4.00-inch bore and stroke, a 10.25:1 compression ratio and a single Rochester 4MV carburetor. It developed 360 hp at 4400 rpm and 500 lbs.-ft. of torque at 3200 rpm. Motor Trend's 3,575-lb. test car had a 3.31:1 axle and moved from 0-to-60 mph in 7.0 seconds flat. The standing-start quarter-mile took 14.9 seconds at 92 mph. Car Life's test car was a bit slower, doing the quarter-mile in 16.2 seconds at 90.1 mph.

With only 2.6 percent of the 1970 Monte Carlos built with the SS 454 option, total production for the year was a mere 3,823 copies of the muscle-car version. That's one reason why a 1970 SS 454 Monte Carlo is now almost worth its weight in gold.

Jerry Heasley

1970 CHEVELLE SS 396

The 1970 Chevelle might have looked a little "fatter" to some critics, but the it was still a hugely popular car and one of the top dogs around with the right engine under the hood.

A horizontally split grille with "blended" dual headlights was new. The SS 396 returned to the product line, but shortly after the manufacturing of 1970 engines started, the bore size of the big-block V-8 was increased from 4.094-inches to 4.125 inches. This increased the engine's actual displacement to 402 cubic inches. In spite of this change, Chevrolet continued to identify the engine as the "Turbo-Jet 396."

The standard version of the "396" V-8 for 1970 was coded RPO L34 and. Despite the modest boost in displacement, it carried the same advertised power rating as in 1969: 350 hp at 5,200 rpm and 415 lbs.-ft. of torque at 3400 rpm. This motor was a $121.15 option.

Also available in the 1970 SS 396 was RPO L78. This optional version of the "396" big-block engine was advertised at 375 hp at 5600 rpm and 415 lbs.-ft. of torque at 3600 rpm. It added $250 to the cost of the car.

The L78/L89 V-8 with large-valve aluminum heads was a pricier ($647.75) option for the SS 396 only. It was also advertised at 375 hp, although that number was used to placate insurance companies and its real output was higher. This solid-lifter engine was rare and adds a lot to the collector value of a Chevelle SS 396 today.

A list of 13 items made up the content of the SS 396 package for 1970. In addition to the 350-hp engine they included: bright engine accents, power front disc brakes, dual exhausts with bright tips, a black-accented grille, wheel opening moldings, a black resilient rear bumper panel, a special domed hood, the F41 heavy-duty suspension, special chassis features, SS identification (including SS emblems on the grille, fenders, rear bumper, steering wheel and door trim), 17 x 7-inch rally wheels (RPO ZL7) and F70 x 14 raised-white-letter tires.

The base price of a 1970 Malibu sport coupe was $2,809 and the cost of the SS package was $445.55. If you added the L78 engine it was $210.65 extra. Chevrolet produced 49,826 of its 1970 Chevelle models with the SS 396 option. With a curb weight of 3,990 lbs., one of the 350-hp cars had to carry about 11.4 lbs. per horsepower. In road testing it was found that it could move from 0-to-60 in 8.1 seconds and cover the quarter-mile in 15.5 seconds.

Jerry Heasley

1970 CHEVROLET CHEVELLE SS 454

Only the good die young. The "bad" cars like the SS 396 kept going, but sometimes even they had to make adjustments to keep up with the competition. By 1970, the SS 396 was becoming a classic. It had been around since 1966 and was no longer the fastest muscle car in town. It was a snappy performer, but muscular newcomers from other automakers were proving to be a bunch faster on the streets and drag strips.

To keep the Chevelle in the muscle car race, Chevy had to do something to swing the balance back in its favor. After some brainstorming, the product planners came up with a simple answer—more cubic inches under the hood. Chevy announced that it would be releasing new 454-cid big-block V-8 for use in the Chevelle. The resulting model was called the SS 454 and is considered by many collectors to represent the pinnacle of the hot Chevelle SS series.

The 454-cid engine had a 4.250 x 4.00-inch bore and stroke. This monster was made available to the public in two different versions. The LS5 edition featured a 10.25:1 compression ratio and a 750-cfm Rochester Quadra-Jet carburetor. It was rated for 360 hp at 5400 rpm and

500 lbs.-ft. of torque at 3200 rpm. This engine was included in the SS 454 option, which had a $503.45 package price.

For a little bit extra, you could get the even more awesome LS6 version of the 454, which used an 11.25:1 compression ratio and a 780-cfm Holley four-barrel carburetor. It developed 450 hp at 5600 rpm and 500 lbs.-ft. of torque at 3600 rpm. To get an LS6 you had to pay the SS 454 package price, plus $263.30.

The LS6 was a super-high-performance engine featuring things like four-bolt main bearings, nodular iron bearing caps, heavy-duty connecting rods, big-diameter exhaust valves and a solid-lifter camshaft. A test car powered by the LS6 engine moved from 0-to-60 mph in 5.4 seconds and did the standing-start quarter-mile in 13.81 seconds at 103.8 mph. Those numbers were racked up with a Turbo-Hydra-Matic transmission and a 3.77:1 rear axle. You could also order either 454-cid engine with one of three available four-speed manual transmissions.

Only 3,773 of the SS coupes and convertibles built in 1970 had the 454-cid V-8s, and only a relative handful were LS6 editions.

1971 CAMARO SS, RS & Z/28

Since Chevrolet Motor Division didn't release the all-new 1970 Camaro until the middle of calendar-year 1970, no major design changes were made to the 1971 models. In fact, about the only way to spot the 1971 edition at a glance is to look in the front compartment for high-back bucket seats with integral headrests.

But there were some equipment upgrades for 1971 models. The Camaro's standard features now included power front disc brakes and steel inner door guard rails, as well as the full complement of General Motors safety features, all-vinyl upholstery, bucket-style rear seat cushions, floor carpeting, a cigar lighter, Astro-Ventilation, E78-14 bias-belted black sidewall tires and a three-speed manual transmission with a floor-mounted gear shifter. The standard 1971 Camaro V-8 was a 307-cid small block engine.

The basic Camaro SS package included a 350-cid/270-hp V-8, a dual exhaust system, bright engine accents, power brakes, special ornamentation, hood insulation, F70-14 white-lettered tires, 14 x 7-inch diameter wheels, a black-finished grille, hide-away wipers with

black arms and Super Sport "SS" emblems. The Rally Sport option package added a special black-finished grille insert with a rubber-tipped vertical center bar and a resilient body-color grille frame, independent left and right front bumpers, a license plate bracket mounted below the right front bumper, parking lights with bright accents molded on the grille panel, hide-away headlights, bright window moldings, bright hood panel moldings, bright body sill moldings, body-colored door handle inserts, RS emblems (deleted when the SS package was also installed), an RS steering wheel medallion, bright-accented taillights and bright-accented back-up lights.

The RPO Z/28 Special Performance package was a factory option that cost $786.75. Standard equipment included an exclusive 330-hp 350 Turbo-Fire 350 V-8, a beefed-up sport suspension, fancier wheels, a rear spoiler, heavy-duty radiator, dual exhausts and special decals and white paint stripes. The manual transmission Z/28 coupe cost $3,841 new, with the automatic version available for $100 more.

Jerry Heasley

1971 CHEVELLE SS 454

The early '70s was the era of low-cost muscle cars and "lick-'em-stick-'em" muscle cars that had the decals, but not the big-cube engines, of the recent past. Chevrolet set things up so buyers could order all of the Super Sport goodies on any Malibu as long as it had a 350-, 400- or 454-cid V-8.

Chevelle models received changes to the front end in 1971. A new twin-level grille was divided by a bright horizontal bar. The front parking lights were moved from the bumper into the fender tips. "Don't panic," says a 1971 Chevrolet sales brochure. Although the muscle car era was in decline, there were still some hot options left. "There's still an SS 454. Any car that was named the best of its kind in Car and Driver's reader's choice (the 1970 Chevelle SS 454) is sure to stay around."

With a V-8 engine, the Malibu coupe sold for $2,980 and weighed 3,342 lbs. The convertible, which came only with a V-8, was base priced at $3,260 and weighed some 3,390 lbs. Only 5,089 Chevelle convertibles were built in 1971.

The RPO Z15 SS package had power disc brakes and lots of other goodies. It sold for $357.

If you wanted a 1971 SS 454 Chevelle, you had to order one of the two big-block engines as an add-on option. This year Chevrolet listed the net horsepower rating and gross horsepower rating for both engines. The LS5 version produced 285 net hp and 365 gross hp. The LS6 version generated 325 nhp and 425 ghp. Both came with a choice of a four-speed manual transmission or a three-speed Turbo-Hydra-Matic transmission.

Chevrolet put together an estimated 80,000 cars that carried the SS option this year. Of those units, 19,292 were equipped with 454-cid V-8s.

Jerry Heasley

1971 CORVETTE

The 1971 Corvette got a new interior and a new resin process for its fiberglass body, but if you were a fan of big horsepower, all you needed to know were three little digits: LS6.

That was the option you wanted in your shark-body Chevy if you really wanted to take flight, and for $1,221 extra you could have it. The LS6 motor had hydraulic lifters, a high-performance cam, an 8.5:1 compression ratio and a four-barrel carburetor. However, the LS6 carb was a big 880-cfm Holley model. The motor was rated 425 hp at 5600 rpm and 475 lbs.-ft. of torque at 4000 rpm.

A 1971 Corvette with the LS5 engine could go 0-to-60 mph in 5.7 seconds, 0-to-100 mph in 14.1 seconds and do the standing-start quarter-mile in 14.2 seconds at 100.33 mph. A 1971 Corvette with the LS6 engine and 3.36:1 rear axle was tested by *Car and Driver* magazine in June 1971. It moved from 0-to-60 mph in 5.3 seconds, from 0-to-80 mph in 8.5 seconds and from 0-to-100 mph in 12.7 seconds. The same car did the quarter-mile in 13.8 seconds at 104.65 mph.

Standard equipment included all-vinyl upholstery, a dual-exhaust system, an outside rearview mirror, carpeting, a center console, wheel trim rings, an electric clock, a tachometer, a heavy-duty battery, front and rear disc brakes with a warning light and tinted glass.

Corvette buyers had their choice of 10 exterior colors: Mulsanne Blue, Bridgehampton Blue, Brands Hatch Green, Steel Cities Gray, Ontario Orange, Millie Miglia Red, Nevada Silver, Classic White, Sunflower Yellow and War Bonnet Yellow. All convertibles came with a choice of black or white soft tops. The interior colors were black, dark blue, dark green, red and saddle.

High-performance engine options included the RPO LS5 V-8. This $295 extra version of the 454-cid big-block now had an 8.5:1 compression ratio. It was rated for 365 hp at 4800 rpm and 465 lbs.-ft. of torque at 3200 rpm.

Another hot option available again to Corvette fans was the small block-based RPO LT1 V-8. This 350-cid engine had a 9.0:1 compression ratio. It generated 330 hp at 5600 rpm and torque was 360 lbs.-ft. at 4000 rpm.

An LT1-powered Vette with the M-21 four-speed manual transmission and a 3.70:1 rear axle was also tested by *Car and Driver* magazine in June 1971. It moved from 0-to-40 mph in 3.4 seconds, 0-to-60 mph in 6.0 seconds and from 0-to-100 mph in 14.5 seconds. The car did the quarter-mile in 14.57 seconds at 100.55 mph and its top speed was 137 mph.

1975-76 COSWORTH VEGA

Was this funky little Chevy a true muscle car? Probably not, but it was certainly a muscular little rascal for its time and one of the more unique vehicles of the 1970s. For a freakin' Vega, it could move!

And if you had one then, you shouldn't have gotten rid of it. The Cosworth Vegas were only around for one year, not many were built, and they are scarce today.

From the start of Vega production in 1971, Chevy capitalized on the new car's sporting character by offering a GT option. This package enhanced the Vega's handling, added a 100-hp engine and provided full instrumentation. By 1974, EPA regs and other factors had reduced the GT to 85 hp.

What the Vega needed was an "image" model that would appeal to high-performance buffs and weekend racers. The result was the Cosworth Vega. Cosworth was the name of a British firm that built racing cars. These cars wore consecutively numbered dashboard plaques for identification.

But the Cosworth package was much more than a plaque. It included twin camshafts and four valves per cylinder. The cams were hidden below covers with the Chevy bow tie, and the Cosworth and Vega names. They helped to boost performance to 140 hp at 7000 rpm. In fact, the hot 2.0-liter four produced 1.15 hp per cube. The torque rating was 105 ft.-lbs. of torque at 6000 rpm.

The launch of the Cosworth Vega was delayed by the EPA until after it passed a 50,000-mile emissions test. It finally arrived in March 1975. As a result, on 2,062 of these cars were built during that model year. With a base price of $5,916, the "Cosworth" had to be of top quality, since a Corvette coupe cost only about $900 more.

In proper tune, the Cosworth Vega could reach 60 mph in 8.7 seconds and do the quarter-mile in 17.6 seconds at a terminal speed of 80.1 mph. Besides going fast, it looked good. Even the engine compartment had a "designer" look with the cam covers finished in black crackle paint and the model names spelled out in raised letters.

For muscle-car history lovers, the Cosworth Vega has a lot of significance. It started a trend, for domestic car makers, towards modern high-performance sport coupes with double overhead cam four-cylinder engines.

1985 CAMARO
5.0-LITER IROC-Z

Just when the aging Camaro needed something good to happen to it, along came the IROC. The timing couldn't have been better.

The International Race of Champions, or IROC, race series originated in 1973, when drivers competed in 15 identically prepared Porsche Carreras. For several reasons, including a desire to expand the series to include oval track drivers, Camaros replaced Porsches in 1974.

TThe IROC-Z was actually a sports equipment package (RPO B4Z). The standard engine was Chevy's LG4 190-hp version of the 305-cid (5.0-liter) V-8. This engine used a four-barrel carburetor and developed 240 lbs.-ft. of torque at 3200 rpm. A more muscular engine was available as the optional LB9 version of the 5.0-liter V-8, with electronic fuel injection and a tuned aluminum intake plenum with individual intake runners for each cylinder. This was dubbed "tuned port injection" and was good for 215 hp

at 4800 rpm and 275 lbs.-ft. of torque at 3200 rpm.

The 5.0-liter H.O. engine also featured a hotter camshaft and a larger-diameter exhaust system. It came only with four-speed manual transmission attachments for 1985. A 3.42:1 rear axle was standard. Other IROC-Z equipment included a lower stance and center of gravity, re-valved Delco front struts, a faster spring jounce rate, front stabilizer bar, re-calibrated performance power steering, Bilstein rear gas shocks, fatter-than-normal rear anti-roll bar and unidirectional 245/50VR16 Goodyear Eagle tires mounted on 8 x 16-inch wheels.

In road tests, *Motor Trend* reported a 6.87-second 0-to-60 time and a 15.32-second quarter-mile run at 89.6 mph. *Popular Hot Rodding* took a little longer (7 seconds) to get up to 60 mph, but ran the quarter-mile in 14.94 seconds at 92.60 mph.

1987 CAMARO
5.7-LITER IROC-Z

According the Chevrolet, the new power train made the 1987 Camaro IROC-Z "a mean hombre in '87 with the arrival of the 5.7-liter TPI V-8 power plant roaring under the hood of the hot IROC-Z."

With the earlier 5.0-liter IROC-Z already accounting for nearly 25 percent of Camaro Z/28 sales (which in turn represented 47 percent of all Camaros sold), the 5.7-liter version was expected to have a strong influence on Chevrolet's overall business. A potential impediment, the unavailability of air conditioning on the 5.7-liter IROC-Z, was only temporary, since it was slated for production beginning in October 1986.

Except for its Camaro LB9 accessory drive belts, exhaust system and electronic control module, the new L98 IROC-Z V-8 was identical to the Corvette 5.7-liter TPI V-8 engine. Its power ratings were 220 hp at 4200 rpm and 320 lbs.-ft. of torque at 3200 rpm. With the exception of its 3.27:1 geared 7.75-inch Australian-built Borg-Warner rear axle, the 5.7-liter IROC-Z shared its running gear with the 5.0-liter version. All IROC-Z models had slightly revised suspensions for 1987.

The price of this engine, which was identified as RPO B2L, was $1,045 over the $13,488 cost of an IROC-Z with the base LG4 engine. Chevrolet required the purchase of a number of mandatory options. These included RPO MX4, a special version of the four-speed 700R4 automatic transmission with an upgraded torque converter, RPO B80, a limited-slip differential, RPO J85, four-wheel disc brakes and the RPO KC4 engine oil cooler. The cost of these features raised the price of the 5.7-liter engine to $1,924..

For the money, the new engine was a steal! Hot Rod magazine, in its January 1987 issue, suggested that "it could be the closest facsimile to a full-bore road racing car you'll ever drive." Chevrolet's acceleration data underscored this perspective. Chevrolet test drivers achieved a 0-to-60-mph time of 6.2 seconds and a standing-start quarter-mile time of 14.5 seconds. Subsequent road tests essentially duplicated these figures.

Also available in limited numbers as a 1987 model was an IROC-Z Camaro convertible conversion done by the American Sunroof Corp. (ASC) of Livonia, Mich.

Jerry Heasley

1990 CORVETTE ZR1

How much anticipation was there for the all-new 1990 ZR1 Corvette? Ninety-five percent of the first-year ZR1s were pre-ordered by March 1988!

People couldn't wait to get their hands on one, and this was one car that lived up to the hype.

This car had been conceived and built to compete in the marketplace with the top cars in the world—at a price that was noticeably higher than other Corvette stickers, but six figures less than the competition! The second thing was the length of time the car took to reach the market. Deadlines were missed and missed again, as Chevy refined the design and waited for necessary government approvals.

The collectibility of the 1990 ZR1 went beyond initial demand for the car, which far outpaced supply. Subtle styling changes that set it apart from the 1990 Corvette coupe, along with low production numbers in its first year, marked the ZR1 as a car collector's target. Estimates from Chevrolet had only 2,000 ZR1 Corvettes being produced for 1990.

The ZR1, at first glance, looked similar to the Corvette coupe, but it was stretched 1 inch and was 3 inches wider to accommodate an increased rear tread width. The telltale difference between the base Corvette and the ZR1 was the high-performance model's revised rectangular taillights.

What really put a stamp of uniqueness on the ZR1, however, was its drive train. The ZR1's all-aluminum 350-cid LT5 V-8 produced enough thrust to launch the Corvette from 0-to-60 mph in 4.3 seconds. The LT5 was rated at 375 hp and was constructed by boat-engine specialists at Mercury Marine. An AZF six-speed manual transmission was mated to the engine. This transmission was also offered as optional equipment on 1989 Corvette coupes, but it was mandatory in the ZR1, which did not have an automatic transmission option.

The factory list price of a ZR1, as shipped with both the automatic climate control and one-piece removable top options, was $62,675. This was compared to the 1990 Corvette coupe's asking price of $37,900. But, because of the great demand for ZR1s, dealers asked for — and got — prices that were out of this world.

1993 CAMARO Z28

The no-excuses 1993 Z28 was an immediate hit with the car magazines. *Car & Driver* pitted it against the Ford Mustang Cobra and declared the Z28 the fastest with a 0-to-60 in 5.3 seconds and a quarter-mile romp of 14 seconds flat at 100 mph. Motor Trend tested several performance cars and noted that the Camaro—with a top speed of 151 mph — represented the "biggest bang for the buck" of the bunch.

Despite the softening of the old pony car market, Chevrolet didn't look for any easy way out when it introduced its fourth-generation Camaro a few months into the 1993 model run. It featured an all-new body, reworked chassis and a Z28 that came only one way—fast.

While the 1982-1992 Camaro (and its close relative the Pontiac Firebird) stuck to rear-wheel drive and solid V-8 power in a changing automotive world of front drive and less cylinders, it still left room for improvement, mainly in handling and structural tightness. The new 1993 Camaro (and Firebird) improved on performance, handling and even comfort.

For the 1993 model year, only a hatchback coupe was offered. It came two ways, in a base model priced at $13,889 with a 3.4-liter, 160-hp V-6, and as a Z28 priced at $17,269.

The body, while much sleeker than the old style, featured a 68-degree raked windshield and steel structure to which composite (plastic) panels were attached. Only the rear quarters and hood were steel. Optional removable glass roof panels retailed for $895.

A new short-and-long arm coil spring front suspension and power rack-and-pinion steering replaced the old struts and re-circulating ball setup. The rear continued with coils with multi-link bars.

By checking the Z28 box on the order form you got a LT1 350-cid V-8 with aluminum heads. It was rated at 275 hp (up 30 from 1992). You also got a standard Borg-Warner T-56 six-speed manual transmission, four-wheel antilock disc brakes, 16 x 8-inch aluminum wheels and Goodyear GA P235/55R16 rubber. Z-rated GS-C Goodyears were optional at $144.

If you kept the standard tires, you also got a governed top speed of 108 mph, which you could hit in fourth, fifth or sixth gear. Going for the Z-rated doughnuts meant the Z28 could do what it wanted, which several magazines found exceeded 150 mph.

1993 CAMARO INDY PACE CAR

A Camaro paced the Indianapolis 500-mile race for the fourth time in 1993, and if you had one, you were definitely going to get noticed.

The previous years for Camaro pace cars were 1967, 1969 and 1982. Chevrolet provided the Indianapolis Motor Speedway with three "Official Pace Cars" and another 125 replicas for track officials. In addition, dealers were to get 500 copies, with another 20 reserved for Canada. The tally puts the 1993 Camaro Indy Pace Car replica squarely in the limited-production class, at least as far as Chevrolets go.

Only the Camaro hatchback coupe was available for 1993. The pace car replica came with a special black-and-white exterior and multi-colored accents. The special interior featured the same color combination with a new 3D knitting process for the seats and door panels. A gold hood emblem topped it all off. Mechanically, nothing special was needed, as the 350-cid/275-hp LT1 Corvette V-8 met Indianapolis Motor Speedway's performance requirements without modification. "Performance-wise, every 1993 Camaro Z28 is capable of pacing Indy," said Jim Perkins, Chevrolet general manager and driver of the pace car for the 500.

Camaro Indy Pace Cars were fitted with automatic transmissions. Chevrolet installed the 4L60 Hydra-Matic with a .70 fourth gear. The rest of the Z28 driveline and underpinnings were just fine for track duty. Camaro Z28s equipped with the optional six-speed manual transmission were clocked in the 155-mph range by magazines in 1993.

Jerry Heasley

1993 CORVETTE ZR1

The ZR1 was still one of fastest production cars in the world in 1993. They were expensive, and not many buyers probably took their new 'Vettes out and really wound up them up, but if they did, they were in for a white-knuckle ride.

Motor Trend tested a '93 ZR1 and found it could do 0-to-60 mph in 4.9 seconds. Quarter-mile performances were 13.1 seconds and 109.6 mph for the ZR. As for top speed, Road and Track did 178 mph in another ZR1.

The ZR1 Corvette's 5.7-liter LT5 V-8 was upgraded this year and featured significant power and torque increases. Improvements in the designs of the LT5 engine's cylinder head and valve train included "blending" the valve heads and creating three-angle valve inserts, plus the use of a sleeve spacer to help maintain port alignment of the injector manifold. These upgrades added up to a 30-hp increase and also produced a higher torque rating.

In addition to the aforementioned improvements, the LT5 engine was now equipped with four-bolt main bearings, platinum-tipped spark plugs and an electrical linear exhaust gas recirculating (EGR) system. Improved airflow from the cylinder head enhancements and the valve train refinements boosted the engine's rating from 375 hp to 405 hp!

A special 40th anniversary appearance package was offered in 1993 and was available on all models. This package included an exclusive "Ruby Red" color exterior.

ZR1s were identified by a YZ in the vehicle identification number. The last six symbols indicate the sequential production number starting with 800001 for ZR1s. The engine code suffix ZVC identified the 350-cid/405-hp RPO LT5 V-8 used in the ZR1 model only.

The 1991 ZR1 Special Performance Package was actually a $31,683 option for the hatchback coupe and brought its base price up to $66,278. In standard trim, the ZR1-optioned hatchback weighed 3,503 lbs. Only 448 cars were built with the ZR1 option this year.

1994 IMPALA SS

From a 1960s perspective, the 1994 Chevrolet Impala SS was an odd duck. It's a four-door sedan, it's big and it caters to comfort as much as performance. However, putting the SS back in context, it ranks as one of the last remnants of the old big-horsepower era. It combines a large-for-its-time V-8 with ample horsepower, rear-wheel drive and full-frame construction.

Chevy went to its retired name farm and revived the Impala SS tag and reaction at the SEMA show and other previews that followed was the same: "Build it!" This is just what Chevrolet Motor Division general manager Jim Perkins wanted to hear and on Valentine's Day of 1994 the first of the new Impala SS models rolled off an assembly line in the GM Assembly Plant in Arlington, Texas.

Unlike some production versions of show cars, the SS was not a watered-down, wimped-out version. The 260-hp version of the 350-cid LT1 came standard and was attached to a 4L60-E automatic transmission. Four-wheel ventilated disc brakes were used at all four corners, as were stiffer coil springs and DeCarbon shocks

similar to those on the Camaro Z28. The result was a 20 percent stiffer suspension, much better handling and a still comfortable ride. From the police car parts bin came front and rear anti-roll bars and other hardware aimed at going fast on straight or curved roads.

Chevrolet listed a 0-to-60-mph time of 7.1 seconds, but a spirited *Car & Driver* crew got a 6.5-second run and a quarter-mile of 15 seconds with a 92 mph trap speed. A couple of SS examples were even quicker. GM put a 502 big-block in a test car and got 0-to-60 mph in 6.0 seconds and a 14.5-second quarter-mile at 98.2 mph. Horsepower was claimed to be 385. Reeves Callaway converted customers' Impalas into the SuperNatural SS with a 383-cid small-block with 404 horses. *Motor Trend* performance figures were 0-to-60 mph in 5.9 seconds and for the quarter-mile 14.0 seconds at 100.3 mph!

The late-model Impala SS cost $22,495 and turned out to be a small-volume niche car in the GM scheme of things. For the model's first year, 6,303 units were built. Of course, instant collector status was assured for the Impala SS.

Jerry Heasley

1996 CAMARO SS

As the modern muscle car era progressed into the late 1990s, Detroit turned to smaller companies to help it create super cars for the enthusiast market niche. These companies were able to upgrade the looks and performance of regular production cars without jumping through all of the hoops the big automakers had to deal with. By "outsourcing" work to these companies, cars like the Camaro SS became available to those willing to pay a bit more to have a muscular ride.

The Camaro SS was built by SLP, which stood for "street legal performance." Ed Hamburger first got involved in the high-performance field by drag racing Mopars in the 1960s. Later, in the 1980s, he created SLP Engineering, in Red Bank, New Jersey. This company converted Pontiac Firebirds and Chevrolet Camaros into "street-legal performance" machines. His 1992 Firehawk version of the Firebird was a successful venture for SLP, as well as for the Pontiac dealers who sold the SLP package.

In 1996, Hamburger started working in conjunction with Chevrolet Motor Division to produce a Camaro muscle car that could be sold by Chevrolet dealers as a high-priced, factory-approved option package.

The secret of the 1996 Camaro SS was a special air-induction system which, when combined with an optional low-restriction exhaust system, boosted horsepower of the 10.4:1 compression 350-cid LT1 V-8 to 305 at 5000 rpm and torque to 325 lbs.-ft. at 2400 rpm. The engine had a cast-iron block and aluminum cylinder heads. It came with a sequential port fuel injection system and was hooked up to a six-speed manual transmission.

Like any real muscle car, the 1996 Camaro SS needed an image and a "feel" to suit its higher-than-standard performance capabilities. Therefore, the SS package also included a special composite hood with an "ant eater" air scoop, 17 x 9.0-inch Corvette ZR1-style wheels, BF Goodrich Comp T/A tires and special SS badges. It also featured a Torsen limited-slip differential, Bilstein shock absorbers, progressive-rate springs and performance-altered lower rear control arms.

The Camaro SS was roughly a $28,000 package. It weighed in at 3,565 lbs. and, while that didn't exactly make it a lightweight, it could accelerate from 0-to-60 mph in 5.3 seconds. It handled the quarter-mile in 13.8 seconds at 101.4 mph.

1996 CORVETTE GRAND SPORT/ COLLECTOR EDITION

The ZR1 Corvette was gone by 1996, but two very cool Corvettes arrived to take its place: the Grand Sport and Collector Edition models.

The 1996 Corvette Grand Sport evoked memories of its 1962-1963 racing predecessors. It sported Admiral Blue Metallic paint, a white racing stripe, red "hash" marks on the left front fender and black five-spoke aluminum wheels.

Powering the Grand Sport model (and also available as an extra-cost option in all other Corvettes) was a 330-hp 5.7-liter LT4 V-8 featuring a specially prepared crankshaft, a steel camshaft and water pump gears that were driven by a roller chain. The LT4 engine was offered only with the six-speed manual transmission.

The 1996 Collector Edition Corvette featured exclusive Sebring Silver paint on its sleek exterior. It also wore special "Collector Edition" emblems and distinctive five-spoke Silver aluminum wheels. A 5.7-liter LT1 V-8 was in-

stalled and was mated with a four-speed automatic transmission. The LT4 V-8 and six-speed manual transmission were both optional, in case you wanted to turn your Collector Edition Corvette into a muscle Corvette.

The Sebring Silver Metallic (code 13) colored cars came only with black cloth tops. Admiral Blue (code 28) Grand Sports came only with white cloth tops.

With sequential multiport fuel injection and a 10.8:1 compression ratio, the LT4 V-8 developed 330 hp at 5800 rpm and 340 lbs.-ft. of torque at 4500 rpm. According to manufacturer's test data, the LT4-powered Grand Sport did 0-to-60 mph in 4.7 seconds and the quarter-mile in 13.3 seconds at 109.7 mph.

The Z15 Collector's Edition was a $1,250 option and was installed on 5,412 cars. The Z16 Grand Sport Package option, was installed on 1,000 Corvettes.

Jerry Heasley

1997 CAMARO Z28 SS AND 30TH ANNIVERSARY EDITION

It was in 1997 that the Camaro observed its 30th anniversary and Chevrolet appropriately marked the occasion by offering a killer 30th Anniversary Package exclusively for the Z28 model.

The $575 option package consisted of Artic White paint with Hugger Orange stripes, a combination patterned after the collectible 1969 Camaro Indy Pace car. Also included in the package were Artic White door handles, Artic White five-spoke aluminum wheels and an Artic White front fascia air intake.

The seats used only inside the 30th Anniversary Camaro were trimmed in Artic White with black-and-white houndstooth cloth inserts. This is another Camaro tradition that dated back to the classic '69 model. The floor mats and headrests had special five-color embroidery.

The Z28 came in coupe and convertible mod-

els for 1997. The closed car sold for $20,115 and weighed 3,433 lbs. The open car had a base retail price of $25,520 and weighed 3,589 lbs.

The Z28 included a 5.7-liter sequential fuel injected V-8 and a six-speed manual gear box.

The 350-cid engine was another marque tradition, as the Chevy "small-block" V-8 powered many Camaros over three decades. This latest version developed 285 hp at 5200 rpm and 325 lbs.-ft. of torque at 2400 rpm.

Also available, as an extra-cost option, was the Camaro SS Z28, which was powered by a 305-hp Corvette LT1 V-8. This car was specially built and sold through selected Chevrolet dealers. It featured a hood scoop, a high-performance exhaust system, a Hurst gear shifter and a sport suspension package with Bilstein shock absorbers.

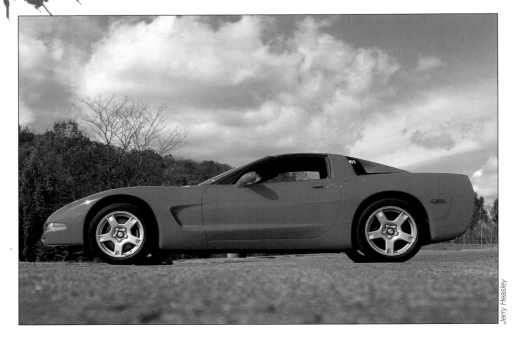

Jerry Heasley

1997 CORVETTE

The awesome 1997 C5 model was the first all-new Corvette in 13 years and only the fifth or sixth (depending upon your viewpoint) major change in the car's history. The "fifth-generation" Corvette was offered only as a coupe in its debut year. It was designed under the direction of John Cafaro.

Among the equipment featured for the C5 was a new, more compact, 5.7-liter LS1 V-8 that produced 350 ponies and 345 lbs.-ft. of torque. A rear-mounted transaxle opened up more interior space and helped maintain a near 50/50 front-to-rear weight distribution. An electronic throttle control system allowed engineers a limitless range of throttle progression.

The 1997 Corvette's underbody structure was the stiffest in the car's history and consisted of two full-length, hydro-formed perimeter frame rails coupled to a backbone tunnel. The rails consisted of a single piece of tubular steel, replacing the 14 parts used previously. The new-design blunt tail section allowed for smoother

airflow and resulting 0.29 coefficient of drag.

The C5 Corvette was offered with a 4L60-E electronic four-speed overdrive automatic as the base transmission and a six-speed manual transmission was optional. Corvettes came in Arctic White, Sebring Silver Metallic, Nassau Blue, Black, Light Carmine Red Metallic, Torch Red and Fairway Green Metallic. Interiors came in Black, Light Gray and Firethorn Red. Standard features included a removable body-color roof panel. Leather seats were standard equipment.

The C5 coupe sold for $37,495 and weighed 3,229 lbs. The car's SFI V-8 engine had a cast aluminum block and heads. Its displacement was 346 cu. in. or 5.7 liters. It had a 3.90 x 3.62-inch bore and stroke, a 10.1:1 compression ratio and 345 hp at 5600 rpm. Torque was 350 lbs.-ft. at 4400 rpm. An automatic transmission with floor-mounted gear shifter was standard equipment.

Chevrolet built only 9,092 of these cars.

Too bad, because everybody should have one.

Jerry Heasley

1998 CORVETTE

In its 45th year, the Corvette returned to offering convertible and coupe models with the debut of an awesome "topless" version of the C5 Corvette. The convertible's glass rear window was heated and the top had an "express-down" feature that released the tonneau cover and automatically lowered the windows part way at the touch of a button.

New for 1998 was a magnesium wheel option featuring lightweight wheels with a unique bronze tone. Standard features included a stainless-steel exhaust system, tires capable of running for 200 miles with no air pressure, dual heated electric remote breakaway outside rearview mirrors, daytime running lamps and 5-mph front and rear bumpers.

For the fourth time (1978, 1986, 1995, 1998) a Corvette was selected to pace the Indianapolis 500. Indy 500 veteran Parnelli Jones drove the Purple and Yellow pace car.

The LS1 V-8 and four-speed automatic transmission were again the standard offering, with the T56 six-speed manual transmission optional. Corvettes were available in Artic White, Sebring Silver Netallic, Nassau Blue Metallic, Black, Light Carmine Red Metallic, Torch Red, Magnetic Red II Clearcoat and Fairway Green Metallic. Leather seats were standard and came in Black, Yellow, Light Oak, Light Gray and Firethorn Red. Convertible tops came in Black, Light Oak and White.

The 1998 Corvette C5 coupe retailed for $37,495 and tipped the scales at 3,245 lbs. It had a production run of 19,235 units. The convertible could be purchased for a minimum of $44,425. It weighed just a pound more than the coupe. Chevrolet built 11,849 ragtops and 1,163 had the Indy pace car package.

Some neat performance options were on the C5 Corvette's list. They included the RPO F45 Continuously Variable Real Time Damping system for $1,695, an RPO G92 performance axle ratio for $100 (not available with six-speed), an RPO JL4 Active-Handling system for $500, the RPO MN6 six-speed manual transmission for $815, the RPO Z4Z Indy Pace Car package for $5,039 with automatic transmission and $5,804 with manual transmission and the RPO Z51 Performance Handling package with Bilstein's adjustable ride-control system for $350.

Jerry Heasley

1998-99 LIGENFELTER TWIN-TURBO CORVETTE

The 1999 Ligenfelter Twin-Turbo Corvette was a 650-hp muscle car that *Motor Trend* (March 2000) described as "The fastest, meanest, street-legal car we've ever tested." Race driver and car builder John Ligenfelter "remanufactured" these cars in his shop in Decatur, Ind.

The Ligenfelter Twin-Turbo Corvette turned 0-to-60 mph in 3.3 seconds and went from 0-to-100 mph in 6.7 seconds (which would have been a great 0-to-60 time for any 1960s muscle car). The standing-start quarter-mile was covered in 11.8 seconds at 132.1 mph with street tires. The test was then repeated with drag racing slicks and the car did the distance in 10.8 seconds at 133.5 mph. Its top speed was 226 mph!

For $43,995 and up, Ligenfelter Performance Engineering would convert a new Corvette into a car with nearly double the factory model's price and performance. The conversion process started with the blueprinting of the stock Corvette LS1 engine. Then Ligenfelter installed a forged steel crankshaft, billet steel connecting rods and forged aluminum pistons, ported the cylinder heads, fitted larger stainless-steel valves, added a new roller-bearing camshaft and installed two Garrett turbos with up to 8.5 lbs. of boost pressure.

The 346-cid engine featured an aluminum block and heads, a 3.90 x 3.62-inch bore and stroke, a 9.5:1 compression ratio and sequential fuel injection. It produced 650 hp at 5800 rpm and 600 lbs.-ft. of torque at 5000 rpm. The engine was linked to a six-speed manual transmission.

Motor Trend tested the car with a 2.73:1 axle ratio for top speed and a 3.43:1 axle for acceleration runs. It also had some minor suspension changes like stiffer anti-roll bars, Penske adjustable shock absorbers, Baer brakes and thinner-than-stock Michelin Pilot Sport street tires (P235/235ZR18 up front and P275/235ZR18 in the rear) to improve its aerodynamics at 200-plus mph.

Wieck Media

2000 CAMARO SS

If the 2000 Camaro SS has a single claim to fame, it may be that it was perhaps the greatest performance car bargain of its era. The 2000 Camaro was offered in a choice of coupe and convertible body styles with prices ranging from a low of about $17,500 to a high of $35,000. Regardless of where you purchased on the Camaro price spectrum, you wound up with a lot of car for your hard-earned bucks!

The base model came with a 3.8-liter 200-hp V-6 that was plenty adequate for the general public. A few rungs up the ladder you got to the Z28, which used a 305-hp version of the venerable 5.7-liter (350-hp) V-8. However, for muscle car lovers, the hot ticket was the SS, which came stuffed with a tweaked 5.7-liter motor that cranked up 320 hp and promised 5.2-second 0-to-60-mph times, even with a 3,306-lb. curb weight.

Chevrolet offered a wide choice of convenience options and handling packages for the Camaro and those wanting to drive quick or fast were well advised to order the optional traction-control system and 1LE performance suspension.

2001 CORVETTE Z06

The Z06 Corvette just kept getting better and faster in the early 2000s, and the 2001 version was no exception.

The Z06 took the place of the previous model known as the hardtop, but it retained that body style as the sole platform for the Z06 model option. Basically, as compared to the 2000 hardtop, the Z06 gained 40 hp and lost 103 lbs. That added up to an amazingly muscular supercar. In fact, in performance terms the Z06 could speed from 0-to-60 mph in just 4.7 seconds.

The new 346-cid LS6 small-block Chevy V-8 under the hood of this impressive car produced 385 hp at 6000 rpm and 385 lbs.-ft. of torque at 4800 rpm. Its special features included modifications to the engine block casting to alleviate crankcase pressures, a special high-air-flow intake manifold, a high-lift camshaft with increased duration, a 10.5:1 compression ratio and over-sized fuel injectors.

To lighten the cars, Chevrolet came up with a weight reduction of 6 lbs. for each tire and wheel, thinner glass in the windshield and backlight, and a titanium exhaust system that was 17 lbs. lighter than a conventional steel exhaust system. The increased power combined with the weight reduction added up to a car that carried just 8.09 lbs. per horsepower!

Other features of the $46,800 Corvette Z06 are a six-speed manual transmission, 12.6-inch-diameter vented disc brakes front and rear with ABS standard, forged aluminum wheels and Goodyear Eagle F1 SC tires size 265/40ZR18 up front and size 295/35ZR18 in the rear.

The interior of the Z06 included black seats with red pleated inserts and matching door panels, but all-black door panels could be substituted. However, you couldn't get any other seats but the red and black ones.

Wieck Media

2004 CORVETTE

The C5 Corvette was in its final season in 2004, but Chevrolet continued to celebrate the nameplate's golden anniversary and keep the car fresh with technologies such as Magnetic Selective Ride Control, Goodyear EMT "run-flat" tires, active handling and a rear transaxle. Standard performance equipment included a 5.7-liter V-8, a four-speed automatic transmission, and a limited-slip rear axle.

The 2004 Commemorative Edition package recognized the success of the C5-R competition coupes campaigned by the Corvette Racing Team. The Commemorative Edition package included a Le Mans Blue exterior, a Shale interior, special badges, special seat embroidery and high-polished, five-spoke aluminum wheels with specific center caps. The Commemorative Edition package was only available with the 1SC package, which was a $3,700 option. It included a Shale convertible top with the convertible.

A 2004 Corvette convertible was selected to serve as the Official Pace Car at the 2004 Indianapolis 500. Very few modifications were made to the Corvette to prepare it for this role.

The Z06 Corvette was still geared for the extreme performance enthusiast. Z06s featured revised chassis tuning for quicker, smoother response in challenging environments. The chassis enhancements were subtle in terms of physical parts, but significant in terms of the car's performance and feel. GM engineers refined the Z06's shock damping characteristics to provide improved handling in the most challenging conditions, while maintaining good ride control for the demands of daily driving. The Z06 Corvette also included a special engine, a unique six-speed manual gearbox, hollow-stem valves, a high-lift camshaft, a low-restriction mass air flow (MAF) sensor, a low-restriction air cleaner, a high-performance exhaust system, a Z06-specific FE4 high-performance suspension system and other goodies.

The Commemorative Edition Z06 was also Le Mans Blue and also included a C5-R Le Mans stripe scheme, special badges, polished Z06 wheels and a lightweight carbon fiber hood. For 2004, the regular Z06 was given two performance-enhancing upgrades. A lightweight, race-inspired carbon fiber hood was used on Z06s with the Commemorative Edition option and all Z06s had the carbon fiber hood that weighed 10.6 lbs. less than the standard hood.

2005 CORVETTE

The sixth-generation Corvette was a slightly smaller and lighter package than the C5, and with a dizzying array of performance and comfort features, it was definitely the most high-tech production 'Vette built to date.

The new Corvette featured dramatic upgrades throughout, a new 400-hp 6.0-liter V-8 and dynamic new styling, the C6 Corvette brought more power and precision to America's performance icon.

The sixth-generation Corvette replaced the outgoing C5 Corvette (1997-2004), but the formula from the C5 era remained: Extremely high performance capabilities in a car that offered great style, value and quality, with surprising comfort for daily driving. The new Corvette added dramatic increases in performance and refinement, wrapped in a new design.

Thanks to an all-new chassis, a strong lightweight body structure and a new 400-hp LS2 V-8, the C6 Corvette raised the bar for performance, with outstanding handling and surpris-

ing ride quality. Equipped with the new Z51 Performance Package, the 2005 Corvette was offered in both coupe and convertible body styles and both nearly matched the Z06 model's track performance.

The sixth-generation Corvette convertible featured an optional power-operated soft top, a feature last seen in 1962. The convertible top reflected great attention to detail. In both manual and power versions, the canvas soft top was available in three colors: Black, Beige and Grey. In its closed position, the canvas top had a smoother, more contoured appearance that concealed the underlying structure better than traditional soft tops.

In an era in which most vehicles seem to grow ever more bulky, the C6 Corvette achieved a lower vehicle weight, even with the addition of numerous new features. The convertible had a base curb weight of 3,199 lbs., 49 lbs. less than the 2004 model.

2010 CHEVROLET CAMARO

"When old becomes new again" certainly sums up the trifecta of modern muscle cars that lean on their predecessors' styling cues. Dodge did it with its Challenger, Ford did it with its Mustang and Chevrolet did it with its Camaro.

In the case of the Camaro, the 2010 version that went on sale to the public in April 2009 recalls the first-generation 1969 version with safety and aero updates. When fourth-generation Camaro production ended in 2002 due to declining sales, it seemed the catalyst for the drop was that Camaro enthusiasts had not embraced the evolution of the car's design, which had gotten far away from the halcyon days of first-geners' desired lines.

What better way to re-launch the fifth-generation of Camaro than through a concept car that, though having a modern design, mimicked the flavor of the '69's lines. What better launch pad than having it debute in "car capitol" Detroit at the Jan. 6, 2006, North American International Auto Show (NAIAS).

This trial balloon, officially dubbed the 2006 Camaro Concept and designed by Sangyup Lee, wowed both the automotive press and show-goers. What eventually landed as the 2010 Camaro in dealer showrooms in April 2009 was not far off from the 2006 concept car. The Camaro staple of two-door, four-place, front-engine, rear-drive pony/muscle car was retained. The car was produced at the Oshawa assembly plant in Canada, which was slated to be closed in 2008, and resulted in saving 2,750 jobs. The intial coupe-only

Camaro was offered in LS, LT and SS versions. Powertrain for the LS/LT was a 3.6-liter V-6, rated at 304-hp, linked to either a Hydra-Matic six-speed automatic transmission with TAPshift or Aisin-Warner AY6 six-speed manual transmission. The SS came with the LS3 V-8 (426-hp) coupled to the TR6060 six-speed manual trans or the L99 V-8 (400-hp) mated to the Hydra-Matic.

The V-6-powered LS or LT ran on regular unleaded and produced 273 lb.-ft. of torque at 5200 rpm. Both of the V-8s in the SS demanded premium fuel and offered torque ratings of 420 lb.-ft. at 4600 rpm or 410 lb.-ft. at 4300 rpm, respectively.

Other key features of the 2010 Camaro included a fully independent four-wheel suspension system, four-wheel disc brakes (four-piston Brembo calipers on SS models) and a RS appearance package available on LT and SS trim levels that offered a spoiler and RS-specific taillamps and wheels.

Rally and "hockey" stripe packages were available in several different colors as well.

1951 NEW YORKER/ SARATOGA FIREPOWER HEMI V-8

The Chysler Saratogas were also the hot ticket in the La Carrera Panamericana (or Mexican Road Race). Non-professional driver Bill Sterling finished third overall in his Chrysler, as well as first among strictly stock cars. Despite such performances, the '51 Saratoga gets little respect from muscle-car buffs or those bidding on high-performance models at classic car auctions.

Too bad, because these were some great performers for their time.

The contribution of the Chrysler FirePower hemispherical head V-8 to the domestic-car horsepower race of the 1950s is widely known and unquestioned. Lesser realized is the fact that, during the first year this engine was produced, Chrysler added a potential "factory hot rod" to its model lineup — the Saratoga.

The FirePower engine made its initial appearance when the new, mildly facelifted models were introduced in 1951. Replacing the flathead straight eight used in previous New Yorker and Imperial models, the engine was a plus in these large cars with their 131.5-inch wheelbase chassis that dated back to late-1949 models.

The 331.2-cid Hemi engine produced 180 hp.

That was equal to the top rating available in the entire industry. The engine featured twin rocker shafts in each cylinder head, which allowed the valves to be canted on either side of the centrally positioned spark plugs. The early Hemi ran a 7.5:1 compression ratio and a Carter two-barrel carburetor, so operation required only regular-grade fuel.

At first it was the New Yorker that showcased the FirePower V-8. Automotive scribe Tom Mc-Cahill tested one of these cars. Despite its Fluid-Matic "semi-automatic" transmission, this car did just over 100 mph in the Flying Mile run at Daytona Beach. *Motor Trend* reported the New Yorker's top speed at 106 mph.

Even with automatic transmission, *Motor Trend* got a 10-second 0-to-60 run out of the Hemi Saratoga.

The new car's racing potential wasn't overlooked. Stock car driver Tommy Thompson piloted a Saratoga to Chrysler's first NASCAR win August 12, 1951, at Michigan Fairgrounds, a dirt oval in Detroit. A bunch of auto industry brass were there and the Saratoga's go power impressed them all.

1960 300-F "LETTER CAR"

When Chrysler took away the 300's Hemi in 1959, its performance image suffered. Even though the "Golden Lion" wedge-head V-8 was shown to be equally as potent (92 mph in the quarter-mile), the loss of the Hemi created a vacuum.

In 1960, the vacuum was filled by providing the swift 300-F with a ram-inducted 413-cid V-8 good for 375 hp in standard form and 400 hp in optional form. Engine hardware common to both included a hot cam, heavy-duty valve springs, low-back-pressure exhaust system, dual-point distributor, low-restriction air cleaner, special plugs and dual quad carbs.

The carbs were mounted on a wild-looking cross-ram manifold that put one air cleaner on each side of the engine. The stacks were 30 inches long and had to be crisscrossed to fit under the hood. At low speeds, the "long" rams worked great, but they hurt performance above 4000 rpm. To solve the problem, engineers removed a section of the inner walls of the manifolds to create the optional 400-hp engine. On the outside, these "short" rams looked the same, but they were effectively 15 inches long.

This option was really intended only for Daytona-bound cars that competed in the Flying Mile there and about 15 "short" ram cars were built. The $800 option also included a rare four-speed gearbox made for the Facel Vega, a Chrysler-powered French luxury car. One of the 400-hp cars, driven by Greg Ziegler, set a Flying Mile record of 144.9 mph. In 1960, a total of 969 hardtops and 248 convertibles, all with ram manifolds, were made.

1963 300-J "LETTER CAR"

The 300-J was a thoroughbred American grand touring car that maintained a tradition of excellence, which today gives it a status unique among performance automobiles. What a pity there aren't enough to go around!

All Chrysler 300 Letter Cars deserve recognition as "beautiful brutes," but the 300-J has the added distinction of also being a rare beautiful brute. Only 400 were produced, so a sighting nowadays is worth celebrating.

Performance of the 300-J paralleled or exceeded that of many smaller and lighter vehicles. Motor Trend, April 1963, reported a 0 to 60-mph time of 8.0 seconds and a quarter-mile time and speed of 15.8 seconds at 89 mph in a Torque-Flite-equipped 300-J running with a 3.23:1 axle ratio. The true forte of the 300-J was its top speed, which was in excess of 142 mph.

Like the original C-300 and 300-B models, the 300-J was available only as a two-door hardtop. Chrysler adopted new styling for 1963 that it said possessed a "crisp, clean and custom look." As applied to the 300-J, a more appropriate description would be "restrained elegance." It's true that the 300-J shared much of its styling with lesser Chryslers, but the 300-J's lack of extraneous trim, its muscular profile and marvelously distinctive grille that evoked memories of earlier

300 models all contributed to make the 300-J one of America's most handsome automobiles.

The 300-J was available in five colors: Formal Black, Alabaster, Madison Gray, Oyster White and Claret. Adding a touch of class were the two pin stripes (in a contrasting color) that ran the length of the body and 300-J medallions situated on the C-pillar and the rear deck. The interior featured the controversial square steering wheel that many drivers found uncomfortable, but the outstanding design of the front bucket seats (finished in claret red leather), plus vinyl door panel trimming, color-coordinated claret carpeting and a center console with a built-in tachometer served as at least partial redemptions for this lapse of judgment by Chrysler.

A feature unique to Chryslers that was found on the 300-J were windshield wiper blades fitted with airfoils to press the blade against the windshield at high speedsOnly one engine was offered for the 300-J — Chrysler's 413-cid wedge-head V-8. This engine, with mechanical lifters and a compression ratio of 10.0:1, had ratings of 390 hp at 4800 rpm and 485 lbs.-ft. of torque at 3600 rpm. Dual four-barrel AFB 3505S carburetors were used on a special cross-ram intake manifold. The dual-exhaust system was designed for maximum flow with minimum restriction.

Wieck Media

1999 300M

This is a car that is hard to define. It's a specialty vehicle and it's chock full of luxury, but is it really a muscle car? With a 0 to 60-mph time of 7.8 seconds, you have to admit it's no rapid-accelerating Camaro SS, Mustang Cobra R or Corvette C5, but then it's not intended to be. On the other side of the coin, it has a top speed in excess of 145 mph!

In a way, that places it squarely in the tradition of earlier Chrysler Letter Cars, which also needed 8 seconds to get from rest to 60 mph, but then kept accelerating when the needle swept past double zeros! If the earlier "beautiful brutes" are muscle cars — and we think they are — this one seems to fit the same image.

The front-engined, front-wheel-drive 300M first bowed in 1999. It featured a single overhead camshaft, 24-valve, 3.5-liter, all-aluminum V-6 that made it scoot pretty good. In 1999, this engine produced 253 hp at 6400 rpm and 255 lbs.-ft. of torque at 3950 rpm. It came linked to an AutoStick dual mode manual/automatic transmission that permitted driver control on winding roads. Differentiating the $29,445 300M from other Letter Cars was an extra set of doors. It was a sedan, while all earlier Letter Cars were two-door hardtops or convertibles.

The 1999 Chrysler 300M's standard equipment list included heated leather seats, 16-inch tires, a premium four-disc changer Infinity sound system and a black-and-white analog clock and gauge cluster. Also featured was Chrysler's "cab-forward styling," driver and passenger air bags and all-wheel ABS disc brakes. Options included a pair of specific suspension settings and two different steering and braking levels that aided high-performance operation.

Phil Kunz

1963-64 "MAX WEDGE" 426 RAMCHARGER

Since the horsepower race was in full gallop, Mopar came out of the gate with the 426 "Max Wedge" V-8 in 1963. Like the 413 version, it came two ways. The tamer version had the 11.0:1 compression ratio and twin Carter four-barrels It stirred up 415 hp at 5800 rpm. The hairier "Max Wedge Stage II" Ramcharger V-8 used the 13.5:1 pistons. It was good for 425 hp at 5600 rpm. Both versions of the engine were designed strictly for racing. Dodge even supplied car buyers who ordered the Ramcharger V-8 with aluminum front end sheet metal to help make their cars lighter and faster. A functional aluminum hood scoop was part of the package, which dropped car weight by some 150 lbs.

The "Max Wedge" 413 was actually released in 1962. It had big intake and exhaust ports, stainless-steel head gaskets, big valves, a hot cam, dual valve springs, solid valve lifters and cast nodular rocker arms. A special aluminum ram-induction intake manifold with no heat crossover passage carried twin Carter AFB four-barrel carburetors. The engine was offered with two different compression ratios — 11.0:1 or 13.5:1 — and TRW built two types of special pistons for it. This potent big block could

be hooked to a three-speed gearbox with a floor shifter or a beefy version of Chrysler's Torque-Flight automatic transmission. The 413 soon made drag racing history in cars such as Dandy Dick Landy's SS/S class Dodge. By the way, Dodge called it the "Ram-Charger 413" while Plymouth dubbed what was essentially the same engine its "Super Stock 413."

Also making its first appearance in 1962 was the 426-cid Wedge-head V-8. That year, you could not order this engine in a Dodge (or Plymouth); it came only in big Chryslers. *Motor Trend's* "Spotlight on Detroit" column (June 1962) said, "You can now order 426 cubic inches on any Chrysler 300 or 300-H. Factory 413-cid blocks bored .060 are available on special order, with component combinations including forged pistons of 12-to-1 compression, 292-degree-duration cam with solid lifters, big exhaust valves, streamlined exhaust headers, and the original dual-four-barrel ram manifolds with passages shortened to "tune" above 4000 rpm. This top engine is rated 421 hp at 5400 rpm. Chrysler Division isn't going in for any dragging like Dodge and Plymouth, but they will supply the hot stuff if you want it."

Doug Mitchel

1963 POLARA 500

With its 119-inch wheelbase and 3,985-lb. curb weight, it is a bit hard to think of the 1963 Dodge Polara 500 convertible as a muscle car, until you see the results that Jim Wright recorded when he test drove such a car for *Motor Trend* magazine.

"Barring the all-out drag-strip engines, there aren't many that can stay with the 330-hp "383" in acceleration," Wright wrote in his article. He noted that the car's times through various speeds and the quarter-mile were "very impressive," especially considering that it used a 3.23.0:1 rear axle.

His ragtop was equipped with the 383-cid/330-hp V-8 and managed to get from 0-to-60 mph in a mere 7.7 seconds. The quarter-mile took 15.8 seconds, by which time the big, open-top Dodge was moving at 92 mph. And we assume that a lighter Sport Coupe would have done even better.

With its 4.25 x 3.38-inch bore and stroke, the 383 was considered a Chrysler big-block engine and it was one of the best for all-around driving. It used 10.0:1 aluminum pistons and the 330-hp version had a Carter four-barrel carburetor that let the engine breathe deeply and rev to a 5,500-rpm redline above its 4,600-rpm horsepower peak. The torque output was a strong 425 lbs.-ft. at 2,800 rpm. Wright's combination attached the 383 to a Borg-Warner T-10 four-speed with a 2.20.0:1 low gear, which didn't hurt its drag-strip performance one bit.

The 1963 Polara was considered the top trim level "Dodge" back in 1963, when the even fancier Custom 880 was thought of as, well, a Custom 880 instead of a Dodge. The basic Polara 500 convertible (which included four bucket seats) listed for just $3,196 and weighed 3,546 lbs. Wright's test car had some 340 lbs. of extras, including a Sure Grip differential, power steering, power brakes, electric windows, an AM/FM radio, a heater, a Sun tachometer and seat belts. The cost was $4,265.79.

Jerry Heasley

1966 HEMI CHARGER

Though the car itself was large, lush and heavy, the availability of the optional 426-cid Hemi V-8 engine made the Charger a genuine contender for the hottest niche in the muscle car market. The 425-hp big-block V-8 featured a pair of four-barrel carburetors, extra-wide dual exhausts and all sorts of heavy-duty performance hardware. The Hemi package also included engine call-out badges, a heavy-duty suspension, larger brakes and 7.75 x 14 Blue Streak racing tires. The use of either a four-speed manual gear box or a TorqueFlite automatic transmission was mandatory. Dodge specified that the Hemi's short 12-month or 12,000 miles warranty would be invalidated by "extreme operation" or driveline modifications.

Fastback styling was back in vogue in the mid-1960s and the Dodge Charger was a participant in the "Dodge Rebellion," an advertising and promotional campaign that pushed high-performance motoring.

The Charger was really based on the Coronet platform and had essentially the same lower body styling, but with a more streamlined look and rich interior appointments and trimmings.

With its low and wide roof line, the Charger showcased a drastic interpretation of fastback styling. Its "electric razor" grille was also quite distinctive looking.

Soon after the Charger arrived on the scene, almost every car enthusiast magazine rushed to take a test drive and publish the results. The Charger was new and exciting and having the car featured on the cover of a magazine was a sure way to pump up circulation and newsstand sales.

Most magazines tested Chargers with the 383-cid V-8, a big-block engine that cranked out 325 hp at 4800 rpm. This combination was actually quite fast, with *Car and Driver* registering a 7.8-second 0-to-60 time and doing the quarter-mile in 16.2 seconds at 88 mph. With the same engine and tranny, *Motor Trend* reported an 8.9-second 0-to-60 time and 16.3 seconds for the quarter-mile at 85 mph. The huffing-and-puffing Hemi could shave 2 seconds or more off acceleration times like those.

Total production of 1966 Chargers hit 37,300 cars. Of these, only 468 had Hemis, of which a mere 218 featured TorqueFlite.

Phil Kunz

1967 HEMI CORONET

Dodge production numbers show only 283 Hemi Coronet R/Ts were built for 1967. That means you better have deep pockets if you want to own a nice survivor today.

You could get the new-for-1966 Street Hemi in the 1966 Dodge Coronet 500, as well as in the Dodge 440 and base models. So when the 1967 pre-production publicity photos showed a couple of Coronet 500 hardtops with 426 Hemi badges, it led to a bit of confusion because press kits and literature said the Hemi engine would only be available as a limited-production option for the top-line Coronet R/T and also for the Charger fastback.

On January 23, 1967, Dodge announced that the Coronet 440 two-door hardtop was being built on a production basis to meet National Hot Rod Association's (NHRA) Super Stock B rules. The WO23 cars — as they are known — were the latest in the Mopar tradition of special lightweight models built for drag racing. A shipping weight of 3,686 lbs. was given for Dodge 440s with Street Hemi engines.

There were two versions of these drag-racing-only Dodges. One came with a modified TorqueFlite automatic using a 2,300 to 2,500-rpm-stall-speed torque converter and 4.86:1 Sure-Grip Chrysler-built 8 3/4-inch differential. The second had a four-speed manual transmission with Hurst linkage, reinforced gearing and clutch and an explosion-proof clutch housing. This second combo drew a 4.88 Sure-Grip Dana differential.

The S/S-B cars could be ordered through your friendly Dodge dealer and came without a warranty of any kind.

To meet the rules, Dodge had to build at least 50 of the cars and when 55 went out the door, enough was enough. Plymouth was also allowed to build 55 similar Plymouth Belvedere II two-door hardtops (RO23).

At least the availability of S/S-B Dodge Coronets was of some consolation to those who missed the Coronet 500 and other lesser-model Hemis. Prices for nice survivors are in the stratosphere today.

Jerry Heasley

1967 CORONET R/T

One of the things the muscle car era did was to bring high-performance driving to streets and drive-ins across America. One no longer had to set aside Saturday or Sunday for a trip to the drag strip to see cars that could get up to 60 mph in under seven seconds! And there was nothing like the thrill of pulling up to a gas pump or a root beer stand and hearing a muscle machine rumble up alongside you.

Many "street" muscle cars were also weekend drag racing cars in the 1960s and the R/T badge was intended to emphasize street-and-strip nature of such beasts. The R/T stood for road-and-track, and we're not talking about a sports car magazine! A Charger-like "electric shaver" grille distinguished the hot mid-size Dodge, although it did not utilize the fastback model's retractable headlights. Other Coronet R/T features included simulated rear fender air vents and non-functional hood scoops.

Standard under the hood was the 440 Magnum V-8 linked to either a four-speed manual gear box or TorqueFlite automatic transmission. The Magnum engine had a 4.32 x 3.75-inch bore and stroke, a 10.1:1 compression ratio and

a single four-barrel carburetor. It developed 375 hp at 4600 rpm and 480 lbs.-ft. of torque at 3200 rpm. One 440-powered R/T did 0-to-60 mph in 7.2 seconds and the quarter-mile in 15.4 at 94 mph. *Motor Trend* drove the same car with racing slicks mounted and did the 0-to-60 test in 6.5 seconds. The fat-tired car required 14.7 seconds for the quarter-mile with a 96-mph terminal speed.

The R/T hardtop listed for $3,199 and a convertible was $3,438. The package also included a stiff suspension, heavy-duty brakes and 7.75 x 14 Red Streak tires. Production amounted to 10,181 cars, including a mere 628 ragtops.

For $907.60, the Hemi V-8 could be special ordered for a Coronet R/T. This powerful V-8 had a 4.25 x 3.75-inch bore and stroke, a 10.25:1 compression ratio and two four-barrel carbs. It produced 425 hp at 5000 rpm and 490 lbs.-ft. of torque at 4000 rpm. *Motor Trend's* stock-tired Hemi-powered Coronet went 0-to-60 in 6.8 seconds and ran the quarter-mile in 15.0 seconds at 96 mph. When shod with racing slicks, it went 0-to-60 in 6.6 seconds and did the quarter-mile in 14.8 seconds at 99 mph.

Jerry Heasley

1968 HEMI CHARGER

The Hemi Charger was a quarter-mile rocket meant to go straight from point A to point B in the absolute minimum amount of time.

By 1968, Dodge had its go-fast fleet in high gear. The King Kong Coronet was its mid-size muscle machine and the jumping-ramp-roofed Charger arrived in '66 to offer the family man with Hi-Po pretensions a good-looking brute of a car that had ample storage space. Out on the streets, when performance was spoken, Hemis could be heard rumbling under the air-scooped hoods of Mopars and Chargers had no problem digesting 426 cubes of bonsai big-block in their engine bay. Then Dodge sealed its deal with the devil and unveiled the second-generation '68 Charger. It was like beauty-and-the-beast combined in one fabulous fastback.

Compared to the '66-'67 Charger, the swoopy '68 was slimmer and smoother. With a 117-inch wheelbase, the Charger was no compact, but it didn't look like Haystacks Calhoun either. A new "Coke-bottle" profile drew your attention to the rear quarters like a mini-skirted gal in the Dodge white-hat ads. The sheet metal tapered to the front and gave the car a thrusting image that made it look fast standing still.

The hood was lower. A spoiler blended smoothly into the rear deck. The integrated bumper-grille had an aluminum molding and in-corporated hidden headlights. Simulated "waste gates" in the hood and sides and a quick-fill gas cap were other fighter-jet touches. Rally-style parking lights hid in the bumper.

A handful of six-cylinder '68 Chargers were built, but the great majority were V-8-powered. The standard V-8 was the 318-cid/230-hp small-block engine. Options included the 383-cid/335-hp two-barrel V-8, the 440 Magnum V-8 with 375 hp at 4,600 rpm and 480 lbs.-ft. of torque at 3,200 rpm and the 426 Hemi V-8 with 425 hp at 5,000 rpm and 490 lbs.-ft. of torque at 4,000 rpm. Performance numbers reported for the '68 Hemi Charger included 0-to-60 mph in 5.3 seconds and a quarter-mile run in 13.8 seconds at 105 mph.

Carrying the high-performance torch was the new R/T (Road and Track) which came standard with a 440 Magnum V-8, heavy-duty suspension and brakes, dual exhausts and fat tires. "Bumble bee" stripes made the R/T buzz louder. The stripes ran around the rear deck and down the quarter panels. The popular new look pushed Charger production to 96,108 (including 908 six-cylinder cars) and 18,307 had the R/T package.

Only a scant 475 Chargers came stuffed with the 426 Hemi.

Phil Kunz

1968 DART GTS

GTS meant GT Sport. It was the name of a sexy new-for-'68 "sawed-off shotgun" that was a whole bunch more than a sporty compact car. "Not to take the edge off the Road Runner, the GTS might be a more sensible package," said *Hot Rod* magazines's Steve Kelly. "The base price is higher, but you get things like carpet on the floor, fat tires, bucket seats and a few other niceties that can make Saturday night roaming more comfortable. The engine's smaller, but that could prove an advantage for drag racing classes."

Two hefty V-8s were available. A 340-cid small-block engine was standard. It was derived from the 273-318-cid Chrysler family of engines and had a 4.04 x 3.31-inch bore and stroke, a 10.5:1 compression ratio and a single four-barrel carburetor. The 340 engine cranked out 275 hp at 5000 rpm and 340 lbs.-ft. of torque at 3200 rpm. A 383-cid big-block engine with a four-barrel carburetor and 300 hp was optional. The 383 added 89 lbs. to the car if you got a four-speed gearbox and 136 lbs. if you got an automatic transmission. A standard 3.23:1 rear axle was supplied, but 3.55:1 and 3.91:1 ratio axles were also available as optional equipment.

Other technical enhancements included a low-restriction dual exhaust system with chrome tips, a heavy-duty Rallye suspension, 14 x 5.5-inch wheels and E70-14 Red Streak tires. Although a column-shifted three-speed manual transmission was standard, most Dart GTS models had either a four-speed manual gearbox with a Hurst floor shifter or a competition-type TorqueFlite automatic transmission.

Also identifying the GTS were hood power bulges with air vents, body side racing stripes, special GTS emblems and simulated mag wheel covers. A bumblebee stripe to decorate the car's rear end was a no-cost option. Vinyl front bucket seats were standard in the $2,611 hardtop and optional in the $3,383 convertible.

The 1968 Dart GTS hardtop with the 340-cid/270-hp power train tested out with a 0-to-60 time of 6 seconds. It did the quarter-mile in a "Scat Pack" time of 15.2 seconds. *Hot Rod* magazine published even better numbers for its 340-cid TorqueFlite-equipped Dart GTS, which ran down the quarter-mile in 14.38 seconds at 97 mph.

1969 CHARGER 500

Sleek, beautiful new styling had characterized the '68 Dodge Charger and had helped to boost the model's sales to 96,100 units — from only 15,800 in 1967. Wind-tunnel testing revealed that the good-looking body's recessed grille and tunneled-in rear window created wind turbulence on the high-speed NASCAR superspeedways. Dodge engineers figured out that a flush grille and flush-mounted rear glass could reduce this wind resistance. Some say that a prototype car with these changes — which was actually the first Charger 500 — was really a modified 1968 model.

The production–type 1969 Charger 500 was issued as a special limited-production model based on the style of the Charger 500 prototype. It was released to the public on September 1, 1968, but as a 1969 model. Dodge Division literature said it was offered specifically for high-performance racing tracks and available only to qualified race drivers. In reality, that was a great promotion, as muscle car lovers flocked to Dodge dealerships trying to buy one of the cars. Chances are pretty good that, if they didn't get one, they at least drove away in another Charger or a jazzy Coronet.

The Charger 500's handcrafted body modifications were actually the workmanship of a company called Creative Industries, which was an aftermarket firm from Detroit, Michigan. A minimum of 500 such cars had to be sold to the public to authorize the changes and make the Charger legal for racing under NASCAR rules. The Charger 500 model designation was based on the number of cars scheduled to be made.

Even though some books say Hemi engines were standard in the Charger 500, at least 392 of these cars have been researched and only about nine percent have turned out to have Hemis. If you didn't get the monster motor, at least you did get a heavy-duty suspension, a four-speed manual gear box (or TorqueFlite automatic transmission), a rear bumblebee stripe, "500" model badges, a special shorter-than-stock rear deck lid and a custom-made rear window package shelf.

Officially, 32 Hemi-powered Charger 500s were built, though experts have tracked down serial numbers for 35 such vehicles. About 15 cars had four-speed manual gearboxes. Charger 500s with automatic transmission covered the quarter-mile in 14.01 seconds at 100 mph. Cars with the optional four-speed manual transmission were significantly faster. They did the quarter-mile in 13.60 seconds at 107.44 mph.

Tom Glatch

1969 CHARGER DAYTONA

Along with its winged cousin, the Plymouth Superbird, the Charger Daytona was certainly among the most distinctive American cars ever dreamed up, and a true fantasy machine for muscle car fans.

Shortly after the Dodge Charger 500 bowed in 1969, Ford Motor Co. launched the Torino Talladega and Mercury Cyclone Spoiler models. Both FoMoCo products had superior aerodynamics, which helped them to outrun the slippery Charger 500s in enough races (including the Daytona 500) to take the National Association of Stock Car Automobile Racing title. The '69 Charger Daytona was designed to get the NASCAR championship back.

A company named Creative Industries received the contract to build 500 Daytonas to legalize the 200-mph body modifications for stock car competition. The rear window was flush, rather than tunneled. The front fenders and hood were lengthened and dipped lower in front. The front air intake was lower. Reinforced-plastic parts were used on the front-end extension and hood parts. The concealed

headlights popped up like bug eyes. The hood featured a fresh air intake similar to the NASA inlets employed on aircraft. The hood and fenders had cooling vents. At the rear was an airfoil/spoiler of fin-and-wing that provided greater aerodynamic stability. Dodge press releases noted the modifications had been submitted to NASCAR for approval.

The winged cars won so many races that NASCAR outlawed the Hemi as well as wedge engines with piston displacements over 305 cubic inches.

Experts say that total production of Daytonas was 503 units. Officially, 433 cars with base 375-hp 440 Magnum V-8s were built for the streets and 70 were turned out with Hemi V-8s under their snout. The breakout as to how many of the Hemi Daytonas had four-speed manual or automatic transmissions was 22 and 48, respectively. One yellow Daytona, with 5,000 original miles, has been documented to be a car with a dealer-installed 440 Six-Pack V-8. Dodge did not, however, offer this set up as a factory option.

Phil Kunz

1969 CORONET R/T

Back in the 1960s, thousands of young car enthusiasts looked forward to weekends at the drag strip — and they didn't go there to watch other muscle car owners run. Instead, they spent Saturday night in the garage, tuning the engine of the car they had driven all week for a couple of quick runs on Sunday afternoon. After that, it was re-tuned for additional street use until the following weekend. The "Dodge Boys" were well aware of how the car world worked, so they used the R/T designation to identify the cars best suited for dual-purpose use. The mid-sized Coronet was one of the favorites.

In 1969, the Dodge Coronet R/T continued to play its traditional role as the high-performance model in the Coronet series. It included all of the features of the upscale Coronet 500 model, plus the Magnum 440-cid V-8, TorqueFlite automatic transmission, a light group option, body sill moldings and R/T bumblebee stripes across the trunk lid and down the fender sides. Two simulated hood air scoops located on the rear fenders, just ahead of the rear wheel openings, were optional equipment.

The Coronet R/T two-door hardtop was designated model WS23. In standard format it

listed for $3,442 and tipped the scales at 3,601 lbs. Also available was the model WS27 convertible, which carried a $3,660 base sticker price and weighed in at 3,721 lbs.

A "Six-Pack" arrangement of carburetors was the big news for the Coronet R/T in 1969. Three two-barrel Holley carbs sat on top of a 440 Magnum V-8 that harnessed 390 horses and 490 lbs.-ft. of torque. A fiberglass performance hood covered the three carburetors. Also available was a Ramcharger fresh-air induction system, which was standard on Hemi-powered cars and extra-cost equipment on others. The four-barrel 440-cid was, of course, the standard motor.

A Hemi was an additional $418 option for 1969 Coronet R/Ts. Model year production totaled 7,238 hardtops and convertibles combined. This included 97 two-door hardtops (58 with a four-speed manual transmission) and 10 ragtops (six with TorqueFlite) fitted with 426 Hemis.

One magazine test-dragged a '69 six-pack R/T (complete with dummy rear fender scoops) to a 105.14-mph 13.65-second quarter-mile run. The Dodge's 0-to-60 time was a blazing 6.6 seconds.

Phil Kunz

1969 DART SWINGER 340

Not every Mopar muscle machine that came down the pike was a fire-breathing, Hemi-powered, big-engine-in-small-body bomber that fit in better at the drag strip than at the strip mall. There were also some compact Dodges and Plymouths fitted with hi-po small-block V-8s that provided enough sizzle for the masses without going overboard on the "high-end" high-performance hardware. The 1969 Dodge Swinger 340 was one example of such a car.

This model qualified as a member of the hot Dodge "Scat Pack" and proudly wore its bumblebee stripes, even though it was really more of a swinger than a stinger. Designed to give muscle car fans more bang for the buck by emphasizing performance over luxury, the Swinger fit right into the "budget muscle car" trend that produced cars like the Plymouth Road Runner and Pontiac GTO Judge. It was like a small-scale counterpart to such models.

As muscle cars went, the Swinger 340 was a bargain and collector's today can still swing a pretty good deal on one of these cars.

"Play your cards right and three bills can put you in a whole lot of car this year," said an advertisement showing a red Swinger two-door hardtop with a black vinyl roof. "Dart Swinger 340. Newest member of the Dodge Scat Pack. You get 340 cubes of high-winding, four-barrel V-8. A four-speed Hurst shifter on the floor to keep things moving. All the other credentials are in order."

Standard equipment for 1969 included the 340-cid/275-hp V-8 engine, four-speed full-synchro manual transmission with Hurst shifter, a three-spoke steering wheel with a padded hub, a heavy-duty Rallye suspension, "Swinger" bumblebee stripes, D70 x 14 wide-tread tires, dual exhausts, a performance hood with die-cast louvers and fat 14-inch wheels. Seven colors were available for the car and four colors for vinyl roofs.

A total of 20,000 were built. Even today, muscle car collectors can find bargains in the Swinger 340 market, since these cars don't look as flashy as a GTS, although they are equally fast.

Jerry Heasley

1970 CHALLENGER R/T 440

In writing about the '70 Challenger R/T, *Car Life* magazine posed the unusual question, "What do you call a car with a 440 Six-Pack, four on the floor, purple metallic paint and an urge to challenge the world? Genghis Grape?"

The new-for-1970 Challenger was Dodge's answer to the Mustang, Camaro, Cougar, Firebird, Camaro and Barracuda. The sports compact model was offered in three body styles: two-door hardtop, formal coupe and convertible. Challengers featured a low, wide look with a full-width, scoop-like grille opening. The body sides had the familiar "Coke-bottle" profile with raised rear fenders tapering down at the tail end. Two large, rectangular tail lamps nearly filled the entire rear beauty panel.

For high-performance buffs, Dodge offered all three models in the Challenger R/T format. The 440-cid Magnum V-8 was one option — at it was a beast!

The standard version of this overhead-valve V-8 was a $250 option. It featured a 4.32 x 3.75-inch bore and stroke, hydraulic valve lifters, five main bearings, a 10.0:1 compression ratio, a Carter AFB four-barrel carburetor and a 350 hp at 4000 rpm output rating. It produced 425 lbs.-ft. of torque at 3400 rpm. A dual exhaust system with reverse-flow mufflers was standard. A 375-hp version of the 440-cid V-8 with a hotter cam was $113 additional. There was also a "Six-Pack" version with three Holley two-barrel carburetors.

Dodge built a total of 14,889 Challenger R/T two-door hardtops, which had a base price of $3,266. The formal hardtop listed for $3,498 and 3,979 were built. Naturally, the convertible was the rarer model. The ragtop had a $3,535 window sticker and a mere 1,070 were made.

The Challenger convertible with the 440-cid 375-hp V-8 could move from 0-to-60 mph in 7.1 seconds. The quarter-mile got covered in 14.64 seconds with a terminal speed of 97.82 mph. The Hemi-powered version of the hardtop was even faster. It did the quarter-mile in 14 seconds at 104 mph.

Jerry Heasley

1970 HEMI CHALLENGER R/T

A muscle car fan could pick up a Challenger R/T hardtop for $3,266 new in 1970. For another, $778.75 you could get the Hemi shoehorned in under the hood.

And it was money well spent! A Hemi could propel this legendar Mopar to 104 mph in the quarter-mile right off the lot.

The 1970 Dodge Challenger came as a beautifully styled two-door hardtop or a ragtop, plus a Special Edition (SE) formal-roofed hardtop. Car and Driver magazine once described the muscular Challenger as "Lavish execution with little or no thought towards practical application."

Quotations like that really sum up the Hemi Challenger. Nobody needed such a car to get to work or run out for a pack of cigarettes. In the winter (and maybe even the summer) you could burn out a set of rear tires without moving an inch. The Hemi Challenger was a race car. It was really fast! It didn't even have to look pretty — but it did! And that made it a very special product within the muscle car market niche.

All three Challenger body styles were offered in the high-performance R/T (Road and Track, if you prefer) series and all R/T models had large-displacement V-8s. A 383-cid engine with a four-barrel carburetor was standard.

The 1970 Challenger R/T hardtop listed for $3,266 and weighed 3,402 lbs. According to Chrysler records, 14,889 were built. The 3,498-pound convertible listed for $3,535 and had a 3,979-unit production run. Only 1,070 Challenger SEs, base priced at $3,498, left the factory. The SE weighed in at 3,437 lbs.

Challenger buyers could add a 375-hp/440-cid Magnum V-8 to the R/T model for just $130.55 or they could get a 390-hp version for only $249.55 more. For those who wanted maximum performance, the Street Hemi was also available at a price of $778.75.

Hemi production included 287 hardtops (137 with four-speeds), 60 SE hardtops (23 with four-speeds) and nine convertibles (five with four-speeds).

All Hemi Challengers were R/Ts. And who cares if they weren't great daily drivers? They were ridiculously fast, they looked great, and chicks dug 'em.

OK, maybe all chicks didn't dig 'em but muscle car fans sure did.

Jerry Heasley

1970 CHALLENGER T/A

The 1970 Dodge Challenger T/A was a kissing cousin to the Plymouth AAR Barracuda. Unfortunately, the "fish car" usually sees more of the limelight than its Dodge counterpart. Too bad. The Challenger T/A was a fast, fast machine that got up to 60 mph in only 6 seconds.

"Wild and woolly" is a good way to describe the '70 Challenger T/A Sport Coupe. Chrysler allowed the Dodge Division to schedule production of 2,500 copies of the model. The plan was to build just enough to meet the requirements for racing its new Challenger "pony car" in the Sports Car Club of America's (SCCA) Trans-American Sedan Championship series.

The Trans-Am was a competitive venue for small-block-V-8-powered two-door hardtops and two-door sedans (coupes). Chrysler's Pete Hutchinson used a de-stroked 340-cid V-8 block as the basis for a competition coupe that ran a small 305-cid V-8, but cranked out 440 hp.

Street-ready T/As had the same snorkel-type hood scoop, side-exit exhausts and lock-pin-secured flat-black hood as the all-out racing cars.

Of course, if you raised the hood you could spot differences in the engine compartment. The street version carried some special underhood goodies including a 340-cid "Six-Pack" V-8 with three two-barrel carburetors. Buyers had a choice of TorqueFlite automatic transmission or a four-speed manual gearbox.

A ducktail rear deck lid spoiler was part of the Challenger T/A package, along with heavy-duty underpinnings. The package also included a Sure-Grip differential. Performance axle ratios, semi-metallic front disc brakes, semi-metallic rear drum brakes, a specific black body side tape stripe and mixed size tires (E60-15 tires were used up front with G60-15s mounted in the rear). To provide clearance for the pipes of the dual exhaust system with the fatter rear tires, the T/As were "jacked up" in the rear through the use of increased rear spring camber.

The 1970 Challenger T/As were good for 0-to-60 mph in a flat 6 seconds. They could hit 100 mph in 14 seconds and do the quarter-mile in 14.5 seconds.

Jerry Heasley

1970 CHARGER R/T

Car Life had a pretty good handle on the '70 Charger R/T when it reported that "They keep making the Charger go like stink and handle better than a lot of so-called sportsters."

For a big car, the Charger R/T packed a big wallop when it came to high-speed performance. *Motor Trend* did a comparison test between a 440-powered Charger R/T, a Mercury Cyclone GT and an Oldsmobile Cutlass SX in its April 1970 issue. The Charger test car had the standard equipment V-8, which produced 375 hp at 4600 rpm and 480 lbs.-ft. of torque at 3200 rpm. It also had a 3.55:1 rear axle. The car did 0-to-60 mph in 6.4 seconds and covered the quarter-mile in 14.9 seconds at 98 mph. It also averaged 14.9 to 15.7 mpg, which was much better fuel mileage than the two other cars.

The 1970 Dodge Charger continued to use the same semi fastback body that it had employed in 1969. Naturally, there were several minor trim changes to set cars of both years apart. The R/T (Road/Track) edition was again marketed as a higher-performance version of the basic Charger. It had a newly designed grille, a new loop-style front bumper, two hood scoops (one near each outside edge of the hood), big bolt-on side scoops (with R/T badges) on the rear quarter panels and a choice of longitudinal or bumblebee racing stripes on the rear. The 440-cid Magnum V-8 engine was standard equipment, along with Mopar's sturdy Torque-Flite automatic transmission. Other Charger R/T features included a heavy-duty 70-amp/hour battery, heavy-duty automatic-adjusting drum brakes, heavy-duty front and rear shock absorbers, an extra-heavy-duty suspension, three-speed windshield wipers, all-vinyl front bucket seats, carpeting, a cigar lighter and F70-14 fiberglass-belted white sidewall tires (or black sidewall raised-white-letter tires). R/T model designations were also carried on the center of the rear escutcheon panel, directly below the Dodge name.

All Charger R/T models included blacked-out escutcheon panels and large bumblebee stripes running across the trunk lid and down the rear fender sides. A hefty jump to $3,711 was seen in the price of the basic 440 Magnum-powered Charger R/T for 1970. Total production this year dropped to 10,337 units, including a mere 42 cars with 426-cid Hemi V-8s.

Doug Mitchel

1970 CORONET R/T

Like most automakers, Dodge offered several flavors of muscle in its mid-size cars and the basis for the hotter models was the Coronet, which was facelifted with a new grille and new delta-shaped taillights. Instead of using a conventional bumper running across the front of the car, Dodge switched to a bumper that consisted of heavy moldings that looped around the grille openings. The smooth split grille tapered towards the center.

The Coronet R/T was a high-performance version of the upscale Coronet 500. On the R/T, there were dummy rear fender scoops above and ahead of the front wheel openings and the air scoops wore R/T emblems. These emblems were repeated on the nose of the car and between each of the segmented, tapering tail lamps. A bumblebee stripe circled the rear end.

The Coronet R/T hardtop was base priced at $3,569 and had a production run of 2,319 units. Only 296 Coronet R/T convertibles (base priced at $3,785) were made. The hardtop had a shipping weight of 3,573 lbs. and the ragtop was about 65 lbs. heavier. It was the last year for the Coronet convertible body style and also the last year for the Coronet R/T model.

Standard R/T equipment included all Coronet 500 features plus the 440-cid Magnum V-8 engine, TorqueFlite automatic transmission, a heavy-duty 70-amp/hour battery, heavy-duty self-adjusting drum brakes, heavy-duty front and rear shock absorbers and extra-heavy-duty suspension.

Engines were essentially the same as before with the "440 Six-Pack" back for the second year with its triple two-barrel carburetors. The 426-cid/425-hp Hemi was priced at $718 and only 14 Hemi R/Ts — 13 hardtops and one convertible — were built. The R/T continued to come in an outrageous assortment of colors, like Plum Crazy (purple), Sublime (green), Go-Mango, Hemi Orange and Banana Yellow. Optional vinyl roofs came in black, white, green or "gator grain."

Five Scat Pack options were available to muscle car fans who wanted to dress up their Coronet R/T a little bit. They included the Showboat engine dress-up kit, the Read-Out gauge package, the Kruncher axle and Hurst shifter combination, the Bee-Liever high-rise manifold and carb setup and the Six-Pack option with a fiberglass hood and other hi-po goodies.

Jerry Heasley

1970 CORONET SUPER BEE

The Dodge Super Bee was an "old school" muscle car created with an emphasis on keeping the price down as low as possible, while still delivering some serious go-fast hardware. But the Super Bee was not a "cheap" car. The hardtop version was in the same bracket as a top-of-the line Coronet 500 hardtop — in fact it was $26 more expensive. In the fancy 500 model, the buyer was getting more chrome, richer upholstery, carpets and a cigar lighter. In the Super Bee, the buyer got less of the comfort and convenience items and more muscle for the money.

Also available for an even lower price was the Super Bee coupe (two-door sedan), which listed for $3,012. Now, that was $167 more than a Coronet 440 Deluxe coupe, but you got a whole lot more under the hood. So the Super Bee was more of a "good value" car than it was cheap. You were just buying hardware, rather than tinsel.

Restyled for 1970 along the lines of the Coronet R/T, the Super Bee did not get the dummy rear fender scoops, at least as standard equipment. It also had horizontally divided (rather than individually segmented) tail lamps. New options included a hood mounted tach and a rear deck lid spoiler. Buyers could get the R/T-type bumblebee stripe or pipe-shaped upper and lower rear fender stripes with a circular Super Bee decal between them.

Still standard ingredients were the 383-cid Magnum V-8, a heavy-duty torsion-bar suspension and a three-speed manual transmission (last year's four-speed manual gear box was optional). Despite the price reduction, production dropped to 11,540 hardtops and 3,966 coupes. Hemis went into only 32 hardtops (21 with four-speed) and four coupes (all four-speeds). Wouldn't you love to own one today?

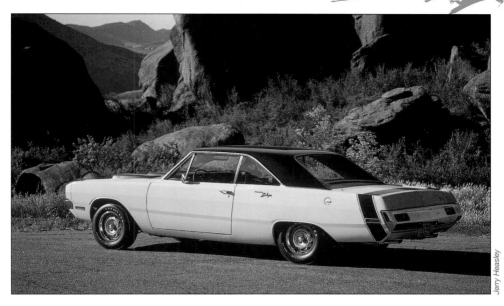

Jerry Heasley

1970 DART SWINGER 340

Even today, in-the-know muscle car collectors will find tremendous bargains in the Swinger 340 market. These cars just don't share the flashy looks of the Dodge Dart GTS, although they are equally as fast. And you know that some people will pay silly money just to get a little flashiness.

Jerry Heasley once wrote in *Car Review*, way back in 1986, "If the Road Runner was the first econo-supercar, then the Dart was very much its counterpart in the compact lineup. Nobody built this car better than the 'Good Guys' in the white hats from Dodge."

When it came to the Swinger 340, the Good Guys advertised the car as "6000 rpm for under $3,000." With a short 97-inch wheelbase and overall length of just 178 inches, the Swinger 340 was a small, light car that used hot versions of the small-block V-8 to the best advantage.

The 1970 Dodge Darts shared revised front and rear cosmetics and the Swinger 340 version even got a slightly reduced $2,808 price tag. A three-speed manual gearbox was on the standard equipment list. Instead of small power vents, the mini Mopar muscle machine now carried two long, narrow hood scoops.

Despite the introduction of the all-new Challenger "pony car" in 1970, the Swinger 340 remained popular enough to generate 13,785 assemblies. One reason for its popularity was that insurance companies considered it a "compact" car. As a result, the insurers charged lower premiums for a Swinger 340 than for other more obvious muscle cars.

Of course, the Swinger 340 was also as fast as — or perhaps even slightly faster than—the 340 powered Dart GT Sport. It accomplished 0-to-60 mph in about 6.5 seconds and did the quarter-mile in around 14.5 seconds with a 98 mph terminal speed. At 3,179 lbs., the '70 Swinger carried about 11.4 lbs. per horsepower and proved to be highly motivated by the 340-cid V-8's "herd" of 275 horses.

1971 HEMI CHALLENGER

For maximum visual impact, as well as an outward statement of purpose, many Hemi Challenger owners selected bright Hemi orange paint trimmed in white. After all, if you put the big engine under the hood, you might as well let the world know it.

Dodge scored a hit with its first pony car, the 1970 Challenger. Up until then, Dodge had relied on special mid-size Chargers and Coronets and compact Darts to uphold its performance image.

The Challenger succeeded so well that it outsold the Barracuda 83,000 to 55,000 in its first year. The next season, though, sales fell off drastically and the Challenger sold 30,000 units. Still, the Barracuda's dropped to 19,000.

With the Challenger, Dodge was clearly selling performance in a package that looked the part. So it's not surprising that 93 percent of the 1971 model run was fitted with V-8 engines, even though the "Slant Six" was avail-able. Nearly 17 percent were optional engines, ranging all the way up to the 425-hp Hemi.

Unfortunately, 1971 would be the last year for the 426-cid Hemi, as emissions, safety and insurance considerations put the horsepower race under a caution flag. However, in 1971, Dodge was definitely promoting power and performance.

The Street Hemi engine, a $790 option on the '71 Challenger, had continued unchanged after its introduction in 1966. It had a bore and stroke of 4.25 x 3.75 inches, a 10.25:1 compression ratio, hydraulic valve lifters and dual four-barrel Carter AFB carbs mounted inline.

On the Hemi Challengers, a flat-black finished air scoop was mounted to the carbs and poked through a hole in the hood. This was the impressive "shaker" hood, so named because you could watch the torque twist the engine as throttle was applied. Some cars also had chrome NASCAR-style hood hold-down pins.

John Lee

1971 CHALLENGER R/T HEMI

Road Test magazine summed up the Mopar muscle car marketplace in 1971 when it said, "For the street racer who doesn't mind sticking close to 6 grand in his toy, the 440 Six-Pack or 426 Hemi will be very hard to beat in the stoplight grand prix." And this was especially true when you ordered the monster motor in the small-bodied Challenger. The result was a machine that was not only sportier, but also snortier, than anything else on the street.

For 1971, the Dodge Challenger R/T sub-series had only one model left. This was the two-door hardtop. It listed for $3,273 and weighed 3,495 lbs. With the muscle car fervor winding down, this rare car found a mere 4,630 buyers. Styling changes for model year 1971 included a new grille, color-keyed bumpers and two dummy scoops in front of the rear wheel wells.

Standard equipment on all 1971 Challengers included Chrysler's Air Control system, front and rear side armrests, a front ash tray, a cigarette lighter (except in the base Chal-

lenger coupe), an evaporative emission control system, color-keyed carpeting, ventless side glass, a glove box with a rotary latch (lockable in convertibles), dual headlights, a heater and defroster, dual horns (except coupe), dome and parking-brake system warning lights, a manual left-hand outside mirror, an inside day-night mirror, roof drip moldings, wheel opening moldings (except Coupe), bucket seats with foam front cushions, a three-spoke steering wheel with simulated woodgrain and a padded hub and electric windshield wipers.

However, the optional performance power plants were still available.

Only 71 of the Challenger R/Ts with the 426-cid Street Hemi V-8 were ordered this season. A dozen of these cars had TorqueFlite automatic transmission. The rest were equipped with a four-speed manual transmission. It was the last year for the Challenger R/T model. The handful of these cars fitted with Hemi engines really went out with a bang!

Jerry Heasley

1971 CHARGER R/T 440/440 SIX-PACK

According to Dodge Division, the 1971 Dodge Charger R/T 440/440 Six-Pack was designed "strictly for adults." It was good for 0-to-60 mph in under 7 seconds. Getting to the end of a drag strip took under 15 seconds. By that time you were moving almost 100 mph!

The Dodge Charger started life in 1966 as a semi-limited-production specialty car, but it caught on and grew to become an important part of the Chrysler division's line. In 1969, more than 70,000 Chargers were sold. For 1971, management decided that it was time to give the Charger an image of its own — one quite separate from that of the mid-sized Coronet.

The Charger name was now applied to two-door hardtops that had a 115-inch wheelbase, while the Coronet name was used only on 118-inch-wheelbase four-door sedans. The re-sized Charger was 2 inches shorter in wheelbase than the 1970 model and more than 3 inches shorter at 205.4 inches. It also had nearly 3 more inches of front overhang and 3 1/2 inches more width.

The new Charger seemed to be the perfect size for a sporty performance car. The R/T model was the quintessential "muscle" model and technically represented a sub-series of the middle-priced Charger 500 series. It included all of the many features of the Charger 500, plus hot stuff like heavy-duty underpinnings and the 440-cid Magnum V-8.

This engine had the same 3.75-inch stroke as the 426-cid Hemi, but a larger 4.32-inch bore size. The base version, with a single four-barrel carburetor, produced 370 hp at 4600 rpm and 480 lbs.-ft. of torque at 3200 rpm. It had a 9.1:1 compression ratio. In a four-Charger test in December 1970, *Motor Trend* drove a 370-hp 1971 Charger SE with automatic transmission and a 3.23:1 rear axle. It did 0-to-60 mph in a flat 7 seconds and covered the quarter-mile in 14.93 seconds at 96.4 mph.

Also featured in the same test was a 1971 Charger Super Bee with the 440 "Six-Pack" engine. This version added three two-barrel carburetors and a 10.3:1 compression ratio. The Six-Pack V-8 developed 385 hp at 4700 rpm and 490 lbs.-ft. of torque at 3200 rpm. The car it was in also had an automatic transmission, but it was hooked to a 4.10:1 rear axle. This cut the 0 to-60 time to 6.9 seconds. The quarter-mile required 14.74 seconds with a terminal speed of 97.3 mph.

Jerry Heasley

1971 CHARGER SUPER BEE HEMI

Not too many 1971 Charger Hemi Super Bees were built. In fact, the total was 22 cars, of which nine had four-speeds and 13 came with TorqueFlite automatic transmissions.

That put these Hemi powerhouses on the short list of the scarcest muscle cars around.

The Dodge Charger was completely restyled for the 1971 model year. It had a semi-fastback roofline with a flush rear window and an integral rear deck lid spoiler. Dodge's Charger Super Bee was manufactured only this one year and used the same restyled body. The Charger Super Bee was aimed at the same market niche as the Coronet Super Bee and represented a value-priced serious high-performance package.

Price-tagged at $3,271, the Charger Super Bee included a standard 383-cid Magnum V-8 that cranked out 300 hp. The engine used a single four-barrel carburetor and came attached to a three-speed manual transmission with a floor-mounted gear shifter. Covering the motor was a "power bulge" hood with flat black finish. The Charger Super Bee had tape stripes and bumblebee decals. The interior was similar to that of the Charger 500, but substituted a standard bench seat for bucket seats. The Rallye suspension components package was used. The standard tires were fat F70-14 black walls with white lettering. The Charger Super Bee's optional equipment list was fat, too.

All Charger Super Bees carried a Mopar V-8. Available engines included the 440 Wedge with "Six-Pack" carburetion or the 426-cid Street Hemi. Unlike the 8.7:1 compression base engine, these muscle car mills had high-test hardware and continued to offer 390 or 425 hp. Other neat extras were a first-for-the-Charger functional Ramcharger hood scoop, color-keyed bumpers, a Super Trak-Pack performance axle (with up to 4.10:1 gearing), a four-speed gear box with Hurst "pistol grip" shifter, a dual-point distributor, heavy-duty cooling aids and bucket seats.

The 440 Six-Pack Charger Super Bee was advertised at 485 hp. It did 0-to-60 mph in 6.9 seconds and the quarter-mile took 14.7. With a Hemi V-8, this 3,640-lb. machine moved into the same bracket as the original Charger 500, needing only 5.7 seconds to get up to 60 mph and a mere 13.7 to reach the traps at a drag strip!

Jerry Heasley

1971 HEMI CHARGER

With an awesome Hemi stuffed under its hood, the Charger quickly developed a bad attitude, especially when GM and FoMoCo muscle cars rolled by. In December 1970, *Motor Trend* road tested a Hemi Super Bee with automatic transmission and a 4.10:1 ratio rear axle. The car did 0-to-60 mph in 5.7 seconds. The quarter-mile was covered in an elapsed time of 13.73 seconds at 104 mph.

The Dodge Charger was given a complete restyling for model year 1971. Its looks were updated with the goal of making it look more distinct from the Coronet. A new 115-inch wheelbase chassis was used to carry the Charger bodies, of which there were two distinct types: semi-fastback coupe and two-door hardtop.

The base Charger was still offered with the choice of a 225-cid Slant Six engine for $2,707. Most buyers preferred to add at least the 318-cid small-block V-8, which brought the price to $2,802. The hotter Charger 500 series included the Super Bee and SE models. The former retailed for $3,271 and up. The SE (or Special Edition) model had prices beginning at $3,422.

The Charger SE came standard with a 383-cid "big-block" V-8.

For high-performance buffs, there was also a one-car Charger R/T series. The R/T (Road/Track) model listed for $3,777 and included a 70-amp-hour battery, heavy-duty front and rear brakes, heavy-duty shock absorbers at all four corners, a pedal dress-up kit, an extra-heavy-duty Rallye suspension and TorqueFlite automatic transmission. A four-speed manual gearbox could be substituted for the automatic for free. The R/T also featured a 440-cid Magnum V-8 and specific R/T identification pieces.

The 426-cid Hemi V-8 was available in Charger R/Ts for $707 extra and in Charger Super Bees for an additional $837. The "Street Hemi" had a 4.25 x 3.75-inch bore and stroke, a 10.25:1 compression ratio and twin Carter AFB four-barrel carburetors. It produced 425 hp at 5600 rpm! According to Mopar authority Galen V. Govier, Hemi Charger production was extremely low. The big engine was bolted into 22 of the 1971 Charger Super Bees and 63 Charger R/Ts.

Jerry Heasley

1971 DART DEMON 340

The 340 was a card-carrying member of the 1971 Dodge "Scat Pack," which boasted many performance cars. It would be the final year for the Scat Pack, however.

After Plymouth experienced a runaway sales success with its 1970 Valiant Duster, the Dodge Division of Chrysler Corp. couldn't wait to get its hands on the 108-inch wheelbase coupe. It became the base for a new mini-muscle car in the compact Dart lineup. Things started cooking in the fall of 1970, when the Dart Demon was added to the 1971 model range.

Like the Duster, the Demon came in two models. The base version had the 198-cid "Slant Six" and minimal standard equipment. It listed for $2,343, only $30 over the cost of a base Duster. The Demon 340, which at $2,721 was a mere $18 upstream from the Duster 340. It came standard with a well-balanced 275-gross horsepower version of the 340-cid small-block V-8. A three-speed, fully synchronized floor shifter was standard along with a Rallye instrument cluster, heavy-duty suspension, E70-14 rubber, stripes and dual exhaust.

Playing the option list was the name of the game with domestic compacts and the 340 had some interesting extras. They included a dual-scoop hood complete with hood pins, rear spoiler and "Tuff" steering wheel. You could also order a four-speed manual gearbox, TorqueFlite automatic transmission or an upgraded interior.

All the tricks worked and the Demon was a success, with 69,861 base models built and the 340 adding 10,098 more. The Dodge Demon returned for 1972, but the name was scrapped after that, in part because the religious community was less than thrilled by the name. Dart Sport nomenclature sufficed from 1973 models through the end of production after the 1976 model year.

1992-93 VIPER RT/10

It all started in a brainstorming session by Chrysler's president Bob Lutz, VP of design Tom Gale, VP of vehicle engineering Francois Castaing, and racing car legend Carroll Shelby. They thought it was time for a successor to the great American sportscars of the 1960s. Shelby's famous Cobra was used as a benchmark.

They envisioned a car that brought back all the memories and emotions of the 1960s roadster, but with the technology and refinement of the 1990s. Their concepts laid out the pattern for the Dodge Viper.

All involved agreed that the new car had to have a smooth, sensuous shape that appealed to enthusiasts who fondly remember the great Cobras. It had to fit equally well in someone's driveway or at the racetrack. It had to be more stunning and more refined than the original Cobra. And all this had to be incorporated into a package selling for under $50,000.

A total of 285 Viper RT/10 roadsters were produced in 1992. All the cars were originally painted red. However, three Vipers used as factory development cars were repainted in three different colors: black, green and yellow. On one car, the standard grey interior was replaced with a black one.

The 1992 models had a retail price of $50,700, plus a $2,600 gas guzzler tax and a $2,280 luxury tax. The 488-cid (8.01-liters) V-10 engine had a bore and stroke of 4.00 x 3.88 inches. It produced 400 hp at 4600 rpm and 465 lbs.-ft. of torque at 3600 rpm.

Plans for Year 2 included several new body colors. Black, green and yellow were announced, although not all of them ultimately arrived in time.

The 1993 Dodge Viper was not a car for the weak of heart (or pocketbook). Its wholesale price was $43,125 and the suggested retail price at your local Dodge dealership was $50,000.

Underhood motivation once again came from the same 8-liter V-10 engine. It was rated for 400 hp.

1994 VIPER RT/10

So, let's do the math ... you could crank the speedometer up to 165 mph in your 1994 Viper RT/10, but it cost ya about $55k to get the keys to one. Hmmm ... if our arithmetic is correct, that comes out to about $333 per mph!

Yup, you could really fly in this venomous Dodge, if you didn't mind ponying up a big pile of greenbacks.

Production nearly tripled in the Viper's third season and Dodge produced a grand total of 3,083 Viper RT/10 roadsters in the 1994 model year.

The 1994 Viper RT/10 roadster accelerated from 0-to-60 mph in 4.6 seconds and did the quarter-mile in 12.9 seconds at 113.8 mph. It had a top speed of 165 mph. Chrysler estimated that 2,189 of the 1994 models were finished in Red, 678 were Black, 133 were Viper Emerald Green Pearl and 83 were Viper Bright Yellow.

An antitheft security system became standard equipment in 1994 Vipers and factory air conditioning was now a $1,200 option. As in the past, all Viper RT/10s still came "wired for air." Other 1994 changes were of a very minor nature, but they included such things as a transmission reverse lock-out function, mesh map pockets on the seats, a passenger-door grab handle and a Viper embossed heat shield and EMI protector attached to the under side of the hood. All cars built this year had a windshield mounted radio antenna and amplifier.

Wieck Media

1995 VIPER RT/10

If the RT/10 roadster was akin to Carroll Shelby's Cobra, the GTS was akin to Enzo Ferrari's "prancing horse" cars. "From the beginning, developing the GTS coupe was a more difficult task than the roadster, because the car evolved with a broader character," said Roy Sjoberg, the executive engineer with the Team Viper development group.

"New exterior design themes" was the terminology that Chrysler Corporation adapted in the fall of 1994 to promote the availability of several new color combinations for the 1995 Dodge Viper RT/10 roadster. In addition to the previously available colors — which were Viper Red, Black, Emerald Green and Viper Bright Yellow used in combination with the standard cast-aluminum directional wheels and forged aluminum wheel caps — buyers could now pick from three new color options. The first combined the Viper Red exterior color with Viper Bright Yellow five-spoke wheels. The second featured a Black exterior with a Silver central racing stripe. The third was a White exterior with a Blue center stripe.

The base retail price for the Viper RT/10 roadster remained at $54,500 and the car's standard equipment list again included the 8.0-liter V-10 engine, a six-speed manual transmission, four-wheel independent suspension, power-assisted rack-and-pinion steering, dual stainless-steel side exhausts and 17-inch wheels. There were now three factory options available: air conditioning, a California emissions system and a Massachusettes emissions system.

Production dropped nearly in half this season, with Dodge Division producing 1,577 Viper RT/10 roadsters during the 1995 model year. This included about 515 Black cars, 458 Viper Red cars, 307 Emerald Green cars and 298 Viper Bright Yellow cars. Grey-and-black interiors were used in 1,005 cars and an additional 572 Vipers had a tan-and-black interior.

The official factory-issued performance figures for the 1995 Viper RT/10 roadster were the same advertised for the 1992 to 1994 models: 0-to-60 mph in 4.6 seconds and the quarter-mile in 12.9 seconds at 113.8 mph. A top speed of 165 mph was also generally quoted again.

By any standard, for a production car, this Viper was an absolute missile.

Wieck Media

1996 VIPER RT/10

What to do with a car that was already probably the fastest car built on American soil? Make it faster, of course!

Motor Trend (November 1995) reported a 0-to-60 time of 5 seconds and a standing-start quarter-mile in 13.2 seconds at 113.4 mph for the 1996 Viper RT/10. *Car and Driver* reported a 4.1-second 0-to-60 run and a 12.6-second quarter-mile at 113 mph and a top speed of 173 mph!

The 1996 Dodge Viper RT/10 roadster received several enhancements including a removable hardtop, sliding rigid plastic side windows, a more robust differential, stronger drive shafts, aluminum suspension control arms and revised spring and shock absorber rates.

The 488-cid (8.0-liter) V-10 engine continued to power the Viper. The 90-degree V-10 had a cast aluminum block with cast iron cylinder liners, aluminum cylinder heads and an alumi-

num crankcase. It had a 4.00-inch bore and a 3.88-inch stroke and a 9.1:1 compression ratio. It was attached to a six-speed manual, fully synchronized transmission with electronic 1-4 skip-shift and reverse-lockout mechanisms.

A new rear-exiting exhaust system replaced the side-mounted pipes used on 1992 to 1995 models. In addition to a cleaner look and quieter operation, this change was partly responsible for extra horsepower, too. New spark tuning and fuel calibration also helped boost the engine's output to 415 hp at 5200 rpm and 488 lbs.-ft. of torque at 3600 rpm.

For the model year, Dodge manufactured 721 Viper RT/10 roadsters. About 231 of the roadsters were black, about 166 were red and about 324 were white. A Dodge Viper was entered in the 24 Hours of LeMans and took a 10th place finish in the GT-1 class.

Jerry Heasley

1996 VIPER GTS

The original Dodge Viper RT/10 roadster had its roots in a visceral back-to-the-basics, uniquely American sports car, but the 1996 Dodge Viper GTS coupe reached into a new, more sophisticated arena, offering more in the way of comfort and amenities than its roadster sibling.

Like the RT/10 before it, the GTS coupe first stole hearts when it was introduced as a concept car. That was at the 1993 North American Auto Show in Detroit. The GTS program was given the green light in May 1993 and just 34 months later the first GTS production car started down the line at the Connor Avenue Assembly Plant in Detroit.

In August, 1995, Dodge displayed a GTS coupe prototype at the second annual Dodge Viper Owner Invitational in Monterey, California, and made an exclusive offer to current owners — a voucher for the first GTS coupes produced. More than three-quarters of the 1996 calendar-year production of 1,700 was instantly spoken for.

The base manufacturer's suggested retail price (MSRP) of the first GTS coupe was $66,700, including destination charge. Additional gas and luxury taxes added approximately $6,330.

While the GTS continued the look of the original Viper roadster, more than 90 percent of the car was new. To start, there was a new body, a new interior and a modified V-10 engine with less weight and increased horsepower.

Horsepower in the GTS was increased to 450 from 415 in the 1996 roadster and torque was boosted 10 additional lbs.-ft., bringing it to 490 at 3700 rpm. A NACA duct design on the hood of the car force-fed oxygen into the V-10's intake and E-type louvers above each of the front wheels prevented air pressure from building under the hood.

Dodge built 1,166 of the GTS coupes at the Conner Avenue assembly plant in 1996. Blue finish was on 1,163 of them and three were done in White. Five cars had white wheels and the rest had polished alloy wheels.

Wieck Media

1997 VIPER RT/10

The "second-generation" 1997 Dodge Viper RT/10 roadster that arrived in 1997 was powered by the same 488-cid V-10 engine originally engineered for the GTS coupe. It produced 450 hp at 5200 rpm and 490 lbs.-ft. of torque at 3700 rpm. It had, by far, the highest output of any American production automobile. The power was channeled by a high-performance six-speed gearbox and transferred to the road via independent front and rear suspension system.

Braking was provided by power-assisted, four-piston, caliper front disc brakes and a single-piston rear disc design. The Viper R/T10 roadster came with high-performance Michelin Pilot SX MXX3 tires on 17-inch rims.

In addition to the soft top, the Viper RT/10 roadster also featured a removable body-color hardtop that has been redesigned for 1997 for increased headroom. The hard top was a "delete option," meaning owners could choose not to equip their Viper with the hardtop for a lower base price. Air conditioning was also a delete option for 1997.

For the first time, both the Dodge Viper RT/10 roadster and GTS coupe were available in either Blue with White painted stripes or solid Viper Red. Silver wheels were standard on the RT/10 roadster in Blue, while Viper Red RT/10 roadsters featured standard Gold wheels. Also available as options were additional wheel choice colors and special badging.

Only 117 RT/10 roadsters were produced in 1997. Of those, approximately 53 were painted Blue and 64 were Viper Red. Black interiors were installed in 114 cars and three had a tan interior. There were also 114 cars with polished wheels and three with gold wheels.

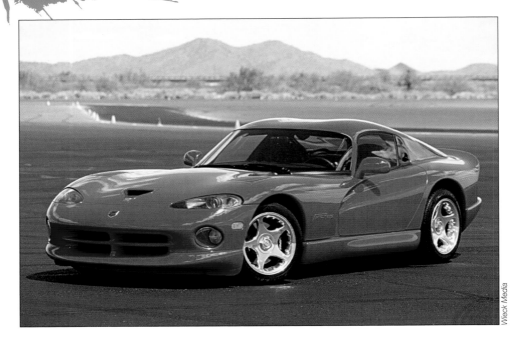

Wieck Media

1998 VIPER GTS

By 1998, the Viper's legend had grown to near mythic proportions since the first concept car version was shown almost a decade earlier.

"Motor Matters" columnist Tom Keane summed up the Viper coupe's personality when he gushed, " I have never been in a car so sensuously thrilling as the all-new Dodge Viper GTS Coupe. Everything about this car excites me beyond my wildest dream. The Viper is not an ordinary sports car. Other prestigious sports cars pale by comparison; collectively, all the other cars are nothing more than also-rans."

The 1998 Viper GTS stayed true to the marque's heritage of delivering the most exhilarating driving experience of any regular American production car. The sleek coupe powered into its third calendar year with several product enhancements and refinements.

The curb weight had been further cut from the 1997 model through the use of new tubular exhaust manifolds. In addition, the use of a low-overlap camshaft helped to reduce emissions and improve fuel economy. A new electronic radiator fan control was adapted to help reduce cooling system noise.

Colors available for the 1998 GTS coupe included White, Viper Bright Metallic Silver and Viper Red. The year's production total included 102 White coupes, 436 monotone Viper Red coupes, 11 Viper Red coupes with Silver stripes, 267 monotone Viper Bright Metallic Silver coupes and 21 Viper Bright Metallic Silver coupes with Blue stripes. Only 837 GTS coupes were made for the model year.

The Viper could move from 0-to-60 in just over 4 seconds and did 0-to-100 mark in under 10 seconds, making it faster and quicker than a Ferrari. And when the prices of these two cars were compared, the Viper GTS looked like a bargain as well.

1999 VIPER GTS

During 1998, an auto industry analysis firm named Strategic Vision took a focused look at how American car owners felt about their automobiles, both domestic and imported. In the nationally syndicated survey, Dodge Viper owners registered the highest level of passion about their new vehicle. Strategic Vision stated that this finding made sense, "Given the financial, and other, sacrifices Viper owners have to make for this raw, heart-stopping performance machine."

The 1999 Dodge Viper GTS was indeed a heart-stopping machine. The annual changes made to this sexy-looking coupe were mostly the same as those that the 1999 RT/10 roadster underwent for that model year. Larger 18-inch aluminum wheels were mounted front and rear. The front wheels were shod with P275/35ZR18 Michelin Pilot MXX3 speed-rated tires. The rear wheels carried the same type of tires in size P335/30ZR18. The wheel and tire updates enhanced the coupe's cornering ability without sacrificing other ride characteristics. Painted wheels were standard equipment, while bright polished wheels were an extra-cost option.

Other 1999 changes included the reintroduction of a Black factory color choice and release of the new Cognac colored Connolly leather interior option.

A grand total of just 699 GTS coupes were built in 1999, with 549 going into the U.S. marketplace, 72 going to Canadian buyers and 78 being shipped to other foreign countries.

The 1999 Viper GTS coupe could move from 0-to-60 in 4.4 seconds and did 0-to-100 in 9.7 seconds. Quarter-mile acceleration was reported as 12.7 seconds. The car's top speed was tested at 185 mph. EPA gas mileage figures for the GTS Coupe were 13 mpg in city driving and 24 mpg on the highway.

Wieck Media

1999 VIPER GTS-R/GT2

Henry Ford once famously noted that customers could have a Model T in any color they wanted, as long as it was black.

Likewise, 1999 Viper GT2 buyers could have a Viper in any color they wanted — as long as it was blinding white with killer blue racing stripes.

Chrysler Corporation competed in and won races with its factory-sourced, factory-sponsored Viper GTS-R competition coupe. This ultra-powerful Dodge muscle car took the FIA's GT2 Manufacturer's Championship in 1997 and 1998 and had a hard-to-forget 1-2 class victory during the French Grand Prix at LeMans in 1998. Race wins like these inspired Dodge to produce the GT2 Championship Edition Viper Coupe for private buyers. This limited-edition Viper carried a hefty $82,500 window sticker and was not for the faint of pocketbook buyer.

The GT2 version of the Viper GTS-R racing car came only in the white-with-blue-stripes combination.

The V-10 engine with an aluminum block and aluminum cylinder heads was a tweaked version of the standard GTS and RT/10 power plant that cranked out an additional 10 hp. The vital statistics showed a stock-looking 4.00 x 3.88-inch bore and stroke and 488 cubic inches of displacement, but didn't tell the whole story. The Dodge boys revamped the intake system with K & N low-restriction air filters, new hoses and an air cleaner housing that had been used on the 1992 to 1996 Vipers. However, the engineers sealed off the regular functional air scoop and the result was a rating of 460 hp at 5200 rpm and 500 lbs.-ft. of torque at 3700 rpm.

Included as part of the GT2 Championship Edition coupe was a special front air splitter, a ground effects package, "dive bomber" spoilers and a carbon-fiber rear deck airfoil that resembled that used on the actual racing cars. The interior featured black leather seats with blue accents. In 0-to-60-mph acceleration testing, the GTS-R coupe pulled a 4.0-second time. It did the quarter-mile in 12.1 seconds at 120.5 mph.

Wieck Media

2000 VIPER GTS COUPE

As the spiritual reincarnation of the Shelby Daytona coupe, the Dodge Viper GTS quickly developed a passionate following and changed very little from one season to the next because there was little motivation to mess with near perfection. A new steel gray color was the main update for 2000.

The base aluminum-block-and-heads V-10 engine was rated at the familiar 450 hp at 5200 rpm and 490 lbs.-ft. of torque at 3700 rpm. With the ACR package it was 460 hp and 500 lbs.-ft. of torque! The engine was linked to a six-speed manual transmission. The 2000 Viper was easily capable of a 4.3-second 0-to-60 times and had a top speed of 185 mph.

The coupe — which first appeared at Dodge dealerships in 1996 — was based on the original RT/10 roadster and had virtually identical specifications, although there were minor differences between the two body styles. The RT/10 was 175.1 inches long, while the GTS was 176.7 in length. Overall height was 44 inches for the roadster and 47 inches for the coupe. The closed car was also a little heavier, at 3,383 lbs., than the 3,319-lb. roadster.

Other minor dimensional differences were a 19.3-sq. ft. frontal area on the RT/10 compared to 20.5 on the GTS. The drag coefficient was 0.495 for the roadster without a top and 0.46 with one. The coupe's was 0.35. The 2000 Viper GTS coupe had a base price of $67,225. You could add the $10,000 American Racing Club (ACR) package that added 10 hp, stiffened the suspension and deleted items like air conditioning, a stereo and fog lights.

Total production of 2000 GTS models was 949, with 804 marketed in the U.S., 92 sold in Canada and 53 going overseas.

Wieck Media

2003 VIPER SRT10

If you wanted a new 2003 Viper back in 2002, you had to act fast! Before the Viper SRT10 was offered at dealerships, Dodge gave the owners of Gen I Viper models the first chance at placing orders for the new car. This worked like gangbusters and the entire first-year production run was sold out almost immediately.

The 500-hp/500 ft.-lbs. formula was carried through in the production version, which did 0-to-100-to-0 mph in about 13.2 seconds, compared to the "old" Viper's time of 14.5 seconds. But Dodge emphasized that the new Viper could also stop faster than the old one.

The improvements didn't stop at that point, either. The new Viper was sleeker, more refined, quieter and better handling than the original. It was not whimpy, however. Dodge said the car was tuned for "tearing up pavement and rumbling out a cool exhaust note."

The 2003 Dodge Viper came only in a single roadster body style (although there were hints that a coupe was in the wings for 2005). Standard equipment for the SRT10 included a manual top with a glass rear window, a six-speed

manual transmission with floor shift, four-wheel anti-lock brakes, a viscous limited-slip differential, power windows and mirrors, intermittent windshield wipers and bucket seats with leather seating surfaces. An alarm system with remote door locks was also included. The only engine available was the 8.3-liter 500-hp V-10.

The new Viper body featured a lowered hood line, swept-back fenders and deep-cut side scallops that took their cues from the original design, while bringing the Viper into the 21st century. Improved aerodynamics and a full-length undertray add functional performance enhancements. The Viper's visceral lines spoke volumes for the passion that Dodge designers could bring to their craft.

The new Viper gave enthusiasts an American sports car offering all-out high performance. The SRT10 was truly a new-age muscle car.

Two 6 1/2-inch low-mass full-range Alpine loudspeakers, one 6 1/2-inch subwoofer with ported enclosure and two 2 3/4-inch fill speakers mounted in the bulkhead.

Wieck Media

2006 SRT10 COUPE

The Dodge Viper legend began with the 1992 Dodge Viper RT/10 Roadster and grew with the introduction in 1996 of the Dodge Viper GTS coupe. Starting in the fall of 2005, history will be repeating itself. Since the debut of the Gen III Viper in 2003, it was a convertible-only series. But on Jan. 9, 2005, the all-new SRT10 coupe made its bow for the Detroit and Los Angeles Auto Shows.

The exterior of the SRT10 Coupe featured "double-bubble" roof styling and unique rear styling with wrap-around taillights reminiscent of those on the Viper GTS Coupe. With the addition of a roof, the Viper SRT10 became more torsionally rigid than the already-sturdy convertible.

Aerodynamically, the SRT10 coupe provides increased downforce and more high-speed stability with its sloping roofline and rear deck lid spoiler. The only bodywork that the new coupe shared with the convertible was the front fascia and fenders, the hood and the doors.

In addition to a new canopy and deck lid, the coupe had a special windshield surrounds, door side glass, rear fascia, quarter panels and taillights.

The deck lid for the Dodge Viper SRT10 coupe was designed for customer convenience as well as for structural integrity. The deck lid opening was deeply integrated into the rear fascia, which offered a low lift-over height for stowing cargo. Gas struts held the deck lid in place when it was open. When closed, the deck lid was secured with a lock that met federal regulations for latch safety.

The SRT10 Coupe was originally available only in Viper Blue with twin Stone White racing stripes. The interior featured a distinctive two-tone color scheme and unique interior pieces in the coupe included various weatherstrip pieces, a headliner, the carpeting and the trim panels. The "double-bubble" roof was promoted as a way to give race drivers additional helmet room.

Under the coupe's hood was an aluminum-block 8.3-liter (505-cid) V-10 that generated 500 hp and 525 lbs.-ft. of torque. The engine was hooked to a heavy-duty six-speed manual transmission.

2010 DODGE VIPER

Make no mistake, the Dodge Viper SRT/10 was, is and will remain a car that makes a bold statement. Even in its final year of production in 2010, with 500 slated to be built, the Viper will go out with a throaty roar and smoking rubber. That cause will be helped by the addition of a very limited edition non-street legal version called the Viper ACR-X that is billed as "the ultimate special edition model of America's ultimate sports car."

According to Dodge Brand President and CEO Ralph Gilles, the ACR-X combines "the best performance attributes of the record-setting, street-legal ACR (American Club Racer) and the safety equipment of the championship-winning Viper Competition Coupe."

The "normal" final-year Viper lineup consists of a coupe, convertible and the ACR-X race-only version. Sticker price on the street-legal editions is approximately $93,000, so budget buyers need to look elsewhere.

Since its inception in 1993, the Viper has always relied on a V-10 engine as its power source. The final-Viper V-10 is the 8.4-liter version coupled to a six-speed manual transmission. Traction is provided via an anti-spin dif-

ferential rear axle and 3.07 rear axle ratio.

Not quite as curvaceous (or what some wags would label as "lumpy") as the first-generation Viper from the '90s, the 2010 Viper continued the more streamlined look that took hold with the 2008 model. This more subtle and aero-friendly design included a larger air-intake hood scoop, a more angular frontal shape and additional louvers to aid cooling of both the engine and brakes.

Additional final-edition Viper features include rack-and-pinion steering, Michelin-shod 18-inch five-spoke wheels up front and 19-inchers in back, four-wheel disc brakes, independent front and rear suspension and a curb weight of 3,430 lbs.

The 640-hp ACR-X racers compete in a series of events held across the country under the banner of the Viper Racing League. It's hoped that keeping a racing Viper on track through the future will appease members of the "Viper Nation" when the last Viper leaves the assembly line. As with many popular models that are discontinued, there's always the possibility that a next-generation Viper may be re-introduced at some future date.

John Gunnell

1957 THUNDERBIRD "F-CODE"

The '57 Thunderbird equipped with a supercharger as a factory option heads the list of classic Thunderbirds for not only being the hottest Thunderbird on the road, but also on the auction block.

Engine options increased in 1957 with high-performance, racing and super-charger options. The supercharged version of the 1957 Thunderbird is the rarest. The first 15 production supercharged Thunderbirds were reportedly built in January, 1957, to homologate the engine for NASCAR competition.

The very first factory-sponsored supercharged Thunderbirds were actually 1956 models built by Peter DePaolo Engineering in Long Beach, California. Several 1957 Thunderbirds were then similarly modified for racing. On the 1957 T-birds, the code letter of each engine type leads off the serial number. Supercharged cars could be either D or F cars.

The "D" cars came with a 312 cid V-8 with a four-barrel carburetor used with automatic and overdrive transmissions — 90 percent of automatics.

Fifteen D-types were fitted with Paxton-Mc-Culloch superchargers and are popularly referred to as "DFs." Their serial numbers will be near 30,000.

1957 Thunderbirds with a serial number of "F" featured the 312 cid V-8 with four-barrel carburetor and a Paxton McCulloch VR57 supercharger. A special head reduced compression to 8.5:1. Production of the 196 F engines began in spring. They were available at a factory invoice price of $340. There were three grooves on the crank pulley and the manual transmission cars used two belts for the supercharger. With an automatic transmission, the front groove was larger and drove the super-charger with a single belt.

Horsepower ratings with fine-tuning ranged from 325 to 340.

The formal total of 211 superchargers in the D and F series is an approximation. Some of the Thunderbirds with an F letter don't have the blower, special heads or manifolds. Many original owners removed the superchargers because they were noisy and not oil-tight. Also a Ford dealer in 1957 would probably have been willing to add a supercharger to a D or E 312-cid engine, or remove one from an F-series car if the buyer wanted it.

Jerry Heasley

1960 GALAXIE 352/360 SPECIAL

"We like the way it looks, we like the way it rides, we like the way it corners, we like the way it stops and we especially like how it goes when equipped with the 360-horsepower engine." That's what *Hot Rod* magazine's technical editor Ray Brock said after road testing the 1960 Ford Galaxie 352/360 special. Back in the early '60s, this was the performer that Ford fans had been waiting for, with a tri-power V-8 engine capable of pushing a stock-bodied coupe way over the 150-mph mark.

Ford got a late start in the new performance sweepstakes, but before the end of 1959 it had released its 360-hp Thunderbird Super V-8, which was based on the 352. It was also called the "Interceptor" or "Super Interceptor" and carried an "R" code. This engine was not initially available with Cruise-O-Matic, but only

with a Borg-Warner T-85 three-speed manual gearbox, with or without overdrive. A Holley 540-cfm four-barrel carburetor, an aluminum intake manifold, new cast-iron exhaust headers, a cast nodular crank, solid valve lifters, a 10.6:1 compression ratio and a dual-point ignition system all helped.

The muscular combination was available on any full-sized 1960 model. Motor Life magazine got hold of a pre-production example and found it capable of going from 0-to-60 mph in 7.5 seconds with a top speed of 152 mph. Obviously, it had been modified a bit over the production version.

The most desirable combination for the 360-hp 352 is with a Starliner two-door hardtop or a Sunliner convertible.

Jerry Heasley

1963 GALAXIE 427

Ford really got its act into gear around the middle of 1963. Its first step was the release of the good-looking 1963 1/2 Galaxie fastback. Then came a new 427-cid V-8 with massive muscle for the street, the drag strip and the NASCAR superspeedways.

To promote the 427-powered 1963 Galaxie, Ford manufactured 50 special cars at its factory in Atlanta, Georgia. These cars were "factory lightweights" made exclusively for going down the quarter-mile faster than the competition. They had fiberglass doors, hoods, trunks and front-end components. The bumpers and other parts were made of aluminum. Virtually everything that wasn't needed for racing was left off the cars.

For motivation, the Galaxie lightweights got a 427-cid V-8 with two Holley 600-cfm four-barrel carburetors advertised at 425 hp at 6000 rpm. The actual output was much higher.

The engine was attached to a special version of Ford's "top-loader" four-speed manual gearbox that had an aluminum case to cut even more weight off. These cars tipped the scales at below 3,500 lbs. and ran the quarter-mile in the low-12-second bracket at just under 120 mph!

In addition to the just-for-racing cars, Fo-MoCo produced 4,978 big Fords with one of two versions of the 427-cid V-8. One was the 425-hp engine tuned for the street. It had dual Holley 540-cfm carburetors on top of a cast-aluminum intake manifold and most owners who took these cars racing on weekends felt that the power rating was very conservative. The second street engine was a 427-cid V-8 with a single four-barrel carburetor. It produced 410 hp. Both of the big engines were available in Galaxie or Galaxie 500 XL two-door hardtops. The dual-quad engine was a $461.60 option.

Phil Kunz

1963 GALAXIE "LIGHTWEIGHT"

The big-block Galaxie "Lightweights" of the early 1960s were definitely members of the all-time "Wolf In Sheep's Clothing" team. They might not have looked like speed burners, but they were some of the meanest machines on the road at the time.

Although some questioned the use of the term "fastback" for Ford's 1963 1/2 model, there was good reason for its existence. By adopting the "sportsroof" for NASCAR competition, by stuffing a 427-cid V-8 under the hood Ford had a car that could maintain 160 mph with 100 less hp.

The lightweight fastbacks were made to let it all hang out on the drag strip. Ford offered these hardtops only in a white-and-red exterior/interior color combination.

Although the drag model's steel body was identical to that of a stock Galaxie, all bolt-on items, such as the doors, trunk lid, hood and front fenders, were constructed of fiberglass. Aluminum was used for the bumpers. The interiors offered only the basics: skinny front buckets, cheap floor mats and absolutely no sound deadening.

With 425 hp, these Galaxies — which the NHRA declared eligible for both super stock and stock eliminator competitions — were capable of quarter-mile marks of 12 seconds and 118 mph.

Before the competition season came to a close, Ford offered a "Mark II" version of the 427-cid V-8 with new cylinder heads. It had larger ports and valves, an aluminum high-rise manifold, stronger connecting rods, a forged-steel crankshaft and a 10-quart oil pan.

The tremendous performance of the 427-cid NASCAR Ford was demonstrated in a road test of a car that stock-car builders Holman & Moody had prepared. It was conducted by *Car Life* magazine. Although rated at 410 hp, the true output of the 427, after the Holman & Moody treatment, was closer to 500 hp. With a 3.50:1 rear axle, the Ford's top speed was approximately 155 mph. Even with this gearing, however, the Ford was a strong sprinter with *Car Life* (February 1964) reporting the following acceleration times: 0-to-30 mph in 2.3 seconds; 0-to-60 mph in 6.3 seconds and 0-to-100 mph in 13.2 seconds. The same car did the quarter-mile in 14.2 seconds at 105 mph.

Wieck Media

1964 FAIRLANE "THUNDERBOLT"

A few years back, we watched in awe as a pack of restored 1964 Ford Fairlane "T-Bolts" blasted down the track during the "Muscle Car Showdown" event at Quaker State Dragway in Ohio. Back in May of 1964, Car Life magazine's Allen Hunt said of the T-Bolt, "Obviously it's a racing car . . . and one calculated to Ford right back in the front row on the drag strips this summer."

These cars had fiberglass fenders, teardrop-shaped hood blisters, Plexiglas windows, lightweight bucket seats, a cold-air induction system, 8000 rpm Rotunda tachometers, modified front suspensions (to accommodate the 427), a long list of equipment deletions and many special competition equipment features. The 425-hp big-block V-8 actually cranked out more like 500 hp. It was linked to a beefed-up Lincoln automatic or a Borg-Warner T-10 four-speed manual transmission.

The 1964 Fairlane Special Performance drag vehicles soon adopted the Thunderbolt name and also became known as "T-Bolts." Demand was strong enough to prompt the ordering of a second batch of 54 all-white cars. Racing driver Gas Ronda dominated NHRA's 1964 World Championship with 190 points by running his T-Bolt through the quarter-mile in 11.6 seconds at 124 mph.

Ford records show that the first 11 cars left the factory painted maroon and 10 of them had four-speed transmissions. The 100 additional cars produced were painted white when they were built and 89 of them had four-speed gearboxes. At least one 1965 Thunderbolt-style car was raced by Darrell Droke. However, the new Mustang soon took over as Ford's best offering for drag-car enthusiasts and the short life of T-Bolts halted at that point.

Jerry Heasley

1964 GALAXIE 427

In 1964, the 427-powered full-sized Fords were still the hot ticket for stock car racing and to get them sanctioned for NASCAR competition the company kept producing big muscle cars.

But, despite their best-ever-for-Ford performances on drag strips and racetracks, the 1963 Galaxie lightweights had not dominated quarter-mile competition the way Ford hoped they would.

At first the hot Fords competed with Pontiac's powerful 421 Super Duty V-8, and later the Chrysler Hemi V-8 came along. To keep up with the Joneses, Ford changed its focus to mid-size muscle by launching its fleet of Fairlane-based Thunderbolts that could run down a drag strip in less than 12 seconds at close to 125 mph.

In addition to looking fast, the new Galaxie offered a big-car-based lightweight drag package as well. The 1964 Galaxie A/Stock dragster package was offered for two-door models. Also

available was a B/Stock Dragster package that added a low-riser manifold for the monstrous 427-cid V-8.

These cars came in white with red interiors. Body sealer, sound deadening insulation and heaters were deleted. Lightweight seats and a fiberglass "power bubble" hood were added. The grilles were modified with fiberglass air-induction vents.

The 427-cid V-8 was also offered in two versions for production-type full-sized 1964 Fords. The "Thunderbird High-Performance" option carried code "Q" and was the 410-hp (at 5600 rpm) version. The "Thunderbird Super High-Performance" engine carried code "R" and added two larger Holley carburetors to boost output to 425 hp at 6000 rpm. A 427-powered stock-bodied Ford was basically good for a 0-to-60 time of just over 6 seconds and a quarter-mile time of just under 15 seconds.

Jerry Heasley

1965 SHELBY-AMERICAN AC/COBRA 289

"When the Cobra is certified for production sports racing, a fox will have been dropped among the chickens," said *Car Life* magazine. Well, we don't know about feathers, but fiberglass was flying all around the hen house after the Cobra arrived in Ford dealerships.

The Cobra is perhaps the ultimate American road warrior because it brought this country its first and only World Manufacturer's Championship in auto racing. The year was 1965 and the car was the 289 Cobra roadster. Despite the British origins of its AC Ace chassis, which was highly beefed-up and modified to accept American V-8 power, the Cobra was by rights its own unique marque. It was built by Shelby-American of Los Angeles, Calif. Carroll Shelby contracted with AC of England for the chassis and body and put the dream together using engines from Ford.

When the Cobra became a reality, AC had its name on the car. So did Ford, thanks to the use of "Powered By Ford" fender badges. However, the Cobra vision belonged to Carroll Shelby and Cobra was officially the name of the marque. A Cobra is not an AC and it is not a Ford. A Cobra is a Cobra. Shelby built small-block-powered versions from 1961 to 1965 and big-block versions from 1965-1967.

The small-block Cobra, which weighed slightly over 2,000 lbs., was easily capable of speeds topping 150 mph, and was quicker than literally any other sports car sold to the public.

Shelby's original idea was to sell a street version of the race vehicle to finance the cars on the track, although any final accounting would certainly reveal that Ford Motor Company backed the Shelby-American racing program to benefit from the on-track publicity associated with its new small-block V-8.

Shelby accomplished the ultimate with his Cobra, beating archrival Ferrari for the World Manufacturer's Championship.

At the end of the production run of the small-block roadster, Shelby-American built about 30 cars with automatic transmissions. Carroll Shelby drove one, and still owns it to this day. He favored the automatic for everyday use, but still also owns a big-block 427 Cobra roadster. Sadly, most of the automatics were changed over to four-speeds, but a few do exist today.

Jerry Heasley

1965 GALAXIE 427

Though the Mustangs and Malibus of the world were better suited to the budgets of the young car buyers most interested in muscle cars, there was always a substantial number of young-at-heart car enthusiasts who needed roomier cars and wanted them to go fast. They were "money-is-no-object" type buyers and Detroit had the hardware available to build what they wanted, as long as they were willing to pay for it. That big-block V-8 shoe-horned under a Fairlane's hood could fit into a Galaxie with a whole lot less hassle. In addition, this kind of full-size "squeeze job" was usually a lot more profitable

Ford continued offering the 427-cid V-8 for the big cars to help maintain Ford's "total performance" image. It didn't fit into other models like the Falcon, Mustang and Fairlane without extensive modifications, but it was a drop-in for the big Galaxie. Fortunately for Ford, NASCAR had kicked the Chrysler Hemi V-8 out of stock

car racing, so FoMoCo's 427-powered stock cars took a record of 48 Grand National wins.

The Galaxie 500XL series was the sport trim version of the Galaxie 500 two-door hardtop ($3,167) and convertible ($3,426) and included all Galaxie 500 trim plus bucket seats, a floor-mounted shift lever, polished door-trim panels and carpeting on the lower portion of the doors. It's likely that the majority of full-sized Fords fitted with the 427 (except for all-out race cars) were Galaxie 500XL models.

A Galaxie 500XL two-door hardtop with the 427-cid/425-hp Thunderbird Super High-Performance V-8 could be purchased for as little as $3,233 in 1965. And even though it was a big car with a 119-inch wheelbase, a 210-inch overall length and a curb weight of 3,507 lbs., it still carried only 9.6 pounds per horsepower with the big-block V-8 installed. It could fly from 0-to-60 mph in 6.8 seconds and did the quarter-mile in only 14.9 seconds.

Jerry Heasley

1965 MUSTANG GT

Though it was far from the fastest car of the '60s, the Mustang GT played a big role in building enthusiasm for muscle cars and rarely gets full credit for its contribution to muscle car history. As *Car Life* magazine put it, "Ford started a round-up of its state-of-the-Total-Performance art to produce the Mustang GT." But before getting into the go-fast details, let's review Mustang history a bit.

It is not often that a car comes along and gets to create its own market segment, but that is what happened when Ford introduced the Mustang sporty compact on April 17, 1964. Mustang initiated the all-new "pony car" segment, and the market for the cars was large and long lasting.

There is argument among purists over whether the Mustangs produced prior to September 1964 are 1964 1/2 or 1965 models. However, when it comes to the interesting and collectible GT equipment group, there can be no question, as it was introduced for the first anniversary of the Mustang's introduction on April 17, 1965.

Combining available mechanical features with new visual pieces made the GT package a fairly thorough upgrade and gave Mustang lovers some more dash for their cash. First, the buyer had to order an optional V-8 engine, which at the time included the 225-hp Challenger Special 289 at $157, or the high-performance 271-hp/289-cid engine for $430.

The GT option included quick-ratio steering, disc front brakes, chromed dual exhaust tips that exited through the rear valance panel, a new grille bar with fog lights built in and GT instrumentation — which replaced the Falcon-based instrument panel with five round dials. Throw in GT badging and lower body striping and you had a bargain for around $150.

Although the exact number of Mustangs built with GT equipment is not available, they had a massive following and the installation rate for this option increased even more when Ford later released the appearance items separately for dealer installation.

Jerry Heasley

1965 SHELBY MUSTANG GT 350 "R" CODE

The "R" is for race, no joke. After serial number 34, Shelby-American began inserting an R as the second digit of the vehicle identification number (VIN). But in the early days, both Ford and Shelby-American were not entirely clear on the direction of this new high-performance Mustang.

The R-model came with the high-performance features of the street GT 350 — the 289-cid 306-hp small-block with a hi-rise aluminum intake manifold, four-speed transmission, No-Spin differential, lowered suspension and lots more — plus special R-model features. The GT 350 R code Mustang was so specialized that a mere 36 were sold. However, they were available to anyone willing to pay the base price of $5,950 to buy an out-of-the-box race winner.

The task of building a hi-po Mustang that could run with the Corvette was turned over to Shelby-American of Los Angeles, which had taken the AC-based Cobra roadster and thrashed Corvettes in USRRC (United States Road Race of Champions) racing.

Ford felt that it made a lot of sense to hire Shelby to turn the Mustang into a car that could beat the Corvette in SCCA B-production racing. The automaker knew this would further reinforce the muscular image of Ford's new pony car.

Shelby-American proceeded to build a street version of a new GT Mustang, which Carroll Shelby himself named the GT 350. It was a rather obvious reference to the 350-cid small-block engine from Chevrolet, although Shelby gave the press some story about walking off 350 steps.

With racing victories a major goal, Shelby-American also built a race-ready competition model that was not meant for street use. It was called the "R" model.

To satisfy SCCA regulations at least 100 cars (race and street versions) had to be built. Therefore, 100 white fastbacks — each fitted with 289-cid high-performance K-code V-8s with solid valve lifters and 271 hp — were lifted off an assembly line at the Ford plant in San Jose, California.

The 1965 GT 350 R was the SCCA B-production national champion in 1965, 1966 and 1967.

Jerry Heasley

1966 FAIRLANE GT/GTA

They could have written a song about this mighty muscle car. It would go, "Little GTA, you really give me a thrill, four-barrel and a Sport shift and a 390 mill . . . wind 'em up, wind 'em out, you wound up like the GTO." The Fairlane GT/GTA was Ford's "Tiger" and brand loyalty dictated that it would hit the streets to prove itself. *Car Life*'s Gene Booth said, "The GTA (do you suppose it will be called 'GeeTAw') plants Ford firmly in the performance market."

The first production Fairlanes able to carry a big-block V-8 were the totally redesigned 1966 models. The size of the Fairlane body didn't change much on the outside, but the increased dimensions under the hood became important in the muscle car era. These cars served as Ford's factory hot rods when they were equipped with the monster V-8s. They competed head to head with the GTO and a Ford advertisement for the high-performance model was titled "How to cook a tiger!"

The Fairlane GT came with a 390-cid/315-hp V-8 as standard equipment. The Fairlane GTA included a 335-hp version of the 390-cid V-8, chrome-plated rocker covers, oil filter cap, radiator cap, air cleaner cover and dip stick, a high-lift cam, a bigger carburetor and the two-way three-speed Sport Shift automatic transmission that could be used like an automatic or like a manual gearbox.

A limited number of Fairlanes were sold with "side-oiler" 427-cid wedge engines. Some of these cars even hit the NASCAR ovals. The 427-powered Fairlanes were characterized by a big air scoop that gulped cold air at the front of the hood. Only about 60 Fairlanes with 427s were produced.

Both Fairlane GT models were part of the fancy 500/XL line. The two-door hardtop sold for $2,843 and 33,015 were built. With the production of 4,327 units, the $3,068 base-price convertible was much rarer.

Included in the GT package were badges, a special hood, body striping, engine dress-up parts, a heavy-duty suspension, front disc brakes, bucket seats, a center console and a sport steering wheel. The base 315-hp V-8 featured a hot cam, special manifolds and a single four-barrel carb.

A 1966 Fairlane GTA two-door hardtop with the 390-cid 335-hp V-8 carried only about 10.5 lbs. per horsepower. It could move from 0-to-60 mph in a mere 6.8 seconds and did the quarter-mile in 15.2 seconds.

Phil Kunz

1966 SHELBY MUSTANG GT 350H

At a cost of only $17 dollars a day and 17 cents per mile (still about twice the rate of a regular Hertz rental at the time) you could rent yourself a 1966 Shelby GT 350H for a weekend of racing.

And after the race, Hertz could take care of any needed repairs!

It came as no surprise — except possibly to Hertz — that these muscular rent-a-cars would create some maintenance headaches after being put into the hands of weekend racers. There are more than a few tales of "Rent-A-Racers" showing up at drag strips. When the remnants of a roll bar were found under the carpeting in one car, it was concluded that it had seen some track time in SCCA competition.

The "H" stood for Hertz and it was a special version of Carroll Shelby's legendary conversion of the Mustang pony car into a true muscle car. The GT 350H was not Hertz's first venture involving rental cars that weren't totally ho-hum. Prior to 1965, Hertz had rented Corvettes.

While Shelby initially hoped to sell a couple dozen cars to Hertz, the ultimate order was larger. The final tally came to 936 GT 350s out of a total run of 2,380 in 1966.

The original Borg-Warner T-10 close-ratio four-speed manual transmissions were a real problem . . . especially when used by inexperienced drivers. Hertz later switched to Ford's C-4 automatic, which became an option on all Shelbys for 1966. Although lacking a stickshift, this was still a rental car with over 300 hp.

With the automatic, the "Cobra-ized" 289-cid H-Po small-block V-8 was fed by a 595-cfm Autolite carburetor that replaced the regular 715-cfm Holley.

The GT 350H had some visual differences from normal '66 GT 350s. Most were finished in black with gold decals (a color scheme Hertz had used when it built its own taxicabs in the 1920s.) A few GT 350Hs were painted white, red, blue and green. Most of these also got gold striping.

After serving Hertz, the GT 350Hs were returned to Ford for minor refurbishing. Then, they were resold to the general public through selected dealers. Unfortunately, during refurbishing, the high-performance parts sometimes got "lost." While there were no special Hertz models in later years, the company did rent GT 350s through 1969.

Jerry Heasley

1967 FAIRLANE 427

If you wanted to go all the way when it came to building a high-performance Fairlane, your FoMoCo dealer had the vehicles and hardware you needed to create a street racer or a weekend dragster. Ford advertisements made this clear when they stated, "The 427 Fairlane is also available without numbers." They weren't talking about meter rates on the side of a taxi cab, either — they were talking about the numbers on racing cars that went brutally fast.

The stock 1967 Ford Fairlane continued to use the same body introduced in 1966 with only minor trim changes. The 1967 grille was a single aluminum stamping used in place of the two grilles that graced the previous model. The 1967 taillights were divided horizontally by the back-up light, instead of vertically, as in 1966.

The fire-breathing 427-cid "side-oiler" V-8 was again available on the Fairlane's options list. The 1967 edition of Car Fax indicated that it came only on non-GT club coupes (two-door

sedans) and sport coupes (two-door hardtops). In the full-size Galaxie, the price for the 410-hp engine, when ordered without the 7-Litre package, was $975.09. Logic suggests that price is probably in the same general ballpark that the 427 would cost in the smaller Fairlane models.

The milder 410-hp single-four-barrel-carburetor version of the 427 was not the only choice. There was the hairier 425-hp version that carried two four-barrel Holley carburetors. Both of these engine options included a transistorized ignition, heavy-duty battery, heavy-duty suspension, extra cooling package and four-speed manual transmission.

Racing versions of the 427-cid V-8 were offered with goodies like a new eight-barrel induction system that put about 30 extra horses on tap. A tunnel-port version of the 427 was available as an over-the-counter kit, with a tunnel-port intake on special cylinder heads and a special intake manifold.

1967 MUSTANG GT/GTA

Ford was hard pressed to improve on the "classic" Mustang it had introduced in 1964, but it had to. The competition was getting very keen, indeed. Lee Iacocca and company did a great job with a tough assignment.

All of the 1966 engines were carried-over, plus there was a new 200-hp version of the Challenger 289 V-8 with a two-barrel carburetor. This motor was standard in cars with the GT option. A new designation used on cars with automatic transmission and GT equipment was "GTA."

Other technical changes included front suspension improvements. A competition handling package was released, but it cost quite a bit extra and didn't go into too many cars. The 1967 Mustang GT 2+2 with the 390-cid/335-hp V-8 could do 0-to-60 mph in 7.4 seconds and the quarter-mile in 15.6 seconds.

The 1967 Mustang, of course, also got a jazzy new body, a wider tread for better road grip and a wider range of engines. Option choices were widened, too. They now included a tilt-away steering wheel, a built-in heater/air conditioner, an overhead console, a stereo-sonic tape system, a SelectShift automatic transmis-

sion that also worked manually, a bench seat, an AM/FM radio, fingertip speed control, custom exterior trim group, and front power disc brakes. Styling followed the same theme, but in a larger size.

On the exterior, the 1967 Mustang was heftier and more full-fendered. Especially low and sleek was the new 2+2 fastback, which featured all-new sheet metal. The roofline had a clean, unbroken sweep downward to a distinctive, concave rear panel. Functional air louvers in the roof rear quarters were made thinner than before. The wheelbase was unchanged, but overall length grew by nearly 2 inches. Front and rear tread widths went up by 2.1 inches and overall width was 2.7 inches wider at 58.1 inches.

All Mustangs had bigger engine bays. This was very necessary because the first "big-block" option was among the many 1967 hardware upgrades. It was a 390-cid V-8 with 315 hp. This small bore-long stroke power plant was related to the Ford "FE" engine, introduced way back in 1958. It provided a good street-performance option with a low $264 price tag, lots of low-end performance and plenty of torque.

Jerry Heasley

1967 SHELBY-MUSTANG GT-350/GT-500

This year, the Shelby GT-350 took on an appearance different from the stock Mustang. At the same time, the Shelby became mechanically more similar to its garden-variety cousin. Shelby dealers liked this change. It created a visually exciting product with as much creature comfort as a basic Mustang, but with no need for specialized maintenance equipment and training.

With the base Mustang redesigned for '67, Shelby created an entirely new appearance that made its fastback look longer and lower than stock Mustangs by the use of more fiberglass than in previous years. A twin-scoop fiberglass hood with racing-style lock-down pins, reached farther than the Mustang's all-steel piece and made the grille appear like a dark, menacing mouth. The grille housed two round high-beam headlights placed side by side in the middle.

The Mustang's optional 8000-rpm tach sat next to a 140-mph speedometer. Shelbys came with power steering and brakes. Suspension enhancements were largely stock Mustang, including the special handling package, front disc brakes, thicker front stabilizer bar, export brace, and adjustable Gabriel shock absorbers. The

15-inch stamped steel wheels had '67 Thunderbird hubcaps with Shelby center caps. Sporty Kelsey-Hayes rims were optional.

The 289-cid K-code engine was used again with very few changes. Tubular exhaust headers were dropped at the beginning of the year and Ford's high-performance cast-iron manifold, was used. The factory continued claiming 306 hp. Options included a Paxton supercharger, SelectAire air conditioning and the Hi-Po C-4 automatic transmission. For the second straight year, GT-350 prices decreased. Shelby dealers sold 1,175 units for $3,995 apiece.

With the new looks came a new family member: the GT-500. Shelby installed the 428-cid big-block V-8 in this top-line offering. It produced at least 50 more ponies than the 390. This "Police Interceptor" engine featured hydraulic lifters and an aluminum, medium-rise intake manifold wearing a pair of 600-cfm four-barrel Holley carburetors. Ford's four-speed "toploader" transmission was standard. The stout "police spec" C-6 automatic was optional. The GT-500, available only in fastback form like the GT-350, retailed for $4,195 and sold 2,050 units.

Jerry Heasley

1968 MUSTANG CJ 428/SCJ 428

The compact Mustang became a really fast car when Ford Motor Company decided to shoehorn the 428-cubic inch Cobra-Jet V-8 under its hood. Such a machine could move from 0-to-60 mph in a mere 6.9 seconds. The quarter-mile took only 15.57 to do and the car's terminal speed at the end of such a run was about 99.5 mph. After one test drive at a drag strip, *Hot Rod* magazine declared the Mustang 428 CJ to be "the fastest running pure stock in the history of man."

Ford introduced the 428 Cobra Jet engine option on April 1, 1968. The new motor was the automaker's big-block performance leader. Production of the 428-CJ engine continued through 1970. Rated conservatively for 335 hp at 5200 rpm, the 1968 Mustang CJ 428 put out a lot more like 375 to 400 gross horsepower. The engine was hot competition for the SS 396 from Chevrolet, the 400 HO from Pontiac, the 440 Magnum from Mopar and literally any other muscle car on the street in 1968.

A high-performance variant of the basic 428-cid V-8, the main features of the Cobra Jet V-8 were revised cylinder heads. They were of a design that was similar to the Ford 427 "low-ris-er" type, but with bigger valve ports, a camshaft from the 390-cid GT engine, a cast-iron copy of the 428-cid Police Interceptor intake manifold and a 735-cfm Holley four-barrel carburetor.

For 1968 1/2, all Cobra Jets were coded "R" in the fifth digit of the vehicle identification number (VIN) and all were Ram-Air cars (featuring an air cleaner and flapper assembly mounted underneath the hood). A small scoop sat atop the hood to admit cold air to the Holley four-barrel.

The 428 SCJ (Super Cobra Jet) V-8s were built with drag-strip duty in mind, which is why Ford beefed up the bottom end and added an oil cooler, but left the top end alone. SCJs came with hardened cast-steel crankshafts (regular CJs had nodular iron cast cranks) and LeMans rods that were externally balanced with a large vibration damper. Of course, the CJ was already stock with a nodular-cased 9-inch differential and 31-spline axles.

SCJs did not have a unique engine code, but they were mandatory with either a 3.9:1 Trac-tion-Lok (code V) or a 4.30:1 Detroit Locker (code W) axle.

Jerry Heasley

1968 MUSTANG GT/GTA

Ford invited 1968 car shoppers to "Turn yourself on, switch your style and show a new face in the most exciting car on the American road," in its advertising for the 1968 Mustang.

The $147 GT option included a choice of stripes. Either the rocker panel type or a reflecting "C" stripe could be specified. The latter widened along the ridge of the front fender and ran across the door, to the upper rear body quarter. From there, it wrapped down, around the sculptured depression ahead of the rear wheel, and tapered forward, along the lower body, to about the midpoint of the door. Other GT goodies included fog lights in the grille, a GT gas cap and GT wheel covers. The fog lights no longer had a bar between them and the "corral" in the grille. Disc brakes were usually extra, but made the standard equipment list when big-block V-8s were ordered. A total of 17,458 GTs were made in 1968. A GT equipped with the 390-cid V-8 is considered a very desirable collector's car.

Many new engine options were offered in 1968. Some reflected midyear changes. There

were no options with the base 289-cid/195-hp V-8. Instead, a 302-cid V-8 was added. This was initially seen with a four-barrel carburetor and 230-hp output rating. Later, a 220-hp version with a two-barrel carburetor came out. Big-block options included two "FE" series engines, the 390-cid V-8 (with 320/325 hp) and the 390-hp/427-cid V-8. This engine was used in only a handful of cars before it was phased out in December 1967. Starting in April 1968, a new 428-cid Cobra-Jet V-8 with 335 hp was put into about 2,817 Mustangs. Cars with four-speed transmissions included strengthened front shock absorber towers and revised rear shock absorber mountings. Ram Air induction was available.

About 5,000 GT/CS "California Special" Mustangs were produced in 1968. Their features included a Shelby-style deck lid with a spoiler, sequential taillights and a blacked-out grille. They had no Mustang grille emblem. The wheel covers were the same ones used on 1968 GTs, but without GT identification.

Jerry Heasley

1968 SHELBY-MUSTANG GT 500KR

Somebody stole the Shelby GT 500KR that *Car Life* magazine was going to test drive. You couldn't blame them — the under-$5,000 fastback had a lot of appeal. With its 428-cid Cobra Jet engine, it was a big temptation to any car-loving cat burglar. After a rough three-day break-in, the LAPD recovered the car, but a Ford public relations guy had to call *Car Life* and admit it was in no shape for a national article. The magazine wound up with a replacement car and a good lead-in to introduce it.

Although it was not the fastest car ever made, the GT 500KR was the fastest Shelby-Mustang made up to its time. Some racers registered ETs below 13 seconds and top speed was around 130 mph. The fastback model was base-priced at $4,473 and ran about $4,900 with a nice selection of options. Production counts were 933 units for the fastback and 318 for the convertible.

Everyone knew what Cobra meant and the

GT 500 designation was well understood by 1968. As for "KR," the folks at Ford and Shelby said it stood for "King of the Road." With a 6.9 second 0-to-60 mph speed and 14.57 second-quarter-mile ET, the GT 500KR wasn't the undisputed king of drag racing. "But, there's more to life than the quarter-mile," Car Life's editors maintained.

Tucked below the hood was a 428-cid Cobra Jet V-8 with 4.13 x 3.98-inch bore and stroke, 10.6:1 compression, special hydraulic lifters, dual branched headers and one extra-big Holley four-barrel. It was rated for 335 hp at 5200 rpm and 440 lbs.-ft. of torque at 3400 rpm. True horsepower, however, was 435-500.

Large, but ineffective, air scoops were attached to the body sides to cool the disc/drum power brakes. During a test drive, the binders got so hot that they started pouring smoke out of the scoops. No wonder *Car Life* rated overall braking performance poor.

Tim Calvert

1968 TORINO GT

The 1968 Ford Torino GT was the sporty version of the Fairlane 500 and was based on that model. Except for some lousy visibility out the back window, the magazine raved about this manly machine, claiming "The new breed of super car from Ford is a full step ahead of its '67 counterpart."

The test car had the 390-cid four-barrel engine, which developed 335 hp at 4800 rpm and 427 lbs.-ft. of torque at 3200 rpm. It had a 10.5:1 compression ratio, three-speed manual attachment and 3.25:1 rear axle. *Motor Trend* reported 7.2 seconds for 0-to-60 mph and 15.1 seconds at 91 mph for the quarter-mile.

The Torino GT actually came in three versions. Model 65D was the two-door hardtop, which sold for $2,768.17, weighed 3,194 lbs. and had a production run of 23,939 units. The convertible — Model 76D — was much rarer and only 5,310 were made. Prices for the ragtop began at $3,020.40 and it tipped the scales at 3,352 lbs. in showroom stock condition. The real

image car was the Model 63D two-door fastback, with its $2,742.84 window sticker, 3,208-lb. curb weight and 74,135 units produced. Dubbed the "SportsRoof" by Ford, this car had lots of buyer appeal in its era.

The optional 390-cid engine came in two versions. The 265-hp edition with a single two-barrel carburetor added just $78.25 to the price of a Torino V-8. The 325-hp four-barrel version was $158.08 extra and also required an extra-cost transmission (either the heavy-duty three-speed at $79.20, a four-speed manual at $184.02 or Ford's Select Shift Cruise-O-Matic at $233.17).

Real muscle car lovers were probably more interested in getting a Torino GT with a 427-cid/390-hp V-8. It was a $622.97 option for all Fairlane two-door hardtops and you could not get it with Select Aire air conditioning, power steering, a 55-amp generator, a heavy-duty suspension or optional tires as extras either because it didn't make sense or these options were already required.

Jerry Heasley

1969 MUSTANG BOSS 302

The Boss 302 was Ford's answer to the Camaro Z/28 and was as likely to wind up in the hands of a hard-working kid as a middle-to-upper income youth who wanted to put a little excitement into his life.

What made the Boss special was a beefed-up 302-cid V-8 with four-bolt main bearing caps, a stronger crankshaft and — most important of all — redesigned cylinder heads that allowed dramatically better breathing. These "Cleveland" heads (as they are called) were also designed to sit atop Ford's 351 Cleveland V-8. In stock tune, a Boss 302 could turn in 0-to-60 times of under 7 seconds and nudge the century mark in a standing-start quarter-mile.

While a Boss 302 in the hands of a collector is likely to be driven a little more gingerly than the paces original owners put these cars through, Ford built an rpm limiter to keep lead-footed types from blowing up the engine. Basically, the limiter worked by counting ignition impulses and not allowing the engine to exceed 6,000 rpm.

Besides the special 302 engine, a Boss can be recognized by the matte black paint on its hood and trunk, Boss 302 name swatches on its sides, a front spoiler and styled steel wheels. Its performance equipment includes front disc brakes and a four-speed manual transmission. The optional rear spoiler was obviously decorative. (If this feature had been functional it would have been standard, right?)

Unlike other performance cars of the period, the Boss 302 had exceptionally good street manners — although the firm suspension did broadcast tar strips and other pavement irregularities.

Open the door and the Boss became just another Mustang. The interior is attractive, but it also features the infamous Mustang "park bench" rear seat. That's okay, though; the Mustang fastback wasn't really designed to be a four-seater.

If you've had a chance to own or drive one of these cars you'd probably agree with its original admirers: "Hey, man, this car is Boss!"

Jerry Heasley

1969 MUSTANG BOSS 429

This was a "he-man" car with testosterone to burn. Horsepower for the Boss 429 was advertised as 375, although real ratings were rumored to be much higher.

Ford Motor Company was delighted to give birth to a set of twins in 1969—the ready-to-race Boss 302 and the Boss 429. Both of these special cars were built around state-of-the-art, high-performance power plants. The main difference is that one championed small-block performance, while the other was aimed at big-block V-8 competition.

The Boss 429 was born because Ford had a second engine, in addition to the 302-cid small-block V-8, that it wanted to place into race track competition. The Boss 302 was designed to compete with the Camaro in Trans-Am racing. The Boss 429 was created to legalize the 429-cid V-8 for use on the NASCAR circuit.

Ford considered doing a 429-powered Torino, but decided to offer the new-for-1969 429-cid

"semi-hemi" big-block in the popular Mustang platform instead. Marketing experts felt that it would be easier to sell 500 big-block Mustangs than the same number of Torino-based supercars. Kar Kraft, an aftermarket firm in Brighton, Michigan, was contracted to build Boss 429s. Since the Mustang's engine compartment was not designed to house such a wide power plant, the job required a big shoehorn and a lot of suspension changes and chassis modifications.

All Boss 429s had the fancy Decor Group interior option, high-back bucket seats, deluxe seat belts, wood-trimmed dash and console treatment, and Visibility Group option. Automatic transmission and air conditioning were not available, but the $3,826 price tag included all of the above.

A total of 1,358 Boss 429s were constructed during the 1969 calendar year. This included 859 of the 1969 models made in early 1969 and 499 1970 models built late in the summer.

Jerry Heasley

1969-1970 SHELBY MUSTANG

There wasn't much that needed to be changed in the Shelby Mustangs for their final two years, so Ford didn't mess much with a good thing. They were still probably the most muscle-bound machines rolling off the FoMoCo assemby lines, so the company was happy to keep their blue prints the same, even if a few minor cosmetic details changed.

The '69 Shelby's exterior camouflage relied on the extensive use of fiberglass. The use of this material for fender, hood, and rear cap panels allowed Shelby designers to make the GT-350 three inches longer than the factory-stretched Mustang.

The Shelby hood had five recessed NASA-type hood scoops. Early in the year, Blue, Green, Yellow and Orange "Grabber" colors and Competition Orange were added to Black Jade, Acapulco Blue, Gulfstream Aqua, Pastel Gray, Candy Apple Red and Royal Maroon. The '69 Shelby used heavy-duty Mustang components straight from the Ford factory. In order to keep the rear axle from suffering during the occa-

sional hard launch, staggered shocks were standard on the GT-500. No longer was the Shelby Mustang a car that could be ordered as a Plain-Jane racing car. Instead of stamped steel wheels, Shelby buyers got 15 x 7-inch five-spoke rims shod with Goodyear E-70x15 wide oval tires (F-60x15 tires were optional). Some Shelbys wound up with Boss 302 "Magnum 500" wheels when a defect in the stock rim forced a recall.

Every GT-350 built in 1969 received Ford's new 351-cid 290-hp Windsor V-8 with a 470-cfm Autolite four-barrel carburetor. It came attached to Ford's four-speed manual transmission. Optional gear boxes included a close-ratio four-speed manual and the FMX automatic.

Sales were brisk, with 1,087 GT-350 fastbacks ($4,434); 194 GT-350 convertibles ($4,753); 1,534 GT-500 fastbacks ($4,709); and 335 GT-500 convertibles ($5,027) going to new owners.

There is no definitive count of how many 1970 Shelbys were created, but some reports say it was 789 units.

Jerry Heasley

1969 COBRA

There was a new snake in the Ford lineup for 1969, and it was a killer. This Cobra line included just two body types, the Model 65A formal hardtop base priced at $3,208 and the Model 6B SportsRoof-base priced at $3,183. The emphasis was on performance when you went Cobra shopping and the standard equipment included a 428-cid/335-hp Cobra Jet V-8, a four-speed manual transmission, competition suspension, wide oval-belted black sidewall tires and 6-inch-wide wheels with hubcaps.

Motor Trend road tested a Cobra with the Ram Air engine and liked the car. The magazine charted 0-to-60 performance at 6.3 seconds and the quarter-mile at 14.5 seconds and 100 mph.

The base Cobra engine featured a 4.13 x 3.98-inch bore and stroke, a 10.6:1 compression ratio, 335 hp at 5200 rpm and 440 lbs.-ft. of torque at 2600 rpm. You could get it with an optional 351-cid/290-hp V-8 if you wanted to save on gas, but few muscle car buffs did. Also optional on the Cobra was the 428 Cobra Jet "Ram Air" V-8, which also carried a 335-hp rating but achieved it at a higher 5600 rpm peak. Its torque output was 445 lbs.-ft. at 3400 rpm and it had a 10.7:1 compression ratio.

The Ram Air engine featured a functional hood scoop to "ram" cold air into its single Holley four-barrel carburetor.

If you did not want to shift yourself, a Select Shift automatic transmission was optional for $37.06 and it came with a floor shift and optional center console. The 3.25:1 rear axle was standard and optional axle ratios included 3.45:1, 3.91:1 and 4.30:1. Power disc brakes were also available for $64.77. A Traction-Lock differential was $63.51 extra and getting a factory tachometer added $47.92 to the price tag.

Jerry Heasley

1969 TALLADEGA

This fastback Ford was the perfect quarter-mile machine for the FoMoCo fan who wanted to go drag racing against Starsky & Hutch. Though the Talladega was a bit heftier and weightier than other Torinos, the 428 CJ still pushed it to mid-14-second quarter-miles. However, it was much better suited to left hand turns on an oval-shaped racetrack.

At the time they were built, the fastback cars that became combatants in the "aerodynamic wars" on the 1969-1970 NASCAR Grand National superspeedways were more of a headache to their manufacturers than the worshipped treasures they are today. Requirements to "legalize" them for racing meant at least 500 examples had to be produced during the 1969 model year. That minimum production level was raised to one car per dealer for 1970.

Ford's hopes rode on the sloped-nosed 1969 Torino Talladega, which was part of the mid-sized Fairlane model lineup. A similar, but not identical, Mercury Montego counterpart was produced and called the Cyclone Spoiler II.

Ford called its fastback-styled two-door hardtops "SportsRoof" models at this point and the Talladega model was one of them. IIn the stock version, power came from a 335-hp Cobra Jet 428-cid "FE" block V-8, which was pretty potent, but came only with a C-6 Cruise-0-Matic automatic transmission. The racing cars ran the 427-cid big-block at the beginning of the season. Beginning in March, they were allowed to use the new 429-cid "semi-hemi" V-8. These engines were not installed in showroom Talladegas, however, since the Mustang Boss 429 was utilized to meet the requirements of the race-sanctioning groups.

Counting prototypes, Talladega production easily passed the required 500 units and wound up at 754. The cars came in Wimbleton White, Royal Maroon or Presidential Blue. They had Black interiors and came only with bench seats.

The 1969 Talladegas proved very adept at racing. In fact, test drivers found that their 1970 replacements were some 5 mph slower on the big tracks. As a result, Ford's factory-backed teams ran year-old models at many tracks during the 1970 racing season.

Jerry Heasley

1970 MUSTANG CJ 428/SCJ 428

In Mustang enthusiast circles, the 428 CJ/SCJ Mustang is legendary for grabbing the Stock Eliminator title at the 1970 National Hot Rod Association's (NHRA) Winternationals. This was the race of the year for high-performance buffs and the Mustang was the monarch that season. In his book Fast Mustangs, marque expert Alex Gabbard observed, "The 428 Cobra Jet engine has been called the fastest-running pure stock in the history of man."

The 1970 Mustang had some distinctions to set it apart from the 1969 edition. The biggest change was a return to single headlights up front. The new headlights were located inside a larger new grille opening. Simulated air intakes were seen where the outboard headlights were on the 1969 Mustang models. The 1970 rear end appearance was also slightly restyled.

In addition to the base sport coupe (two-door hardtop) and convertible, Mustangs came as the hot Mach 1 fastback, the luxurious Grande hardtop and the race-bred Boss 302 fastback. With different engine option selections, you could change the Boss 302 into a Boss 351 or a Boss 429. In total, Ford offered nine Mustang engines to pick from and the lineup was the same as 1969, except that the 390-cid V-8 was discontinued.

While the pre-packaged Boss models were the hit of the enthusiast magazines this season, the CJ 428 and SCJ 428 engines were both back. The former listed for $356 in all Mustang models except the Mach 1, which offered it for $311 over the price of its standard 351-cid V-8. The Ram-Air version was $376 extra in the Mach 1 and $421 extra in other models.

The 1970 Mach 1 featured the new year's front end styling and had its taillights recessed in a flat panel with honeycomb trim between them. Ribbed aluminum rocker panel moldings with big Mach 1 call-outs and a cleaner upper rear quarter treatment without simulated air scoops at the end of the main feature line were seen. A black-striped hood with a standard fake scoop replaced the completely matte-black hood. New twist-in hood pins held the hood down.

Doug Mitchel

1970 TORINO COBRA

Though conceived as the answer to the winged Dodge Charger Daytona and Plymouth Superbird, the '70 Torino Cobra SportsRoof was more of a street muscle car. And it was a darn good one, too.

Muscle Torinos were nice-sized cars that you could cruise in all day — or you could speed like hell and dare the cops to catch you.

Ford had its intermediate cars on a two-year styling cycle at this time, so no matter how good the 1968 and 1969 Fairlane fastbacks looked or how fast they were in stock car racing competition, by the time the 1970 model year rolled around, it was time for a new batch of sheet metal.

Ford also had its intermediates (and most other lines) on a growth binge and the wheelbase measurement for the new '70 Torino increased from 116 to 117 inches. The length of the car also went up half a foot and its width was increased by about two inches.

A full line of models was again available. At the top of the heap was the Torino Cobra. At

$3,270 it had the most expensive base price in the line, even more than the sole remaining convertible — the GT at $3,212.

Part of the cost could be attributed to its new standard power plant, the 385 series big-block 429. The 428 was gone from the intermediates for the new year. Torinos got the milder 360-hp engine with a single four-barrel carburetor. Cobras came with Ford's top-loader four-speed manual transmission (capped by a Hurst shifter), a competition suspension with staggered rear shocks, 7-inch wide steel wheels, F70-14 wide oval tires, a black hood with locking devices, black-out trim and Cobra badging. Bench seats were standard. Engine options included the 370-hp Cobra 429 or Cobra Jet Ram Air 429 with the same rating. For $155 you could get the Traction-Lok differential, and for $207 the 4.30:1 Detroit Locker rear axle was available.

Production was 7,675, which was overshadowed by the 56,819 Torino GTs produced. The Torino GTs, which were flashier and cheaper at $3,105, thanks to a standard 302 cid V-8.

Jerry Heasley

1971 MUSTANG BOSS 351

What red-blooded American male didn't want one of these back in the day?

When you were "working for the man" back in 1971, a car like this could make you look forward to the weekend — especially your Sunday afternoon trip to the drag strip. Road Test magazine observed in March 1971 that the Boss 351 was the "Sophisticated Mustang." The magazine said, " The '71 Boss is 40 hp bossier than last year's 302 (and) still gives fine handling coupled to straightaway performance." With the base 330-hp V-8, the Boss 351 did 0-to-60 in 5.9 seconds and the quarter-mile in 13.98 seconds at 104 mph.

Ford Mustangs grew to their all-time largest for the 1971 model year. Wheelbase was up an inch to 109 inches, length increased 2.1 inches to 189.5 inches and width grew 2.4 inches to 74.1 inches. The latter was accompanied by a tread increase that permitted the 429-cid big-block V-8 to fit in the engine compartment with ease. Although the 429-powered cars were the most muscular, the Boss 351 was perhaps the most interesting.

The Boss 429 was curtailed early in the 1970 model run, and the Boss 302 was of no more use after it was gone. Racing rules had changed and engine size was no longer critical to racing legalization. As a result, the Boss 351's purpose was just to tap what was left of the declining high-performance market.

Like its predecessors, the Boss 351 was based on the SportsRoof or fastback model. It was considered an option package and brought the base Mustang price of $2,973 up to $4,124. The heart of the new Boss 351 package was a 351-hp Cleveland V-8 with four-bolt main bearings, solid valve lifters and a four-barrel carburetor. The 1971 models were the last for Ford high-compression engines and the last for gross advertised horsepower numbers, which were 330 hp for the Boss 351.

Other mechanical features included a four-speed "top-loader" manual transmission with a Hurst gear shifter.

Only about 1,800 Boss 351s were made, which adds up to rarity today.

1971 MUSTANG MACH 1

You may not be able to break Mach 1 in a Mustang Mach 1, but it's the kind of car that looks — and feels – like it could do just that if you pushed it real hard. "For those interested in owning a sporty car which reflects up-to-the-minute design, Mustang (Mach 1), an all-around vehicle without a significant flaw, can't be a bad choice," opined *Road Test* magazine in September 1970.

Car Life (July 1969) tested a 375-hp Boss 429 with a four-speed manual transmission and 3.91:1 axle. It did 0 to 60 mph in 7.1 seconds. The quarter-mile took 14.09 seconds with a terminal speed of 102.85 mph. Top speed on the car was about 116 mph.

For 1971, Ford completed its fourth redesign of the Mustang. This created a bigger car. It had the basic Mustang look, with a longer wheelbase, a stretched length, more width, wider front and rear tracks and a heavier curb weight. A raked windshield, bulging front fenders and aerodynamic enhancements were evident.

The Mach 1 package returned. It included color-keyed mirrors, a honeycomb grille, color-keyed bumpers, sport lamps, a new gas cap, special decals and tape stripes and black or argent silver finish on the lower body perimeter. A special hood with NASA-style air scoops was a no-cost option with the base 302-cid V-8 and standard otherwise.

Available for the last time was a 429-cid big-block engine, which came in Cobra-Jet Ram Air and Super-Cobra-Jet Ram Air versions. Ford put together 1,255 of the CJ-R equipped Mach 1s and 610 of the SCJ-Rs.

Basically a de-stroked Thunderbird/Lincoln 460-cid V-8, the 429 had a wedge-head-shaped combustion chamber derived from up-to-date performance technology.A Ram Air induction system was included. Advertised horsepower for the 429 CJ-R was 370 at 5400 rpm.

The 429 SCJ-R put out 375 hp at 5600 rpm. A Drag Pack option with either a 3.91:1 Traction-Lok differential or a 4.11:1 Detroit Locker axle was mandatory.

Both Cobra Jet engines had 11.3:1 compression and produced 450 lbs.-ft. of torque at 3400 rpm. The SCJ-R had a bit more camshaft duration (200/300 degree versus 282/296 degrees).

Jerry Heasley

1978 MUSTANG II "KING COBRA"

While scorned by today's standards, the King Cobra wasn't all that inferior compared to the rest of the visual muscle cars of its time. Not everybody wants, can afford or even relates to the muscle cars of the 1960s or the new ones out today.

During the fuel shortage-scared, federal regulation-oppressed mid- to late-'70s, a number of "visual" muscle cars were offered by domestic manufacturers. Their mission was to drum up enthusiasm in the youth market and to snare what was left of the old performance buyers.

Exemplifying this was the 1978 Ford Mustang II King Cobra option. It dressed the not-universally-loved lines of the hatchback in its most garish (or garnished, depending on your point of view) trim yet.

The King Cobra followed the Cobra II option that came out midyear in 1977. Huge side stripes, lettering, front and rear spoilers probably did more to anger purists of the order of the sacred snake than attract serious performance seekers.

The Cobra II returned for 1978, but at the start of the model year we got the King Cobra. It featured a more complete front air dam, similar rear spoiler, wheel flair treatment, the same fake hood scoop and different graphics from the Cobra II.

Subdued lettering on the sides and rear spoiler contrasted to the giant Cobra hood decal that the King carried. Its $1,293 was in addition to the hatchback's base of $4,011.

Mechanically, first the good news. Power front disc brakes, power steering and heavy-duty suspension were part of the package. Also good was a standard four-speed manual gearshift. Its clutch was attached to the 302-cid V-8, which came standard, too.

With around 5,000 KCs made, they are getting rare, offer somewhat unique styling touches, have salvage yards full of mechanical replacement parts and bring a 50 percent premium over the regular hatchback '78 Mustang II prices today.

Jerry Heasley

1980 SVO-MCLAREN TURBO MUSTANG

Loaded with good looks and outstanding performance capabilities, the McLaren exudes collector appeal as well. It has always been a special and rare machine that few people have owned.

The McLaren Mustang was created by Ford Motor Co.'s newly formed Special Vehicle Operations (SVO) group. The car represented a very obvious indication that Ford was finally turning the performance-car battleship around to chase the enthusiast market. "The bright orange police magnet was a bit too obvious to thrash about on residential roads," wrote Bob Nagy in Motor Trend.

This "semi-aftermarket" modern muscle car hit the market in late 1980. It represented the ultimate-for-the-era, small-displacement street performance car. Unfortunately, its price tag of $25,000 was anything but small.

Under the car's hood was a high-tech 2.3-liter turbocharged four-cylinder engine. It had a special variable-boost turbocharger that provided from 5 to 11 psi. This provided optimum road and track driving performance.

Compared to the stock Ford turbo four, with its set pressure of 5 psi (and an estimated 131 hp), the McLaren Mustang was a screamer. It was rated for 175 hp at 2500 rpm with the turbocharger boost running 10 psi.

Flared fenders and a functional air dam were among body changes that set the McLaren apart. Designers Todd Gerstenberger and Harry Wykes went after an International Motor Sports Association (IMSA) racing car image. They did a great job of achieving just the look they wanted. The air dam directed cold air to the front disc brakes through the hairy-looking wastegate hood.

Part of the SVO concept was to showcase high-performance components in cars such as the McLaren—which was virtually hand-built—and determine the most popular equipment. The favorites could then be made available through the performance parts aftermarket at a later date.

No more than 250 examples — including the prototype — were believed put together. Some experts think that the real number was substantially lower than that.

1984 MUSTANG SVO

According to Ford, the SVO could do 0-to-60 mph in 7.5 seconds and had a top speed of 134 mph. *Motor Trend* called the SVO "the best driving street Mustang the factory has ever offered." *Road & Track* said "the SVO outruns the Datsun 280ZX, outhandles the Ferrari 308 and Porsche 944 and it's affordable."

On April 17, 1984, Ford distributed a letter noting the Mustang's 20th birthday and mentioning two hot cars the company was offering that year. One was a more powerful midyear GT with a 5.0-liter V-8 that wound up being delayed. The other was the Mustang SVO, which was named after the automaker's Special Vehicle Operations team.

Featuring a touch of European-inspired technology, the $15,596 SVO model (about $6,000 more than a regular Mustang Turbo GT) was promoted as a "machine that speaks for itself." Special features included multi-adjustable articulated bucket seats, a performance suspension with adjustable Koni gas shocks and a 2.3-liter port-fuel-injected turbocharged four-cylinder engine with an air-to-air intercooler. The engine had an 8.0:1 compression ratio and produced 175 hp at 4400 rpm and 210 lbs.-ft. of torque at 3000 rpm. A functional hood scoop designed to "ram" cold air into the engine was also part of the package.

The SVO engine was linked to a five-speed manual transmission with overdrive fifth gear and a Hurst shift linkage. It had a Traction-Lok rear axle with a 3.45:1 final drive ratio. Disc brakes were fitted on all four corners, as were Goodyear NCT steel-belted radial tires on 16 x 7-inch cast-aluminum wheels.

Only the three-door Hatchback body was delivered as an SVO. Identification features included unique single rectangular headlamps, a front air dam with integral spoiler, a functional hood scoop, rear wheel opening "spats" and a dual-wing rear spoiler.

Brad Bowling

1984 SALEEN MUSTANG

Ford turbocharged the four-cylinder Mustang off and on, but high costs, low power when compared to the cheaper V-8 and reliability issues killed that program. It was the re-introduction of the 5.0-liter HO V-8 in the 1982 Mustang GT that put Ford back on the muscle car highway.

Steve Saleen, a business school graduate with a background in Sports Car Club of America (SCCA) Formula Atlantic and Trans-Am racing, was thrilled by Ford's first assault on the early '80s horsepower war. Saleen (pronounced like the last two syllables of "gasoline") had owned '65 and '66 Shelby GT-350s and a '67 GT fastback with a 390-cid V-8. He was aware of how Carroll Shelby had turned garden-variety Mustangs into world-class performance cars.

To meet federal laws, Saleen established a formula he applied, at least initially, to all of his Hi-Po Mustangs: Rather than make engine modifications that required expensive and extensive testing for emissions, fuel consumption and warranty standards, Saleen left the engines stock and enhanced performance through suspension,

brake, chassis and aerodynamic improvements.

In 1984, Saleen Autosport produced three 175-hp Mustang hatchbacks with Saleen's own Racecraft suspension components including specific-rate front and rear springs, Bilstein pressurized struts and shocks, a front G-load brace and urethane swaybar bushings. He lowered the car and improved the Mustang's handling to near racetrack levels. Those first three cars wore 215/60-15 Goodyear Eagle GTs wrapped around 15x7-inch Hayashi "basketweave" wheels. A custom front air dam, sides skirts, clear covers for the recessed headlights and a rather showy spoiler created a smoother aerodynamic package. The interior featured a Saleen gauge package, a Wolf Racing four-spoke steering wheel and an Escort radar detector.

For $14,300 ($4,526 more than a standard Mustang GT), the Saleen was quite reasonable when parked next to a comparably equipped Camaro Z-28 ($14,086), Pontiac Trans-Am ($15,100) or Toyota Supra ($16,853). Even the SVO Mustang was more expensive at $15,585.

Brad Bowling

1987 MUSTANG GT

The well-thought-out and attractive styling revamp made the 1987 Mustang look more changed than it really was. Although it was not an all-new car, a package of new front and rear body fascias, aero style headlights and a prominent lower feature line with heavy moldings made it seem like a different car. It also sported a redesigned instrument panel, pod-mounted headlight switches and a center console.

With the Mustang SVO model and its sizzling turbocharged four-cylinder engine gone the way of the doo-doo bird, the 5.0-liter HO V-8 took over as the top Mustang performance option. The ante was upped with a pair of hot new cylinder heads that added 25 hp. The engine's compression ratio remained at 9.2:1, but the revised heads and sequential fuel injection system boosted output to 225 hp at 4000 rpm and 300 lbs.-ft. of torque at 3200 rpm.

The Mustang GT was again offered in two body styles. One was a three-door hatchback with an $11,835 price tag and curb weight of 3,080 lbs. The other was the convertible, which listed for $15,724 and weighed in at 3,214 lbs. GT models had a lower front air dam with integrated air scoops and "Mustang GT" lettering formed into the flared rocker panel moldings and rear fascia. Also added were so-called alert lights and a Traction-Lok rear axle. The GT hatchback also had a large spoiler with a high-mounted stoplight. The wide tail lamps on the GT models were covered by a louver-like appliqué. The sport-tuned exhaust system carried dual outlet exhausts.

Brad Bowling

2000 SVT COBRA MUSTANG

SVT pulled the plug on its 2000 Cobra street models, but they more than made up for that move with the decision to unleash the 2000 Cobra R — the most powerful, brutal Mustang since the Boss 429.

The 3,590-lb. R could do 0-to-60 mph in less than 5 seconds, with a top speed of more than 170 mph! A total of just 300 of the $54,995 SVT Mustang Cobra R models were sold., so if you can get your hands on one, don't let it go!

SVT developed an all-new engine for the 2000 R. The cast-iron 5.4-liter DOHC, 32-valve V-8 was tweaked until it turned out an awe-inspiring 385 hp and 385 lbs.-ft. of torque. The 5.4-liter's bore was the same as the 4.6-liter's, but the stroke was 15.8mm longer. Peak airflow was increased by 25 percent over the standard Cobra. Stainless-steel short-tube headers led to a Bassani X-pipe, '98 Cobra catalytic converters, Borla mufflers and dual twin-pipe side exhausts.

A Tremec T56 six-speed manual transmission was specified to handle the 5.4-liter's tremendous torque. An aluminum driveshaft measuring 4 inches in diameter led to the 8.8-inch aluminum-case differential. Induction-hardened GKN halfshafts are the final link to the rear wheels. Final drive ratio was a short 3.55:1 for increased acceleration.

Eighteen-inch five-spoke wheels were fitted with 265/40ZR-18 BFGoodrich g-Force tires, which contributed somewhat to the R's astounding 1.0g of lateral acceleration. The Cobra R's rear deck and fascia were from the base V-6 Mustang, as rear-exit dual exhaust cutouts were unnecessary with the R's side-exit setup. The front of the R included a specially designed front air splitter that, in concert with the large rear wing, reduced front lift and increased rear downforce. Because it also reduced ground clearance to a few inches, the splitter was shipped with the cars and installed at the customer's request by the dealer.

Racing Recaro seats, a thickly padded steering wheel, and a B&M Ripper shifter were used.

Coming from SVT, the Cobra R wasn't exactly a standard issue production car, but it was low-production, super-fast and a throwback to the golden age of muscle.

Wieck Media

2003-2004 SVT COBRA MUSTANG

Packing a supercharged 4.6-liter double overhead cam engine below its hood, the 2003 SVT Cobra was in a league of its own. Factory spec sheets showed engine output rated at 390 hp and 390 lbs.-ft. of torque. Eaton supplied the Roots-type supercharger, which was tuned to produce 8 lbs. of boost. A water-to-air intercooler reduced the temperature of the charge for maximum mixture volatility in the combustion chamber. To strengthen the power train against such violent internal forces, the new Cobra engine was built around a cast-iron block. In the interest of saving weight and speeding up heat dissipation under the hood, SVT retained an aluminum cylinder head. A six-speed Tremec T-56 manual gearbox was the only transmission available. An accelerator-friendly 3.55:1 rear axle backed it up.

With driver and passenger airbags, anti-lock braking on four-wheel discs, traction control and independent rear suspension all as standard equipment, the new Cobra was also safer and better handling than its legendary predecessors. (As a yardstick of how far the Cobra name had come since the dark days of the 1970s, realize that this model put out more than three times the horsepower of the 1976-1978 Cobra II and King Cobra V-8s and it more than quadrupled the output of the four-cylinder version.)

Just when fans of the nearly 40-year-old Mustang thought it couldn't get any better, SVT released its 10th Anniversary Edition SVT Cobra later that summer. It was available in either coupe or convertible body styles with 17 x 9-inch Argent Silver wheels, Red leather seating surfaces, carbon fiber-look interior trim, and special anniversary badging on the floor mats and deck lid. Only 2,003 of the anniversary Cobras — to be painted Red, Black or Silver— were produced.

In all, SVT produced 8,394 2003 Cobra coupes (at $34,065 each) and 5,082 Cobra convertibles ($38,405).

In 2004 every Mustang fan on the planet was eagerly awaiting the all-new Mustang design promised by Ford for 2005, so SVT carried its 390-hp coupes and convertibles into a second year without any serious changes.

2007 FORD SHELBY GT500

For many reasons, the years beginning with 1965 and ending in '70 are the most revered among muscle car enthusiasts. One of the main reasons is this span saw the creation of the Shelby Mustang in its differing, desirable forms: GT350, GT350-H (Hertz), GT500 and GT500-KR (King of the Road). On the heels of creating what is considered THE muscle car, the Shelby Cobra 427SC roadster, Carroll Shelby was brought onboard to power-up Ford's new pony car.

Some 35 years after the last Shelby Mustang was produced in 1970, FoMoCo decided to re-skin its 2005 Mustang to evoke the retro look of the 1967-'69 models. Enthusiasts of the pony car didn't need telepathic powers to realize that sometime soon after, Ford would again woo Mr. Shelby back into the mix.

By the summer of 2006, the product of that inevitable re-merger debuted, called the Ford Shelby GT500 and available in both fastback and convertible body styles.

Built at the Ford-Mazda joint venture plant, AutoAlliance, in Flat Rock, Mich., Shelby had help in the form of Ford's Special Vehicle Team (SVT) in the launch of the new GT500. The retro-rocket's powertrain consisted of a DOHC, 32-valve 5.4-liter V-8 mated to a Tremec TR6060 six-speed manual transmission. The engine, fitted with a Roots-type surpercharger and air-to-water intercooler, was rated at 475-hp and provided an equal number 475 lbs.-ft. of torque.

The two-door, four-place, rear-drive GT500 fastback weighed 3,920 lbs., while its drop-top counterpart tipped the scales at 4,040 lbs. Wheelbase was 107.1 inches. Stopping power was supplied up front via Brembo disc brakes with four-piston calipers and 14-inch vented rotors while the disc brakes in back utilized single-piston calipers and 11.8-inch vented rotors.

Doug Gaffka, design director for Ford SVT summed it up best in 2006, when he explained, "The GT500 takes a huge leap forward by combining the modern Mustang muscle car with the classic Shelby performance look."

Jerry Heasley

1965 COMET CYCLONE

Mercury's 1965 Comet Cyclone was as whiplashingly fast as the Coney Island roller coaster that it shared the Cyclone name with. Auto writer John Ethridge said, "The Cyclone's 225-hp engine had what you'd consider a healthy feeling at any speed between idle and 3000 rpm. Then it felt like four more cylinders were added and came on very strongly."

In May 1965, *Motor Trend* printed a road test titled "2 Comets: Hot & Cool" that compared the Caliente and Cyclone two-door hardtops. The Caliente had the 289-cid, 200-hp engine and Merc-O-Matic transmission. It did 0-to-60 mph in 11 seconds and ran down the drag strip in 18.1 seconds with a 76-mph terminal speed. Its top speed was 96 mph. The Cyclone had the 225-hp version of the "289" and a four-speed gearbox. It trimmed 2.2 seconds off the other car's 0 to 60-mph time and the quarter-mile took 17.1 seconds at 82 mph. Its top speed was 108 mph.

The Comet Cyclone series consisted of a single two-door hardtop priced at $2,683. That made it the second-most expensive Comet (the Villager station wagon was the priciest model).

The 1965 Cyclone had a special grille with only two groups of horizontal blades and blacked-out finish around its perimeter. Cyclones had all the equipment that came on Calientes, plus bucket seats in front, a center console, a tachometer, unique deluxe wheel covers, curb moldings and a 289-cid "Cyclone" V-8 engine with a two-barrel carburetor. A distinctive twin-air-scoop fiberglass hood was optional.

The 195-hp "Cyclone V-8" engine was a $108 option for non-Cyclone models. It had a 9.3:1 compression ratio. In addition, there was a 220-hp "Super Cyclone 289" with a 10.0:1 compression ratio and a four-barrel carburetor. This engine cost $45.20 extra in Cyclones and $153.20 additional in other models.

A three-speed manual gearbox was standard with all engines. A four-speed manual transmission was $188 extra, and Multi-Drive Merc-O-Matic ran $189.60 additional. This was, again, a three-speed automatic, comparable to the Ford Cruise-O-Matic.

Racing promotion for the 1967 Cyclone was limited to its body lines being used atop funny cars for drag racing, but better things were ahead for Cyclones. They would become the NASCAR superspeedway stars of 1968 and beyond, finally helping Mercury's intermediate-sized models to establish a name for themselves.

1967 COUGAR GT 390

There was just flat out a lot to love about the Merc' Cougar GT 390. It was probably one of the most underappreciated pavement pounders of its time.

"The Mercury Cougar's fascination is in finesse in fabrication," *Car Life* said of this well-built Mercury.

Although the optional big-block 390-cid/335-hp power plant was equipped with hydraulic lifters, a fairly mild cam and street-type valve timing, it produced a 1:10 power-to-weight ratio that was good for some driving excitement.

The Cougar GT 390 was good for 0-to-60 mph in 8.1 seconds and 16-second quarter-miles. And it did it with style and manners.

The Cougar, said *Car Life*, was best described as a "Mustang with class." It had a shapely, graceful appearance and jewel-like trimmings. Only the two-door hardtop was available at first. A convertible would come along later.

While based on the Mustang platform, the Cougar received some upgrades to its suspension componentry. They included a hook-and-eye joint in the lower front A-frames to dampen ride harshness, 6-inch-longer rear leaf springs and better-rated rear spring and axle attachments.

The GT, however, came more firmly sprung with solid rear bushings, stiffer springs all around, bigger 1.1875-inch shocks and a fatter .84-inch anti-roll bar. Power front disc brakes, 8.95 x 14 wide oval tires and a 390-cid 335-hp V-8 were included, as well as a low-restriction exhaust system and special identification features.

A Holley C70F carburetor with four 1.562-inch venturis and vacuum-operated secondaries sat on the 390-cid engine. With a 10.5:1 compression ratio, it required premium fuel. The horsepower peak came at just 4800 rpm. A husky 427 lbs.-ft. of torque was produced at 3200 rpm. Transmission choices included three- or four-speed synchromesh gearboxes or a three-speed Merc-O-Matic with manual shift capabilities for downshifting to second below 71 mph or to first below 20 mph.

Cougars were not widely promoted back in 1968 and very few were made, making the survivors highly prized by collectors today.

Jerry Heasley

1969 COUGAR ELIMINATOR

The Cougar Eliminator was one of the true "big rigs" of the muscle car wars, and when Mercury rolled out the ferocious 1969 Eliminator with an optional 428 the company had itself a real burner that buyers could wrap in a bunch of different cool paint colors.

The 428-cid/335-hp could get to 60 mph in a swift 5.6 seconds and clock 14.10 in the quarter-mile while hitting the century mark at the end of the strip. "The Eliminator name was perfect for a muscle pony car," said *Car Review* in December 1986. "And the bright colors created the desired effect at the drive-in."

The 1969 Mercury Cougar that the Eliminator package was based on was wider, longer and heavier. Attractions for model year included the nameplate's first convertible. As a midyear muscle car offering the Eliminator came only in two-door hardtop form.

The Cougar two-door hardtop ($2,999) and convertible ($3,365) were the base models. A GT appearance group option included: Comfortweave vinyl bucket seats, a rim-blow steering wheel, a remote-control left-hand racing mirror, turbine wheel covers, GT decals, a GT dash nameplate and F70 x 14 fiberglass belted tires for $168.40.

Standard in the Eliminator was a four-barrel version of the Windsor 351 cid V-8, rated at 290 hp. Other Cougar options were available, including the last of the 390-cid V-8s and the 428 CJ with and without Ram Air. Both of these were rated at 335 hp, far under their true output on a dyno. Another notable engine option — the Boss 302 — was new and came in "street" and "racing" versions. The former had a single four-barrel carburetor and was advertised at 290 hp, a fraction of its actual output. The latter had two four-barrel carburetors, but its horsepower rating was never advertised.

Visuals with the Eliminator package included front and rear spoilers, a blacked-out grille, a hood scoop, argent styled steel wheels similar to the Torino GT type, appropriate side striping and a rally clock and tachometer. With the CJ 428-cid engine option you got a hood scoop, hood hold-down pins, a competition handling package and hood striping.

Doug Mitchel

1969 CYCLONE SPOILER II

Cars like the Cyclone Spoiler II were designed to put some Viagra into Mercury's high-performance image in the muscle car era.

When Cale Yarborough drove the Wood Brothers' Cyclone to victory in the Daytona 500 in February 1968, the battle of the NASCAR aerodynamic noses was on. Dodge countered with the Charger 500 for 1969. Ford forces fought back with the Torino Talladega and Mercury Cyclone Spoiler II. Both featured flush grilles and extended noses.

The Talladega was fairly simple, but the Cyclone Spoiler was not. Mercury announced the Spoiler as a midyear model to go on sale in January 1969. The main feature in early information was a spoiler bolted on the trunk deck. It was nice, but the device was not legal in NAS-CAR at the time. Originally, an extended nose similar to the Talladega was to be an option.

After considerable confusion, the long-nosed Spoiler came to be known as the Cy-clone Spoiler II. A total of 519 were made, all with the 351-cid four-barrel V-8 despite an announcement that there also would be a 428-cid Cobra-Jet Ram-Air option. At least 500 needed to be produced to qualify the car as a production model so it could be raced.

Cyclone Spoilers came in two trim versions. A "Dan Gurney" Spoiler had a dark blue roof, dark blue striping and a signature decal on the white lower portion. A "Cale Yarborough" edition featured red trim similar to his Wood Brothers stock car. It, too, had a signature decal.

As it turned out, the Spoiler wasn't declared legal in NASCAR until the Atlanta 500 on March 30. This put Cyclone pilots in Talladegas for the Daytona 500 race, which was won by Lee Roy Yarbrough in Junior Johnson's Talladega.

The Cyclone II Spoiler was good for 0-to-60 mph in 7.4 seconds or a 14.4-second quarter-mile at 99 mph.

Jerry Heasley

1970 COUGAR ELIMINATOR

The term Top Eliminator was familiar to drag racing buffs, but to Mercury fans the term simply meant "hot Cougar." *Car Life* recommended, "Think of it as a family car with guts and you'll be happy with it."

One car enthusiast magazine of the era tested a 1970 Cougar Eliminator with the 290-hp version of the "Boss 302" V-8. It carried 12.4 lbs. per hp and did 0-to-60 mph in 7.6 seconds. The quarter-mile took 15.8 seconds.

Evolutionary design changes characterized the 1970 Mercury Cougars. They included a new vertical grille and a forward-thrusting front end. Promoted as "America's most completely equipped sports car," the new Cougar grille had a center hood extension and an "electric shaver" style insert. Its design was reminiscent of the 1967 and 1968 models' grilles.

The Eliminator returned for one final time. Now standard was the new 351 Cleveland four-barrel V-8 that was rated at 300 hp. There were options galore for the muscle car's engine com-partment including the Boss 302, the 428 CJ and a new version of the 385 series big-block 429. This "Boss 429" package included Ram-Air induction and a 375-hp rating. "Call it the road animal," said Cougar literature. A rear deck lid spoiler, body graphics and a restyled scooped hood returned as part of the Eliminator's image.

Features for the basic Cougar models included upper body pin stripes, wheel opening moldings, roof moldings and windshield and rear window chrome accents. The sporty interior featured high-back bucket seats, courtesy lights, carpeted door trim panels, a vinyl headliner and a rosewood-toned dash panel. The Cougar convertible had a Comfortweave vinyl interior, door-mounted courtesy lights, a three-spoke steering wheel and a power top with a folding rear glass window. There was a two-door hardtop with a base retail price of $2,917. Prices for the convertible started at $3,264. Only 2,322 ragtops were made.

Jerry Heasley

1971 COUGAR GT CJ 429

This big ol' Cougar was definitely no pussy-cat. Of course, all you had to do was see its menacing hood scoop and paint-matching rims to know that this machine meant business!

The '71 Mercury Cougar is certainly an interesting automobile and the 429 CJ V-8 adds about as much performance as you might find in the waning years of the muscle-car era. "Driving the Cougar in whatever version you choose is still a fun proposition," Motor Trend opined in September 1970.

For 1971, the Cougars had the most dramatic changes seen since the marque's introduction in 1967. There was a lower silhouette, interior refinements and a muscular new GT option to fill up the gap left by the no longer offered Eliminator. The styling inspiration for the Cougar's thinner roof and windshield pillars was said to have come from European cars.

The 1971 models were "horse-sized" ponies,

based on the big, new Mustangs. They were 4 inches longer (113 inches) in wheelbase and 7 inches longer (197 inches) in overall bumper-to-bumper length. With their new radiator-style grille, they looked even heftier than they actually were.

The Cougars had better manners than the Mustang, with more sound-deadening materials and nicer trim and interior appointments. Only big V-8 engines went under the hood. The power train options included a 351-cid engine with a two-barrel carburetor and 240 hp, a 351-cid V-8 with a four-barrel carburetor and 285 hp and a 429-cid four-barrel job with 370 hp.

There were two Cougar series, each offering both hardtop and convertible body styles. The XR-7 was the sporty version with front bucket seats, full instrumentation and a vinyl half-roof. Cougar list prices started at $3,289 and went to $3,877.

1965 4-4-2

If you wanted to buy a muscle car that gave you the thrill of a GTO or an SS 396 without the headline-high pricing, the "4-dash-4-dash-2" was the way to go in 1965.

Said *Car and Driver,* "Summed up, the Oldsmobile 4-4-2 is another one of those 'special purpose' American cars that should really be sold as the all-purpose car. It really isn't a sports car, and it isn't exactly like the imported sports sedans — even though that seems to have been the aim of its manufacturer — but it does approach a very worthwhile balance of all the qualities we'd like to see incorporated in every American car."

The F-85 Cutlass line was mildly face lifted for 1965 and the 4-4-2 performance and handling package gained in popularity. Noting the runaway success of the Pontiac GTO with its 389-cid engine, Oldsmobile engineers saw the need to cram more cubes into their creation. Reducing the bore of the new Olds 425-cid engine

from 4.125 inches to an even 4.0 produced an engine ideally sized for the 4-4-2 at 400 cid.

This year the 4-4-2 package was offered with an optional Hydra-Matic transmission. Since the second "4" in the 1964 model designation had stood for "four-speed manual transmission," Oldsmobile had to explain the 4-4-2 name a different way. The company now said that the first four (4) stood for the new 400-cid V-8, the second four (4) meant four-barrel carburetor and the two (2) meant dual exhaust. This sounded a little awkward, since "4" and "400" aren't the same, but who cared?

With the 400-cid engine, power rose by 35 horses to a total of 345 hp at 4800 rpm and torque increased by 85 ft. lbs. to 440 at 3200 rpm.

Car and Driver test drove a 1965 Olds 4-4-2 convertible with a four-speed manual gearbox and a 3.55:1 axle in May 1965. Its 0 to 60-mph time was recorded as 5.5 seconds and the quarter-mile run took 15.0 seconds at 98 mph.

Jerry Heasley

1967 CUTLASS SUPREME 4-4-2

The Cutlass Supreme might not be on the list of cars you think of when it comes to 1960s muscle machines, but if you had yourself a '67 Cutlass with the 4-4-2 badging on it, you could run with the best of 'em.

The original 1964 Cutlass 4-4-2 option was a quick, midyear answer to the GTO option for the Pontiac Tempest. It utilized parts and pieces from the police package available at the time. By 1967, Olds and its competitors were turning out nicely packaged hot intermediates with good looks and mechanical performance galore.

The 1967 Cutlass 4-4-2 option was available for the top-of-the-line Cutlass Supreme series, which grew from a single four-door hardtop in 1966 to a full model range for 1967. You could add the 4-4-2 package to all of the series' two-door models. They came with a standard 330-cid/320-hp V-8.

Checking option box L78 brought the 4-4-2 option and added only $184 to your bill. For that small sum came the 440-cid 350-hp V-8, heavy-duty suspension, and other go-fast stuff.

Using factory ducting from the front of the car, the 1967 W-30-optioned version was advertised at 360 hp, the same as the 1966 Tri-Power Cutlass 4-4-2. Performance tests of the 1966 and 1967 Cutlass 4-4-2s, however, revealed nearly a second lost in the 0-to-60 runs and quarter-mile sprints were down about the same for the 1967s. However, that doesn't prevent a 30-percent price premium today for W-30-equipped 1967 4-4-2 examples.

Jerry Heasley

1970 4-4-2

The W-30-equipped 4-4-2 was Oldsmobile's response to the lifting of General Motors' ill-conceived mandate prohibiting the use of engines exceeding 400-cid in its A-bodied automobiles.

On a limited scale — and well beyond the reach of GM's authority — this wall of separation had already been breached by the Hurst Corp.'s 1969 Hurst/Olds. Either in a "bandit" Hurst or a W-30-optioned Olds 4-4-2, the division's 455-cid V-8 represented a major advance in straight-line performance. And it did not adversely affect the 4-4-2's handling, since it weighed about the same as the smaller and less-powerful 400-cid V-8 used in 1969 Olds 4-4-2s.

The 4-4-2 had, since its introduction in 1964, enjoyed a deserved reputation for handling far above the existing norm for American super-cars. The W-30 version, along with its stature as a powerful 370-hp automobile, maintained the tradition of being a handler. There was nothing magical or exotic about the W-30 Olds 4-4-2 suspension, which consisted of front coil and rear leaf springs. Like all 4-4-2 Oldsmobiles, the W-30 was equipped with a rear stabilizer bar. Car Life magazine, in its March 1970 issue said, "At last people who want more power, but still want their car to handle, have a car that does both."

Also adding to the W-30 Olds 4-4-2's performance profile were standard 10.88-inch front power disc brakes that were optional for standard 4-4-2s. At the rear, 9.5 x 2.0-inch drum brakes were utilized. This setup wasn't flawless, but Car Life noted that on its W-30 test car, "The front disc brakes came through the brake fade test smoking, but working well."

The source of all the kinetic energy in the W-30 was, at least officially, only slightly different from the standard 4-4-2 engine. Both engines displaced 455 cubic inches and had 10.5:1 compression ratios, but the standard 4-4-2 engine developed 365 hp at 5000 rpm and the W-30 was said to put out 370 hp at 5400 rpm.

Virtually identical to the one used on the 1969 Hurst/Olds was the 1970 W-30 model's fiberglass hood. Unlike the air ducts installed on the W-31, which were mounted under the front bumper, those for the W-30 were mounted on the hood. The twin intakes rammed a flow of cool air through a mesh filter and were linked to a low-restriction air intake by a sponge-like material that acted as a gasket seal with the hood.

The W-30's standard transmission was identified by Oldsmobile as the "Muncie Close Ratio." *Car Life* described it as "Oldsmobile's version of Chevy's M22 'Rock Crusher.'"

Jerry Heasley

1969 HURST/OLDS

In 1969, if you were a geek, you could give yourself an image transplant overnight just by heading down to your local car dealer and plunking down a big stack of George Washingtons on a hot new muscle car.

And one car that should have been at the top of your list if your life really needed help was the spectacular Hurst/Olds. Yup Skylar, even you could be cool in one of these babies.

"Ah yes friends, there really is a supercar without lumps in it," advised *Super Stock* magazine in July of 1969.

Olds 4-4-2 styling was based on the midsized Cutlass and it was altered only slightly for the 1969 model year. Essentially, each pair of lenses in the quad headlight system was brought closer together. This, along with some modification of the central grille and bumper area contributed to an overall smoother, less-cluttered frontal appearance. The package was finished off with an eye-popping White-and-Gold color scheme and featured an attention-grabbing, strut-mounted rear deck spoiler.

With a shipping weight of 3,716 lbs., it was not the lightest muscle car in the mix, but the awesome power train made up for a lot of the added mass.

The number of Oldsmobiles that Hurst modified nearly doubled for 1969, with a total of 906 making it to the pavement. For this year, all Hurst/Olds were based on the 4-4-2 Holiday two-door hardtop body style.

Stimulated by a special 455-cid 380-hp "Rocket" V-8, this year's Hurst/Olds was slightly lighter (3,715 lbs.) than its '68 counterpart (3,870 lbs.) and therefore bettered the original version's 0-to-60-mph acceleration times (5.9 seconds versus 6.7 seconds). However, it took slightly longer to cover the quarter-mile (14.0 seconds versus 13.9 seconds).

At a price that ranged from $4,500 to $4,900, the Hurst/Olds buyer had to part with a few more pennies than it took to buy Oldsmobile's factory hot rod, the 4-4-2 model.

But once they got one home, it's hard to imagine any buyer feeling sorry that they had spent the cash on this legendary Olds.

Jerry Heasley

1970 RALLYE 350

While not the brawniest muscle car ever built, the Oldsmobile Rallye 350 was surely one of the brightest. Its smart Sebring Yellow paint makes it stand out wherever it's seen. So does the fact that its urethane-clad bumpers and Rallye spoke wheels are done in the same color. In addition, it's trimmed with bold orange and black stripes along the tops of rear fenders and over the backlight.

If looks alone counted in a street race or drag race, the Rallye 350 had the image that it could send feathers flying like a "screaming yellow honker." And the car had more than looks. "Beneath that gaudy paint and wing lurks bargains in performance and handling," said Car Life magazine.

Introduced in February 1970, the car was initially planned as a Hurst/Olds, but Lansing wound up marketing it as a new option that combined the looks of a limited-edition muscle car with a more "streetable" power-train package. It could be added to either the F-85 coupe or the Cutlass 'S' coupe or hardtop.

The base engine, of course, was the 350-cid V-8 with a 4.057 x 3.385-inch bore and stroke. This version developed 310 hp at 4200 rpm. A W-31 Force Air package was available for cars with the Rallye 350 option. It boosted compression from 10.25:1 to 10.5:1 and gave 325 hp at 5400 rpm. Also included on W-31s were aluminum intake manifolds, a heavy-duty clutch, front disc brakes, a special hood and decorative touches such as decals, paint stripes and specific emblems.

Only 3,547 of these cars were assembled: 2,527 were Cutlass S-based and 1,020 were F-85s. Many of the cars came with a rear deck lid spoiler, which cost $74 extra.

In February 1970, *Motor Trend* tested a Rallye 350 with the 310-hp engine, three-speed manual transmission and 3.23:1 rear axle. It did 0-to-60 mph in 7.7 seconds and covered the quarter-mile in 15.4 seconds at 89 mph.

GM photo

1979 HURST/OLDS

The first Hurst/Olds model had been built in 1968, when Oldsmobile used the back-door approach and hired George Hurst's company to stuff the big 455-cid engine into the intermediate Cutlass model. Later versions ended up being more for dress than speed, with the last offering prior to 1979 being the 1975 model.

For 1979, the downsized Cutlass Calais needed some extra dressing and excitement. Uncle George went back to the drawing board and supplied the much-needed ingredients with a Hurst/Olds package. For an extra $2,054 tacked on to the $5,631 base price you got option W-30. There was decal calling out this option kit on each front fender. The extra-cost package included Gold paint trim, Gold aluminum wheels, Gold sport mirrors, Hurst/Olds emblems on the sail panels, a Hurst Dual-Gate shifter on the mandatory Turbo Hydra-Matic 350 and the Oldsmobile 350-cid V-8 (which was not available on some other models at the time).

The output of 170 net hp was nothing to brag about, but it bettered by far the 130 hp being put out by the 305-cid V-8 used in most other GM vehicles at the time.

In the past, Hurst/Olds cars had been shipped to a separate factory for the Hurst conversion, but the 1979 examples were set up for conversion right at the Oldsmobile factory. That didn't seem to bother the buyers in 1979, since a total of 2,499 were made, just a hair short of the 2,535 record set by the 1975 model. Of the 1979 total, 1,334 were finished in black and 1,165 were done in white. Optional T-top roofs ended up on 537 Hurst/Oldsmobiles.

Despite little promotion, the sales tally wasn't enough for the Hurst/Olds to return immediately and the Hi-Po model wasn't seen again until the 1983 model year. A second so-called energy crisis in the 1979-'80 period also was a factor.

1963 MAX WEDGE 426

The Max Wedge Plymouths of the early 1960s were some of the most insane go-fast-in-a-straight-line cars ever built. Today, they are considered some of the granddaddys — or at least great-uncles — of the factory muscle car family tree.

The massive Max Wedge engines were "wedged" into an under-hood space often occupied in Savoy/Belvedere models by off-center inline sixes in earlier years. "Wedge" also indicated the design of the engine. Its cylinder heads had wedge-shaped combustion chambers that greatly enhanced Plymouth's reputation as a muscular automobile.

In 1963, the National Hot Rod Association (NHRA) and the National Association for Stock Car Auto Racing (NASCAR) and several other groups that sanctioned automobile racing established an engine displacement limit of 7 liters or 427 cubic inches. As a reaction to this, in June of 1963, Plymouth announced its development of a 426-cid "Max Wedge" V-8 engine for Super Stock class drag racing. The 426-cid engine block had been introduced only in upper-level Chryslers in 1962 and had not been tuned for drag racing.

This changed in 1963. The so-called Stage II version of the motor brought out that year was intended for sale only to those competing in supervised drag racing and stock car racing. At 1 cubic inch under the new limit, this engine increased Chrysler's ability to win in both drag and oval-track racing. By the end of the year, a total of 2,130 Plymouths and Dodges with this motor would be built.

The new Max Wedge 426 engine looked identical to the previous Max Wedge 413 V-8 on the outside, but it had a larger bore size of 4.25 inches. The power plant came in three different versions. The first version, fitted with a single four-barrel carburetor, was designed to be "legal" under stock-car racing rules. It put out 400 hp. The second version, with an 11.0:1 compression ratio, was made for dragging. It had dual four-barrel carburetors on a cross-ram manifold and produced 415 hp at 5600 rpm and 470 ft.-lbs. of torque at 4400 rpm. The third version (also for drag racing) 425 hp at 5600 rpm and 480 lbs.-ft. of torque at 4400 rpm.

Many of the Max Wedge 426s also carried a new Super/Stock package designed for drag racing. It included lightweight aluminum front-end sheet metal, a large air scoop for the hood and some trim deletions to shave off pounds.

Jerry Heasley

1964 426-R/426-S

Somewhere, sometime, somebody probably drove a Stage III Max Wedge-equipped car to the grocery store to buy some grub. But there might have been a few broken eggs in the bag by the time they got home.

This was a car made for the dragstip. Doing anything more than that with it was not really recommended. As *Musclecar Review* said about the Plymouth Max Wedge in February 1989: "The Super Stock was not designed for milk and egg runs to the 7-11."

In 1964, Plymouth continued offering the "Super Stock" Max Wedge Stage III 426-cid engine. Dodge offered the same motor of course, the only difference being the Plymouth version had a black cooling fan and the Dodge engine had a chrome-plated fan blade. It was a competition-only option and carried the code 426-R, with the "R" indicating "racing." It had an option price in the $500 range.

The 426-R engine was again available in 415- and 425-hp versions. The former had the 11.0:1 compression ratio and the latter had the 13.5:1 ratio. The more powerful version also had nifty "Tri-Y" exhaust headers.

New this year was a 426-S "street" version of the 426-cid V-8 that was rated for 365 advertised horsepower, but actually produced around 410 hp. This engine did not include most of the Max Wedge hardware, but because of the similar displacement numbers, many buyers thought it was nearly the same engine. Most of the 426-R engines went into cheap Savoy two-door sedans because they were the lightest-weight full-size models made by Plymouth and thus went the fastest with the big engine. The NASCAR racing cars carried four-barrel carburetors. The drag racers went for the dual-quad setups and many had the lightweight aluminum front-end sheet metal, large hood scoops, etc. They were plain-Jane machines, but amazingly fast with performance in the same range as 1963.

The street version of the 426 could be had in any model from the Savoy to the Sport Fury hardtop or convertible. A 1964 Sport Fury two-door hardtop with the 426-cid/365-hp V-8 carried about 9.5 lbs. per horsepower and could turn in 6.8-second 0 to 60-mph runs. The same combination was good for a 15.2-second quarter-mile run.

Jerry Heasley

1967 PLYMOUTH BELVEDERE GTX

Having a big-inch performance model in your lineup was mandatory if you wanted to market your muscle in the mid-1960s. Pontiac started it with its GTO option for the intermediate Tempest in 1964. One by one the competition followed: GT, GTA and so on. One of the last to arrive was the 1967 Plymouth Belvedere GTX. The mid-size Belvedere already had a hot-car image, thanks to race driver Richard "The King" Petty. The GTX took it one step further as an official factory street machine with all the show-them-off-at-the-drive-in goodies on the outside and under the hood.

With its lightweight Super Stock models and its big Wedge and Hemi V-8 engines, Plymouth built limited-production cars that were far faster than the GTO.

Two vital elements of the Plymouth GTX story resided under the hood. In the middle of the 1966 model year, the company introduced the 426-cid Street Hemi and it then followed up with the release of the 440-cid "Super Commando" Wedge V-8 in 1967. When either of

these powerful motors was combined with the Belvedere's 116-inch wheelbase and lighter weight, you had a potent combination. When you tossed in top-of-the-line front bucket seats, a couple of fake hood scoops and stripes, the GTX was ready to go cruising the boulevard.

For $3,178 in two-door hardtop form and $3,418 in convertible format, you got a 375-hp/440-cid V-8. If you plunked down an extra $564, you got the Street Hemi.

Magazine tests proved that the Super Commando GTX was capable of 0-to-60 mph spurts in 7 seconds or less.

The exact number of GTXs sold during the model year is not known, since that total was combined with the output of Satellite models. What is known is that the Hemi-optioned GTXs are rare, with only 720 of the approximately 12,500 GTXs that were built being equipped with a Hemi. Of those, 312 had four-speed transmissions and 408 were attached to Torque-Flite automatics. Estimates put the number of Hemi convertibles built at only 17.

1968 BELVEDERE GTX

Car Life magazine called the 1968 Hemi GTX "the fastest standard car on the market." Nobody will ever really be able to prove that claim, but the GTX was a take-no-prisoners machine, particularly with a Hemi in it.

The Belvedere GTX never wavered from its mission of being a high-content muscle car with a nice assortment of big-block power plant offerings. However, since it was only a year old when the redesigned 1968 Plymouth models were introduced, it didn't have a loyal following to see it through. It shared the new Belvedere body — including the special high-performance hood — with the Road Runner.

For 1968, the Super Commando 440-cid V-8 again came as standard equipment in the GTX. Even this was a mighty mill with a 4.32 x 3.75-inch bore and stroke, hydraulic valve lifters, a 10.1:1 compression ratio and a single Carter AFB four-barrel carburetor (model No. 4326S). This engine developed 375 hp at 4600 rpm.

Car Life road tested a 440-powered GTX with automatic transmission and reported a 0-to-60 time of 6.8 seconds. It did the quarter-mile in 14.6 seconds with a 96-mph terminal speed. Its top speed was about 121 mph.

Base prices were $3,329 for the coupe and $3,590 for the soft top. Production figures were kept and with 17,914 hardtops and 2,026 ragtops built, the numbers were surely higher than those for the 1967 GTX models. However, these figures paled by comparison to the 44,599 Road Runners that came off the assembly line.

For $605 extra, you could get the 426-cid Street Hemi stuffed into your GTX. Hemi-equipped GTXs continued to be rare, with only 410 hardtops and about 36 convertibles believed to have been made. The Hemi shaved a half a second off the 0-to-60 time and shrunk the quarter-mile time to 14 seconds with a 96.5-mph terminal speed.

Jerry Heasley

1968 ROAD RUNNER

The Road Runner followed such a simple formula, and it was brilliant! You could get a new "beep-beep" car for as little as $2,870, then for a few bucks at a time keep working your way up the options list and buy as much muscle and flash as you could afford.

And regardless of how many bells and whistles you ordered, this Plymouth squeezed the most punch out of your pennies.

The idea of putting a powerful engine in the cheapest, lightest model available was not a new one and wise users of the option list had been ordering "Q-Ships" for years. What Plymouth did with the new Road Runner was to do all the work for the customer. The company gave the car a low price that youthful buyers could more easily afford and wrapped it all up in a gimmicky fashion — using a popular Warner Bros.

cartoon character as the car's namesake.

The first Road Runner's standard engine was a 335-hp version of the 383-cid Chrysler B-block. It was rated at only 5 hp more than the regular 383, but it probably had more power than that due to the use of cylinder heads, intake and exhaust manifolds and a camshaft from the Chrysler 440-cid V-8. Added to the mechanical goodies were a standard four-speed manual transmission, a heavy-duty suspension, 11-inch drum brakes and Red Stripe tires.

If you wanted to kick the toy image, you had to ante up $714.30 extra for the 426-cid/425-hp Street Hemi.

A two-door hardtop was added midyear and its 15,359 production run was added to the coupe's 29,240 tally to make the Road Runner a winner. Of those, 1,019 were Hemi-powered.

Jerry Heasley

1970 AAR 'CUDA

The Plymouth AAR 'Cuda was one very fast small-block muscle car. Though its name evolved from Trans-Am racing, the AAR had a split personality. "Everything makes sense if you forget all about Dan Gurney and think of it in terms of the Burbank Blue Bombers," said the July 1970 issue of *Car and Driver*. "The new AAR 'Cuda is every inch a hot rod."

Having a player in the Sports Car Club of America (SCCA) Trans-American sedan racing series was a must for the Detroit purveyors of pony cars in 1970. There were factory-backed efforts from American Motors, Ford, Dodge and Plymouth. Chevrolet and Pontiac had back-door programs.

Plymouth could legalize its Trans-Am racing equipment by building 1,900 or more special models. The result was the 1970 AAR 'Cuda.

Powering the AAR 'Cuda was a 340-cid small-block V-8 with high-performance heads and thicker webbing in the block to allow the racing team to use four-bolt mains. Even though only a single four-barrel carb was allowed in racing, that didn't prevent triple two-barrel Holleys from being used in the production model. A fiberglass, cold-air-induction hood let the carburetors breathe fresh air.

Jerry Heasley

1970 HEMI 'CUDA

Plymouth's resounding message in the case of the Hemi 'Cuda was: "Damn the insurance company torpedos — full speed ahead!" The car tested out like a rocketship. As Chrysler maven Cliff Gromer's *Mopar Muscle* magazine put it, "The new E-bodies offered a home for ol' King Kong hisself — the 426 Hemi."

When the redesigned 1970 Plymouth Barracuda came to the muscle-car market, there would be no excuses for not putting a big engine in the gaping crater under its wide hood. Any Chrysler Corporation engine would fit in the engine bay, right up to the street version of the "Monster Masher" racing power plant — the 426-cid Hemi.

The Hemi was an $871.45 option for the muscular 'Cuda sport coupe (which was base priced at $3,164) and the convertible (which carried a $3,433 window sticker total). The 'Cuda came standard with another big-block mill—the 383-cid/355-hp V-8. No wonder Chrysler listed the 'Cuda as a member of its "Rapid Transit System."

Street Hemis got new hydraulic valve lifters for 1970, but a new cam profile gave the Mopar engineers no reason to alter the 425 advertised hp rating. The Hemi's two Carter AFB four-barrel carburetors breathed through the Air Grabber "shaker" hood scoop.

In short, power was the Hemi 'Cuda's long suit. Not long was the list of buyers. Insurance companies did not look kindly on Hemi 'Cudas and did not care if they could do 0-to-60 mph in 5.8 seconds and run down the quarter-mile in 14.1 seconds at 103.2 mph. By the time the 1970 run came to an end, only 652 hardtops had left the factory with Hemi power and 284 of them had four-speed transmissions. Far more spectacular in terms of rarity was the convertible with only 14 being made, five with a manual gearbox.

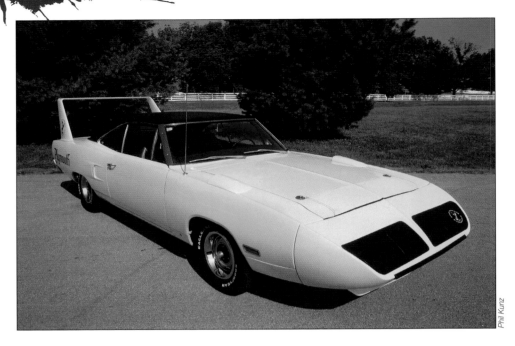

Phil Kunz

1970 ROAD RUNNER SUPERBIRD

The legendary 1970 Plymouth Road Runner Superbird was the final volley in the battle of muscle car aerodynamics. With a 7.0-liter engine-displacement limit, competing automakers armed themselves with more wind-cheating body designs, culminating with the "winged warriors" from Chrysler — the 1969 Dodge Charger Daytona and 1970 Plymouth Road Runner Superbird. Designed for use on the NASCAR Grand National superspeedway oval tracks, these Mopars featured a long, peaked nose and a high airfoil on struts above the rear deck.

Rules in 1969 called for only 500 copies of each model to be made to make it "legal" for racing. For 1970, manufacturers had to build one for each dealer. Experts believe that, when it was all over, a total of 1,971 Superbirds were built.

The most popular engine was the 440-cid

Super Commando V-8 with a single four-barrel carburetor. It was rated at 375 hp and priced at $4,298. A total of 1,120 Superbirds came this way. Another 716 cars were equipped with the 440-cid/390-hp V-8 with three two-barrel carburetors. That leaves just 135 cars that were equipped with the 426-cid/425-hp, twin four-barrel Street Hemi (77 with automatic transmission and 58 with four-speed manual transmission). The racing cars used the Hemi racing engine.

Plymouth intermediates were redesigned for 1971 and, with the performance market shrinking and budgets for racing being shifted to meeting Federal safety and emission standards, there was no follow-up to the Superbird. That made the limited-edition Mopar winged machines among the first muscle cars to start climbing in collector value.

Jerry Heasley

1971 HEMI 'CUDA

"The '71 Hemi 'Cuda is pretty beyond comparison and potent beyond imagination," according to Paul Zazarine, a name well known to muscle car lovers. In *Musclecar Review* magazine, he wrote: "If you're looking for the ultimate Mopar, look no further than the Hemi 'Cuda."

Drag racers like Sox & Martin and PeeWee Wallace were burning up the drag strips in Barracudas back in 1971 and also helping to generate interest in Plymouth's "fish car." A lot of that interest went to non-Hemi-powered cars, however, as the $884 Hemi option was ordered for just 108 hardtops (60 with four-speed manual trans-

missions) and a mere seven convertibles. Two of the ragtops also had the four-speed gearbox.

Seven other engines were offered for 1971 Barracudas and a number of those mills fit into the muscle car category. The 440-cid "Six Pak" version climbed up to 385 hp and 490 lbs.-ft. at 3200 rpm, which wasn't bad. Then came the snortier, top-of-the-hill Hemi, which had 426 cubic inches, 425 hp and 490 lbs.-ft. of twisting power at 4000 rpm.

After model year 1971, Plymouth continued to offer Barracudas, but Hemi versions and convertibles didn't make the cut after the season came to its end.

Jerry Heasley

1972 PLYMOUTH ROAD RUNNER

Plymouth's popular bargain bomber struggled valiantly in 1972 to keep alive the dwindling interest in high-performance motoring.

As in 1971, the model RM23 Road Runner was offered in only a single body style. The two-door hardtop had a $3,080 list price and a 3,495-lb. curb weight. Production dropped nearly 50 percent to 7,628 cars.

The Road Runner equipment list started with all features that were considered standard on the Plymouth satellite, plus the following additions or substitutions: three-speed manual transmission with floor-mounted gear shifter, heavy-duty suspension, heavy-duty brakes, front and rear sway bars, pile carpets, a performance hood, a low-restriction dual exhaust system, a beep-beep horn, a rallye instrument cluster with a 150-mph speedometer, Road Runner trim and ornamentation, F70-14 white sidewall tires and a 400-cid four-barrel V-8.

The Code E86 440-cid V-8 with a single four-barrel carburetor was optional in the Road Runner for $152.70, but could not be ordered in combination with the three-speed manual transmission.

Performance numbers were published for the '72 Road Runner with the 340-cid/240-hp V-8. It went from a standing start to 60 mph in 7.8 seconds. The quarter-mile was eaten up in 15.5 seconds at 90 mph.

Jerry Heasley

1962 SUPER-DUTY CATALINA

I once went to photograph one of these rare cars owned by Dimitri Toth of Pontiac, Mich. He "lit it up" early on a Sunday morning and all of his neighbors woke up immediately. The Super-Duty Catalina shook the asphalt like a barrel of maniacal monkeys playing catch with a can of ammonium nitrate. "The '62 Catalina lightweight sings precious memories from the pre-GTO performance era," said Jerry Heasley in the December 1985 issue of *Car Review*.

Pontiac Motor Division was the first automaker to build factory lightweight drag racing cars. Ever since its NASCAR engine options were issued in mid-1957, the company found that racing on Sunday sold cars on Monday. By 1960, the "Poncho" performance image had made Pontiac the third-most popular American car nameplate for the first time in history. Chevy's new-for 1962 409-cid engine was a threat, though. Pontiac's best match for a 409-powered Chevy was the 1961 Super-Duty 389 Catalina, which had 368 hp with Tri-Power. Perhaps 25 of these cars were built.

More power and less weight was needed to keep the Pontiacs competitive, so Pontiac put its lightest, most powerful car on a diet with a horsepower supplement. Extensive use of aluminum body parts and a special 421-cid/405-hp V-8 created the 3,600-lb. 1962 Super-Duty Catalina.

The new 421-cid V-8 featured four-bolt main bearing caps, forged pistons and twin Carter four-barrel carburetors on a special intake manifold linked to either a Borg-Warner T-85 three-speed manual transmission or a T-10 four-speed manual gear box. Actual output from this massive motor was over 500 hp.

Lightweight parts, in addition to the front-end sheet metal like the fenders, hood and grille sections, included an aluminum back bumper and dealer-optional Plexiglas windows. Many of the Super-Duty Catalinas used a functional hood scoop that was actually a Ford truck part that Pontiac purchased in quantity and issued a GM parts number for. An unusual Super-Duty option was a set of cast aluminum Tri-Y exhaust headers.

Pontiac promotional expert and racing personality Jim Wangers found the 1962 Super-Duty Catalina to his liking and turned in performances like a 12.38-second quarter-mile at 116.23 mph at Detroit Dragway. In all, 225 of the 421-cid motors were built in 1962. They went into 162 cars and 63 engines were made as replacement motors. Not all cars that got the 421-cid Super-Duty engines had factory lightweight body parts.

1964 GTO

If you ran a poll of old car buffs and asked which car gets top billing as "The First Muscle Car," the 1964 GTO would probably take the title.

Certainly, it had the necessary ingredients for a truely great muscle machine: a midsize car with not too many bells and whistles a big-block V-8 engine that was probably too big for its own good.

Late in October of 1963 the Grand Turismo Omologato package was announced for the Le-Mans coupe, hardtop and convertible as a $295 option. GTO equipment included a 325-hp/389-cid V-8 with a special camshaft, special hydraulic lifters and 421-style cylinder heads.

Desirable GTO options included a center console, Hurst-Campbell four-speed manual shift linkage, custom exhaust splitters, no-cost whitewall tires, special wheel covers and a Tri-Power engine option with three two-barrel carburetors. The Tri-Power version of the 389-cid V-8 produced 348 hp at 4900 rpm.

In January 1964, *Motor Trend* magazine found a four-speed GTO convertible capable of doing the quarter-mile in 15.8 seconds at 93 mph. The same car's 0-to-60 performance was 7.7 seconds and it had a 115-mph top speed.

By the year's end, the GTO was considered a huge sales success. Pontiac records showed production of 7,384 GTO coupes, 18,422 two-door hardtops and 6,644 convertibles.

1965 CATALINA 2+2

Along with the GTO, the 2+2 further contributed to Pontiac's mid-1960s performance image that has become a modern day legend. Exciting to look at, exciting to drive and, most of all, exciting to own, the Catalina 2+2 was in a class by itself among American automobiles.

The second 2+2 was available again in either two-door hardtop or convertible body form. The 2+2's performance was given a strong starting point thanks to the 1965 Pontiac's bold "ship's prow" front end with its stacked headlights and a fresh variation on the neo-classic divided grille. Providing sufficient identification were front fender louvers and 2+2 emblems on the hood, rear fenders and rear deck.

The Catalina 2+2 base engine was now Pontiac's 421-cid V-8 with a 10.5:1 compression ratio and four-barrel carburetor. Its ratings were 338 hp at 4600 rpm and 459 lbs.-ft. of torque at 2800 rpm. The standard transmission was an all-Synchromesh close-ratio four-speed. Pontiac specified a 3.42:1 standard axle ratio for the 2+2. It provided excellent all-around performance as reflected in the car's 0-to-60 time of 7.2 seconds, its 0-to-100 time of 20.5 seconds and a standing-start quarter-mile completed in 15.8 seconds at 88 mph.

If a Catalina 2+2 of this caliber didn't satisfy a buyer's performance desires, Pontiac offered a 421 HO version. *Car Life*, April 1965, quoted one happy 421 HO owner as saying "I will say this is the finest road machine I have ever driven — foreign cars included. It has comfort, performance and, in my opinion, handling that should satisfy anyone but a road course driver."

With a list price of $3,287, the Catalina 2+2 was a tremendous performance bargain. Even when equipped in its Royal Oak form, it listed for just over $4,200.

Jerry Heasley

1965 GTO

Put this on your "Top 10 Cars I Want To Own Before I Kick The Bucket" list and you probably won't ever second-guess yourself.

After all, how could anybody not like a lethal "GeeTO," from its second year in existance — especially a ragtop!

Pontiac Motor Division held the price of the GTO option at $295.90 for 1965. The package included most of the same items it did in 1964, except that a single dummy hood scoop was used in place of two. The 421-style cylinder heads were re-cored to improve the flow of gases.

The standard 389-cid GTO V-8 was a four-barrel-carburetor job with 10.75:1 compression and 335 hp. It was good for 16.1-second quarter-mile acceleration runs at 89 mph. Its 0-to-60-mph time was 7.2 seconds. For only $115.78 extra buyers could add Tri-Power carburetion with a special 288-degree camshaft that provided 360 hp from the same block.

The GTO convertible was available for as little as $3,092.90 and 11,311 were made. The coupe had a base price of $2,786.90 and 8,319 assemblies. The sales leader was the two-door hardtop, which could be had for as little as $2,854.90. It was the choice of 55,722 buyers.

Phil Kunz

1967 FIREBIRD 400

Now here was a rookie muscle car that didn't mess around!

Pontiac got right down to business when it offered a fire-breathing 400-cid engine in its debut Firebird. The most potent of the five new Pontiacs, the Firebird 400 paired that 400-cid mill with a single four-barrel carburetor and 10.75:1 compression ratio. It developed 325 hp at 4800 rpm and 410 lbs.-ft. of torque at 3400 rpm.

Car Life dubbed the Firebird 400 "the enthusiast's choice" and discovered that it could deliver a 0-to-60-mph time of 6.5 seconds with the four-speed all-synchromesh transmission and a 3.36:1 axle. Aside from its engine, the 400 option included (as standard equipment) a chrome air cleaner, chrome rocker covers, a chrome oil cap, a dual exhaust system, red or white E70

x 14 wide-oval tires, a heavy-duty battery, a heavy-duty starter, a de-clutching engine fan and dual hood scoops.

When the Ram Air option was ordered it added direct-air induction, a longer-duration cam with more overlap, a more efficient cast-iron exhaust manifold and different valve springs with flat metal dampers. The carburetor was also recalibrated. Power ratings with the Ram Air option were deliberately understated at 325 hp at 5200 rpm and 410 lbs.-ft. of torque at 3600 rpm. Firebirds with this option were truly rare birds, as only 65 400s were so equipped.

The 400 convertible listed for $3,346.53 and the coupe for $3,109.53. With the rare Ram Air option the prices were $3,609.39 and $3,372.36, respectively.

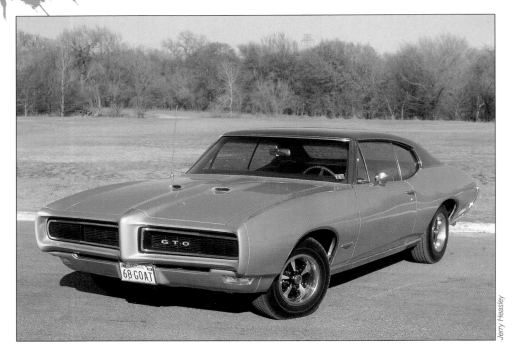

Jerry Heasley

1968 GTO

When the 1968 Pontiacs hit the market in the fall of 1967, it was clear that the "King of Woodward Avenue" was back on the throne for another 12 months.

Motor Trend named the 1968 GTO as its "Car of the Year" and tested two different versions. The first car had the 400-cid/350-hp V-8, a 3.23:1 rear axle and Turbo Hydra-Matic transmission. It did 0-to-60 mph in 7.3 seconds and the quarter-mile in 15.93 seconds at 88.32 mph. The second car was a 360-hp Ram Air model with a four-speed manual gearbox and a 4.33:1 rear axle. It went from 0-to-60 mph in 6.5 seconds and covered the quarter-mile in 14.45 seconds at 98.20 mph.

A long hood and short deck highlighted a more streamlined-looking Tempest line. Two-door models, including all GTOs, were on a shorter 112-inch wheelbase. GTOs added dual exhaust, a three-speed transmission with a Hurst shifter, heavy-duty underpinnings, red line tires, bucket or notchback bench seats, a cigar lighter, carpeting, disappearing windshield wipers and a 400-cid/350-hp V-8. New and highly touted was the unique Endura rubber-clad front bumper (a GTO exclusive). GTO emblems, distinctive taillights and hood scoops rounded out the GTO goodies.

Base prices for the two 1968 models (there was no more "post" coupe) were $3,101 for the two-door hardtop and $3,996 for the convertible. Production of these body styles was 77,704 and 9,980, respectively.

Jerry Heasley

1969 1/2 FIREBIRD TRANS AM

If we had to pick just one muscle car to be stranded on a desert island with, the Trans Am would have to be it.

Pontiac had firmly established itself as an expert in making muscle cars by 1969, having already minted the GTO, Catalina Super-Duty and 2+2 and the Firebird. But the Poncho boys took things to bold new heights with the fabulous T/A.

This mucho macho version of the Firebird started out as a sports-racing car. It was originally conceived of as a sedan racer that could compete in the Sports Car Club of America (SCCA) Trans-American Cup series. The racing version was supposed to be powered by an ultra-high-performance, 303-cid small-block V-8.

The new engine's displacement figure of 303 cubic inches came in under the 305-cid maximum that the Trans-Am racing formulas allowed. However, only 25 of these engines were ever made. They were sold to competitors to replace the 400-cid big-block V-8s their cars left the factory with. Production versions of the Trans Am (the car name is spelled without the hyphen) stuck with the 400-cid engine size.

The base 400 HO engine (which Pontiac engineers called the "Ram Air III" V-8) was used in 634 cars (including all convertibles, which was a rare body style with only eight assemblies). Of these Ram Air III cars, 114 units (including four of the convertibles) had a four-speed manual gearbox. Fifty-five other cars (all coupes) came with a Ram Air IV engine, which cost $390 extra. Of these, nine cars had Turbo Hydra-Matic transmissions and all of the others had stick shift.

The WS4 Trans Am package for base Firebirds included the Ram Air III engine, a three-speed heavy-duty floor shifter, functional hood scoops, heavy-duty running gear, special interior and exterior trim.

The Ram Air III V-8 produced 335 hp at 5000 rpm and 430 lbs.-ft. of torque at 3400 rpm. The Ram Air IV engine cranked up 345 hp at 5400 rpm and 430 lbs.-ft. at 3700 rpm. With its higher output and lower production, the Ram Air IV is definitely the engine preferred by most muscle car collectors. They could do the quarter-mile in 14.1 seconds at 101 mph!

Jerry Heasley

1969 GTO "THE JUDGE"

Any muscle car inspired by the "Here Come 'de Judge" skits on Rowan & Martin's "Laugh In" TV show was sure to be a bit crazy and the GTO Judge was crazy in a very fast way. As *Car Life* magazine once put it, "Pontiac inspired the supercar for this generation . . . and The Judge is one of the best."

"The new model of the GTO was designed to be what *Car and Driver* magazine called an "econo racer." In other words, it was a heavily optioned up muscle car with a price that gave you a lot for your money! It was a machine that you could take racing, pretty much "as is," and for a lot less money than a purpose-built drag racing car cost. It was seen in many street races, too.

At first, "The Judge" came only in bright orange with tri-color striping, but it was later made available in the full range of colors that were available for other '69 GTOs. Special standard features of the Judge package included a blacked-out radiator grille, Rally II wheels (minus bright trim rings), functional hood scoops and "The Judge" decals on the sides of the front fenders

and "Ram Air" decals on the hood scoops. At the rear of the car there was a 60-inch wide "floating" deck lid airfoil with a "The Judge" decal emblem on the upper right-hand surface.

The standard "The Judge" engine was the Pontiac-built 400-cid/366-hp Ram Air III V-8. It came linked to a three-speed manual transmission with a floor-mounted Hurst T-handle shifter and a 3.55:1 rear axle. A total of 8,491 GTOs and Judges were sold with this motor and only 362 of them were convertibles. The more powerful 400-cid/370-hp Ram Air IV engine was installed in 759 cars in the same two lines and 59 of these cars were convertibles.

"The Judge" option was added to 6,725 GTO two-door hardtops and only 108 GTO ragtops. The editors of *Car Life* magazine whipped a Judge through the quarter-mile at 14.45 seconds and 97.8 mph. Supercars Annual covered the same distance in a Judge with Turbo Hydra-Matic transmission and racked up a run of 13.99 seconds at 107 mph!

1970 GTO

This GTO's massive 455 mill was enough engine for a "daily driver" GTO. Though big, it was docile enough to take the family out to dinner at McDonald's. But the Ram Air 400 was the engine you wanted when you went to the drag strip. *Car Life* pointed out: "It got to the end of the drag strip first and it was going faster when we arrived, so the Ram Air 400 does have more power than the 455."

Standard hardware for the two GTOs included: front bucket seats, a padded dashboard, a functional air-scoop with a handle under the dash for manual control, a heavy-duty clutch, sports-type springs and shock absorbers, courtesy lights, a dual exhaust system, a 350-hp V-8 and a heavy-duty three-speed transmission.

It was $3,267 for the base hardtop and 32,737 were built. The base 400-cid/350-hp V-8 was put in 27,496 of these cars, including 9,348 with stick shifts. Priced at $3,492, the convertible saw only 3,615 assemblies. The base engine went into 3,058 of the ragtops.

The 1970 GTO engines had several innovations, including special spherical-wedge cylinder heads and a computer-perfected camshaft design. Ram Air III engines with 366 hp were used in 1,302 hardtops and 114 convertibles with stick shifts and 3,054 hardtops and 174 convertibles with Turbo Hydra-Matics. Ram Air IV engines with 370 hp were used in 140 hardtops and 13 convertibles with stick shifts and 627 hardtops and 24 convertibles with Turbo Hydra-Matic. Also available in non-Judges was a 455-cid/360-hp V-8. This engine was installed in 2,227 stick-shift cars (241 ragtops) and 1,919 cars with Turbo Hydra-Matics (including 158 ragtops).

A 1970 GTO hardtop with the 400-cid/366-hp V-8 did 0-to-60 mph in 6 seconds flat and covered the quarter-mile in 14.6 seconds. With a 455-cid/360-hp V-8 the same model was actually slower, requiring 6.6 seconds for the 0-to-60 run and 14.8 seconds to cover the quarter mile.

Jerry Heasley

1971 FIREBIRD TRANS AM

You had to be a helluva muscle car to get top billing over the iconic GTO in the Pontiac lineup, and the 1971 T/A was certainly that.

With the biggest engine ever stuffed into a pony car, the T/A took no backseats to anybody in its own Pontiac family, or any of the competition.

The biggest change in the Trans Am for the model years was the new high-back bucket seat. The lower-level models like the Firebird, Espirit and Formula also had new front fender air extractors and a few other detail changes, but the 1970 and 1971 Trans Ams looked virtually identical, except for the new bucket seat design.

The style No. 22887 Trans Am hardtop coupe had a base sticker price of $4,590. It weighed 3,578 lbs. and only 2,116 were made. Standard equipment in Trans Ams includedan Endura front bumper, body-colored mirrors, honeycomb wheels, functional front fender air extractors, a rear deck lid spoiler, a black tex-

tured grille with bright moldings, front and rear wheel opening flares, concealed wipers, identification badges, a performance dual exhaust system, F60-15 white-lettered tires, a close-ratio four-speed manual transmission with floor shift and — most important of all — a big 455 HO four-barrel V-8.

With a change to lower compression ratios in 1971 (thanks to future leaded gas requirements), Pontiac found it prudent to substitute the 455-cid V-8 for the 400-cid engine. The 455 HO version had a 4.15 x 4.21-inch bore and stroke and used a single four-barrel Rochester carburetor. With 8.4:1 compression, it developed 335 hp at 4800 rpm and 480 lbs.-ft. of torque at 3600 rpm.

According to one enthusiast magazine of the '70s, the 445-cid/335-hp Trans Am could move from 0-to-60 mph in just 5.92 seconds and did the quarter in 13.90 seconds at 103 mph.

Phil Kunz

1973 TRANS AM/FORMULA SUPER-DUTY 455

Only 43 Formula Firebird Super-Duty monsters made it onto the American roadways carrying the powerhouse hi-po LS2 engine for 1973. So if you're dying to steal somebody's muscle car, this one would be a real challenge.

While many enthusiasts prefer the sano-looking '70-'71 versions of the Gen II Firebird, it was the '73-and-up models with all the bells and whistles that sent the sales charts into the black. Those who drove these cars thought they were buying a true sedan racer, but those who wanted the real McCoy added the required sizzle by popping the SD 455 V-8 below the Formula's double-scooped hood. As Paul Zazarine once pointed out in *Muscle Car Review*: "When every other maker had forgotten about muscle cars, Pontiac introduced the '73 455 Super-Duty."

In the early 1970s, the Formula was Pontiac's street racing version of the Firebird. As a result of this model's image and reputation, the Formula Firebird was a great platform for the hottest options available from Pontiac Motor Division. This was obvious and the hottest engine was what Pontiac decided to make available under the Formula model's hood. It wasn't a cheap option, but for those who wanted to keep the muscle car magic going, it was one of the few choices left.

The SD 455 mill was a very special big-block V-8. This awesome engine had actually been a spin-off of Pontiac's small-block racing program of 1970. PMD had put a lot of effort into developing a powerful small-displacement motor that would be legal under Sports Car Club of America sedan racing formulas, which had a 305 cubic inch limit. Only a few of these engines were sold on an in the crate basis. However, much of the racing technology embodied in them was then transferred to the RPO LS2 455-cid V-8.

The optional super-duty engine was the same one used in Trans Ams. All SD 455 V-8s featured a special block with reinforced webbing, large forged-steel connecting rods, special aluminum pistons, a heavy-duty oiling system, a high-lift camshaft, four-bolt main bearing caps, a special intake manifold, a dual exhaust system and upgraded valve train components. It had an 8.4:1 compression ratio and 310-hp rating.

Jerry Heasley

1973 TRANS AM

By 1973, there just weren't many new cars around that could really wake up your neighbors — or impress the chicks. It was nice to know that you could still count on Pontiac to fill both bills.

When the muscle car market began to evaporate in the mid-1970s, PMD did the only sensible thing: it unleashed the screaming chicken!

The large new hood decal showed the American Indian Firebird icon that the base car was named for. Most Trans Ams displayed it.

Like other Trans Ams that came before it, the 1973 model had special front fender air extractors, a rear deck lid spoiler, body flares and air inlet openings. The hood scoops were now sealed and no longer functional. A new feature was a large hood decal showing the American Indian Firebird icon that the base car was named for. Enthusiasts soon dubbed this graphic the "screaming chicken" and most Trans Ams displayed it. On 1973 models, the flaming bird was always black in color, but the hue of the background varied. The background was Orange on Red cars, Black on White cars and Light Green

on dark Brewster Green Trans Ams.

The base engine used in the Trans Am was a big-block 455-cid V-8 with a single four-barrel carburetor. With an 8.0:1 compression ratio, it produced 250 net horsepower. Pontiac built 4,550 cars with this engine and 1,420 of them had a manual gear box. For real muscle, buyers could add a 455-cid super-duty engine derived from Pontiac's experience in Trans-Am racing. The SD 455 V-8 featured a special engine block with reinforced webbing, large forged-steel connecting rods, special aluminum pistons, a heavy-duty oiling system and other stuff. It had an 8.4:1 compression ratio and cranked out 310 hp.

The SD 455 Trans tested by *Hot Rod* magazine turned the quarter-mile in 13.54 seconds at 104.29 mph. Going from 0-to-60 mph took all of 7.3 seconds. Car and Driver also tested an SD 455 and registered a 13.75-second quarter-mile at 103.56 mph. The SD 455 engine designation appeared on the side of the hood scoop on these cars. Only 252 SD 455 Trans Ams were built and 72 had stick shifts.

Jerry Heasley

1974 PONTIAC TRANS AM SD 455

To quote Bluto from "Animal House": "Over? Did you say over? Nothing is over until we say it is!"

And so it was in 1974, when Pontiac refused to go quietly to the big muscle car industry funeral, instead coming out with another in-your-face dream machine, the final 455 Super-Duty T/A.

The new front end created by well-known Pontiac designer John Schinella introduced an integrated "soft" bumper treatment, which was repeated at the rear of the F-cars. The front of all Firebirds carried a new, slanting "shovel-nose" grille cap with an "electric shaver" grille insert made up of slanting, vertical blades. Black rubber bumper-face bars were featured. An air-scoop-like front valance panel contributed to a more massive overall look. Slimmer, wider front parking lamps without chrome protective grids were used. They carried textured, amber-colored lenses.

The Trans Am model option included a For-mula steering wheel, rally gauges with a clock and a dash panel tachometer, a swirl-finish dash panel trim plate, a full-width rear deck lid spoiler, power steering, power front disc/rear drum brakes, a limited-slip differential, wheel opening air deflectors, front-fender air extractors, a dual exhaust system with chrome extensions, Rally II wheels with bright trim rings, a special heavy-duty suspension, dual outside rear view sports mirrors, F60-15 white-letter tires, a four-speed manual gearbox and a 400-cid/225-hp V-8.

The regular 455-cid/215-hp V-8 was $55 above the price of the 400-cid engine and the SD 455 V-8 was $578 extra. The SD 455 was installed in 212 Trans Ams with four-speed manual gearboxes and 731 with automatic transmission. Although it was relatively rare, the engine was popular with the editors of enthusiast magazines, who said it made the Firebird the hottest car of the year and slightly faster than the Corvette!

Tom Glatch

1977 CAN AM

Can Ams were constructed on an off-line basis by a specialty car company named Motortown Corp. The overall design was taken from a Pontiac factory concept car, exhibited in 1975. The show car was called the All-American Grand Am. Motortown started with a specifically equipped Lemans sport coupe and handled the conversion process.

The Can Ams had a flamboyant and competition-like appearance. Just one body style — the Colonnade coupe — was available with Can Am features. The package constituted a model option, rather than a separate series. It was introduced as a midyear addition to the line and was available for only a few months. This makes the Can Am a rare find.

Some ingredients of the Can Am option package were the same as Grand Am equipmen, but the 400-cid V-8 engine was not the two-barrel version used for base Grand Ams. Instead, the Trans Am's "T/A 6.6-liter" four-barrel V-8

was used. It was rated at 200 nhp. The Can Am had about the same 10-second 0-to-60 time as a 1975 midsized Pontiac with the 455-cid V-8.

Can Ams that were sold in California and in high-altitude counties used a different 403-cid 6.6-liter V-8 built by Oldsmobile.

Other elements of the $1,589 Can Am model-option included: Cameo White body paint, a blacked-out grille assembly, black-finished rocker panel moldings and window moldings, special identification badges and a "shaker" style hood scoop. The graphics package for the Can Am was really an eye catcher. It used fade-away lettering and stripes with an orange base, red lower accents and yellow upper accents. The model name appeared in these colors on the front fenders behind the wheel openings and on the right-hand side of the deck lid.

Alas, the model option was killed after 1,130 cars had been assembled.

1992 FORMULA SLP FIREHAWK

In 1992, Pontiac Motor Division and SLP Engineering teamed up to make the hot new Formula Firehawk available through the factory dealer network as a special 1992 Firebird model-option. The Firehawks were offered in "street" and "competition" versions. The street version produced 350 hp at 5500 rpm and 390 lbs.-ft. of torque at 4400 rpm.

When *High Performance Pontiac* magazine reported that only 250 copies of what it called the "Quickest Street Pontiac Ever" were going to be made, it got ahold of a test car that did 0-to-60 mph in 4.6 seconds and covered the quarter-mile in 13.20 seconds at 107 mph.

The factory-built Formula Firebird that served as the basis for SLP's Firehawk carried the 5.0-liter TPI V-8 and a four-speed automatic transmission (both upgraded to 1LE specs) plus air conditioning. Externally, the main difference from a stock Formula model was the use of five-spoke aluminum alloy wheels and a Firehawk decal on the right-hand side of the rear fascia.

The factory Formula had a $19,242 base price and the Firehawk street package was $20,753 for a total delivered price of $39,995. The Firehawk Competition package was $9,905 additional, raising the total bill to $49,990.

When a Firehawk was ordered, Pontiac shipped a new Formula from its Van Nuys, California, factory to SLP Engineering in Toms River, New Jersey. The aftermarket company then extracted the entire drive train and added a Corvette ZF six-speed gearbox with computer-aide gear selection (CAGS), a Dana 44 rear axle with 3.54:1 gears, a shortened input shaft and a 16-lb. flywheel.

SLP Engineering targeted production of five cars per week starting in July 1991, but only produced actual cars on a build-to-order basis. In the end, SLP Engineering wound up building only 25 street versions, at least one of which was a Trans Am convertible with serial No. 27. That could raise questions in the future, but the reason for the high number was that cars 18 and 25 were ordered but never built.

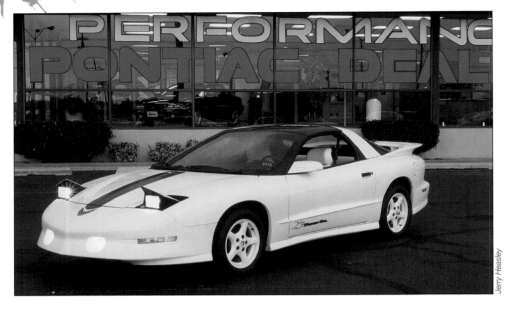

Jerry Heasley

1994 25th ANNIVERSARY TRANS AM

If ever a muscle car car deserved to be honored for surviving 25 years, the T/A was it.

Pontiac Motor Division never did very much to mark milestones years for its "Firebird" brand of pony cars, which started life in 1967. However, the automaker was very faithful about marking anniversaries of its Trans Am model, which first became available in the middle of model year 1969.

At first, the 25th Anniversary package was announced as something available only for the Trans Am GT coupe. About a month later, at the Chicago Auto Show, the Firebird convertible was introduced and a 25th Anniversary Trans Am GT convertible was also put on display. From then on, the Pontiac fans had two special edition Trans Ams to choose from.

The cars' theme was obviously taken from the original 1969 1/2 Trans Am, since the package featured a Bright White exterior that was decorated with a Bright Blue stripe down the center. There were also anniversary logos and door badges. The special 16-inch aluminum wheels were done in White, as were the Prado leather seating surfaces with blue embroidery logos that matched those on the door panels. Owners also got a special portfolio commemorating their purchase.

The price for all of this was only $995. Of course, you had to come up with the base price $22,309 for the GT coupe or $27,279 for the GT convertible. "The result is a white-on-white stunner of a car, with the highest profile in traffic this side of a presidential motorcade," said *Car & Driver*.

Despite its 3,668-lb. curb weight and automatic transmission, the 25th Anniversary convertible was good for a 0-to-60 run in 6.1 seconds.

Seeing that it is part of a set of special editions, this T/A's collector value is still fairly high.

1998 FORMULA FIREBIRD

Pontiac was one of the last marques to give up the ghost when the golden age of muscle cars wound down, and with cars like the hi-po Formula Firebird, PMD seemed determined to bring back "the good old days" in 1998.

A beefed-up LS1 5.7-liter V-8 engine generated 305 hp at 5200 rpm and 335 lbs.-ft. of torque at 4000 rpm. The WS6-equipped Ram Air LS1 V-8 boasted 320 hp And it was mated to a six-speed manual transmission, which made this car 10 tons of fun.

Revisions to this power plant provided enhanced mid-range responsiveness. That translated into 20 more horsepower and 10 more lbs.-ft. of torque than the previous Firebird V-8 delivered. The WS6-equipped Ram Air LS1 V-8 boasted 320 hp.

Leading PMD's stable of aggressively styled cars, the bold new Formula Firebird had a new outer appearance guaranteed to turn heads and continue its legendary status among sports car enthusiasts. It now shared its front fascia design with the base Firebird. The front-end design incorporated twin center ports below the hood and restyled, round, outboard-mounted fog lamps. Two new paint colors, Navy Metallic and Sport Gold Metallic were available. The Formula Firebird also had new styling lines on its rear end. Inside there were new gauges with clear white characters on black analog faces to help keep drivers informed of what was going on with their car.

In addition to standard Firebird features, the Formula model added or substituted a power radio antenna, power operated door locks, dual power sport type outside rearview mirrors with blue glass, a 500-watt peak-power "Monsoon" radio with CD and seven-band graphic equalizer and 10-speaker audio system.

1999 TRANS AM FIREHAWK

Motor Trend's Jack Keebler (April 1999) described his bright red SLP Trans Am Firehawk as "All Detroit muscle all the time." The "Street Legal Performance" Firebird's 16-valve 5.7-liter V-8 produced 327 hp at 5200 rpm and 345 lbs.-ft. of torque at 4400 rpm. The car could do 0-to-60 mph in 5.3 seconds and covered the quarter-mile in 13.6 seconds at 105.6 mph.

Keebler was comparing the $31,000 heated-up Firebird to nine other super cars, including the $140,000 Mercedes Benz CL600 and the $299,900 Bentley Continental R. It was the lowest-priced car in the pack, but was right up there with the top performing models.

The reworked 346-cid LS1 block was attached to a Borg-Warner T-56 six-speed manual transmission. A set of meaty P275/40ZR17 Firestone tires "attached" it to the road and helped it slide through a slalom course at 66 mph while pulling a strong 0.89 Gs on a skid pad. The car built by SLP Engineering could still be ordered directly through Pontiac factory dealers.

The contents of the WU6 Firehawk package included the 327-hp LS1 V-8, a composite hood with fiunctional air scoops, hood-mounted heat extraxtors and an underhood forced-air induction system, a Firehawk badge on the front fasciaA total of 719 Firehawks were assembled in 1999. This includes 622 cars for the U.S. market and 97 for Canada. The total included 34 Formula coupes, 72 Formulas with T-tops, 538 Trans Ams with T-Tops and 75 Trans Am convertibles. The MN6 manual transmission was fitted to 317 Trans Am T-Tops, 40 Trans Am convertibles, 22 Formula coupes and 39 Formula T-tops. The MXO automatic transmission was used in 221 Trans Ams with T-tops, 35 Trans Am convertibles, 12 Formula coupes and 33 Formulas with T-tops.

In terms of color, of the 719 cars 38 were Artic White, 311 were Black, 169 were Bright Red, 37 were Bright Silver, 84 were Navy Blue and 80 were Pewter Metallic.

Drew Phillips

2000 SHELBY SERIES 1

In the late 1990s, Carrol Shelby came up with a new idea: to build a sleek, lightweight roadster with the performance of a real muscle car. Okay, so it wasn't a new idea, but the car was great looking and the use of an Oldsmobile engine was a little bit of a twist on history.

Shelby's $174,975 Series 1 roadster took a long time to become a reality, but when it finally debuted, many people were happy they had filled their penny jar, instead of buying a used Sunbird convertible to run around in.

The non-supercharged version of the Oldsmobile Aurora V-8 delivered 320 hp and 290 lbs.-ft. of torque at 5000 rpm. The engine sported double overhead camshafts and four valves per cylinder. It was linked to a six-speed manual gearbox.

A Vortec supercharger was merchandised as a dealer-installed extra. The system included special camshafts, a larger-than-stock throttle body and tweaked engine control system software. It brought the Series 1 roadster's price up to around $195,000.

With the supercharger and related goodies installed, the 244-cid Oldsmobile Aurora V-8 produced 450 hp at 6800 rpm and 400 ft. lbs.

at 5300 rpm. In the lightweight (2,650-pound) Series 1 roadster it produced amazing performance figures. The Shelby could rocket from 0-to-60 mph in an amazing 3.71 seconds. The quarter-mile required 12.14 seconds. In that brief amount of time, the roadster could get all the way up to about 120 mph. The car could pull .98gs on the skid pad. Top speed was 175 mph.

The Series 1 roadster was 168.9 inches long, 76.5 inches wide and 47 inches high. Underneath the Series 1's sleek, race-car-style body was a competition-style suspension with upper and lower control arms, coil springs and front and rear anti-roll bars. Vented disc brakes were used front and rear with 13-inch vented discs up front and 12-inchers at the rear. Braking from 60 mph to 0 required 129 feet.

Production of the Series 1 was originally supposed to have been limited to 500 cars. Eventually, the price of the Series 1 soared over $200,000, a factor that drove away some potential buyers. According to reliable sources, 280 cars were eventually assembled. But, knowing Carroll Shelby, there might be a few tucked away for the future.

1963 STUDEBAKER R2 AVANTI

As a symbol of change and fresh thinking, the Studebaker Avanti was intended to help save Studebaker from oblivion by shaking it loose from its rather musty and stodgy image. Although this effort ended in failure, the Avanti has gained recognition as an outstanding example both of styling excellence and performance competence.

Three engine alternatives were offered for the 1963 Avanti: the base R1 power plant, the supercharged R2 and the seldom-seen and expensive R3. The R1 was a nice, if somewhat unexciting, 280-cid/240-hp V-8. The R3, although garnering a great deal of publicity, was an extremely rare commodity. The R2 was readily available and (at $210) not terribly expensive. It offered a brand of performance rather different from that of the 400-plus-cid V-8s generally available in the mid-1960s.

While the R2 lacked the brute force of other muscle cars, the use of a supercharged and relatively small V-8, along with clever and resourceful use of existing Studebaker components, resulted in a car that needed no apologies or alibis for either its acceleration or handling.

Officially listed as a 1963 model, the Avanti received a tremendous publicity boost through the successful assault upon existing American records by an R3-engineered Avanti in August. Among the new marks established was a two-way Flying Mile mark of 168.15 mph. Early in 1963, a four-speed-equipped R2 Avanti that was almost completely stock, except for its exhaust system, averaged 158.15 mph through the measured mile.

Output of the R2 was impressive: 289 hp at 5200 rpm and 330 lbs.-ft. of torque at 3600 rpm. Aside from having an engine that developed 1 hp per cubic inch, the Avanti was the first full-size American car to be endowed with front caliper disc brakes.

The performance and top-speed capability of the R2 was superb. *Road and Track*, October 1962, reported a 0-to-60 time for the four-speed model of 7.3 seconds. *Motor Trend*, July 1962, noted that a power-shift model needed 8 seconds for the same run.

With a total 1963 model year run of just 3,834 units, the Avanti was truly a limited-edition vehicle.

1964 STUDEBAKER DAYTONA

With a top speed of 132 mph and 0-to-60 acceleration of 7.8 seconds, the R4 Daytona could show its tail lamps to any production sedan. Its performance was rivaled only by that of the Pontiac GTO, which was also released in 1964.

Designer Brooks Stevens effected more than a facelift when he created the new Studebaker Daytona hardtop in 1964. The crisp, squared-off roof that Stevens grafted onto the now 4-year-old Lark body looked every bit as up to date as Chevy's equally angular Impala. Of course, the Daytona was narrower than a full-size Chevy but its size fit nicely with the new intermediates.

What really made the Daytona stand out were the performance options available. Lacking money for frequent styling changes, Studebaker had attempted to garner attention through performance with its Hawk coupes and the stunning Avanti. Studebaker's overhead-valve V-8, first introduced in 1951, had been a farsighted enough design that more than a dozen years later it was being boosted to outputs exceeding 1 hp per cubic inch.

Studebaker designated its high-output V-8s as the R-series engines. The "base" R1 engine developed 240 hp from a 289-cid displacement. Next came the R2, also a 289, but equipped with a supercharger for a rated 289 hp. The R3, also supercharged and with a slightly larger displacement of 304.5 cid, gave a power rating of 335 hp. The final engine in this series, dubbed the R4, ran two four-barrel carburetors without supercharging for a rated 280 hp. It was this engine that Studebaker selected to create a street "sleeper" from its docile-looking Daytona hardtop.

To give the Daytona some measure of road-handling ability, Studebaker fit it with an Avanti suspension package that consisted of stiffer springs and shocks, anti-roll bars front and rear, and front disc brakes. To glue the engine's power to the pavement, these performance cars came standard with traction bars and a limited-slip differential.

Not many performance Daytonas were built (besides the R4, other R series engines could also be optioned) making them one of the least known and rarest of muscle cars — a real "sleeper" even today.